D1507538

DISCARDED

BOWLING GREEN STATE UNIVERSITY

LIBRARY

National Purpose in the World Economy

A volume in the series

Cornell Studies in Political Economy

EDITED BY PETER J. KATZENSTEIN

A full list of titles in the series appears at the end of the book.

National Purpose in the World Economy

Post-Soviet States in Comparative Perspective

Rawi Abdelal

Cornell University Press

Ithaca and London

BOWLING GREEN STATE
UNIVERSITY LIBRARIES

For Traci

Copyright © 2001 by Cornell University

All rights reserved. Except for brief quotations in a review, this book, or parts thereof, must not be reproduced in any form without permission in writing from the publisher. For information, address Cornell University Press, Sage House, 512 East State Street, Ithaca, New York 14850.

First published 2001 by Cornell University Press

Printed in the United States of America

Library of Congress Cataloging-in-Publication Data
Abdelal, Rawi. 1971–
    National purpose in the world economy : post-Soviet states in comparative perspective / Rawi Abdelal.
        p.cm.—(Cornell studies in political economy)
    Includes bibliographical references and index.
    ISBN 0-8014-3879-9 (cloth : alk. paper)
    1. Former Soviet republics—Foreign economic relations.   2. Former Soviet republics—Economic integration.   3. Former Soviet republics—Commercial policy.   4. Nationalism—Former Soviet republics.   I. Title.   II. Series.
    HF1557 .A23 2001
    338.947—dc21   2001002552

Cornell University Press strives to use environmentally responsible suppliers and materials to the fullest extent possible in the publishing of its books. Such materials include vegetable-based, low-VOC inks and acid-free papers that are recycled, totally chlorine-free, or partly composed of nonwood fibers. For further information, visit our website at www.cornellpress.cornell.edu.

Cloth printing   10 9 8 7 6 5 4 3 2 1

Contents

Preface

The idea for this book originated with a puzzle: Why did the regional economy of post-Soviet Eurasia disintegrate among some states and re-integrate among others? After the Soviet Union collapsed in late 1991, its constituent republics became independent states, and all fifteen formed a distinct region commonly known as Eurasia. Russia stood out as the largest and most powerful, and the other fourteen were economically dependent on it. Because they had recently been part of the same carefully planned and tightly integrated statewide economy, their mutual dependence at the start was pervasive. Post-Soviet states inherited a material reality that was similar for all of them.

By the end of the 1990s, ten years after the breakup of the USSR, post-Soviet states had sorted themselves into three groups defined by their stance toward Russia and what they considered to be the "West." Some sought to reintegrate their economies with Russia's. Others sought to reorient their economies, to integrate them into the economy of the European Union (EU), and to reduce their dependence on Russia. Still a third group was ambivalent; these states rejected reintegration with Russia but failed to pursue a coherent policy of reorientation. Why did the governments of post-Soviet states choose such divergent foreign economic policies?

When I first formulated this research question some years ago, I was quite pleased to have stumbled on such an interesting empirical puzzle as it was just emerging. Unfortunately, I remained truly puzzled for a long time. As a scholar of international political economy, equipped with the theories and analytical tools of the field, I had been sure that I could construct an answer that was both theoretically sophisticated and, even better, right. I began with the theoretical traditions that dominate international political economy—Liberalism and Realism. I tested the theories of economic cooperation and discord derived within those broad perspectives and found that they were not adequate to explain the variety of choices made by post-Soviet governments. Not infrequently, the expectations I derived from Liberalism and Realism were the opposite of the actual behavior of the governments. I began to worry that I had chosen too puzzling a puzzle.

Then I turned to the history of the region and found a few surprises. One was that post-Soviet societies differed a great deal in their interpretations of a common Soviet past. According to some, the Soviet Union had been an empire that subjugated their nations and attempted to crush their distinctive identities. For others, the Soviet era was more benign, even a moment of glory for those that excelled within the Soviet family of nations. Another surprise was that these interpretations of history were linked to contemporary debates about the meaning and purpose of post-Soviet nationhood, statehood, and the economy. I eventually realized that what post-Soviet societies wanted depended on who they thought they were. Differences in the national identities of post-Soviet societies led to their divergent policy choices. I had at least found the right answer.

This answer created a theoretical problem, however. The field of international political economy did not have a way to explain how nationalisms and national identities affect economic relations among states. The concept of economic nationalism and Robert Gilpin's "Nationalist perspective," though standards in the field, were actually Realist ideas framed in the language, but not the substance, of nationalism. A distinct tradition of scholarship had dealt with issues of nationalism in the world economy, but scholars working in the Realist tradition had subsumed this Nationalist tradition. In this book I have attempted to distinguish the Nationalist perspective from the Realist perspective and to advance the Nationalist perspective as an important explanatory paradigm in its own right. Thus, this book's theoretical contribution is an explanation of how nationalisms and national identities interact with the world economy.

My theoretical agenda is at once ambitious and modest. The ambitions are straightforward enough. The field of international political economy lacks a fully articulated framework for understanding the influence of national identities on international economic relations. In the pages that follow, I propose such a framework, which builds on the work of scholars ranging from Friedrich List to E. H. Carr as well as on recent constructivist theorizing in international relations. I hope to reinvigorate an older theoretical tradition as well as link it to the emerging consensus that collective identities, themselves social constructions, influence the political-economic practices of governments. I argue that national identities matter in ways that scholars have not yet fully appreciated. Moreover, an appreciation of the influence of national identities requires that scholars depart from the assumptions and causal logics of Realism and Liberalism. The logic of the Nationalist perspective is distinct.

I also show that the Nationalist perspective is useful. In addition to examining Lithuania, Ukraine, and Belarus in detail, I apply the Nationalist perspective to all fourteen peripheral post-Soviet states. Then I consider parallels throughout the twentieth century—the moments after the collapse of empire when the societies of successor states had to discern their interests and choose economic reintegration or reorientation. The parallels in the economic relations among the successor states of the Habsburg, Dutch, and French empires are remarkable. In all, the book covers four continents, twenty-four countries, and most of the twentieth century. Not only were the countries' choices consequential; so, too, were the postimperial moments when societies often chose trajectories that guided their policies for decades. Thus, in this book I seek to establish for the Nationalist perspective a space among some of the most important empirical questions, as well as the most influential theories, of international political economy.

But I do not claim the entire universe of cases for a theoretical framework based on national identity. Scholars of international political economy have sometimes pitted the field's broadest theoretical perspectives against one another in an abstract contest for analytical superiority and priority. International political economy has not, I think, been well served by the idea underlying such a contest—that paradigms can and should apply to all empirical questions regardless of context. In contrast, I suggest that the theories scholars use must depend on the empirical questions they ask. The question that motivated this book required a Nationalist perspective, as do many other important questions of international political economy. But not all questions require a focus on national identity, just as they do not all require an emphasis on the incentives and regulatory institutions of Liberal theory or the statism and power balances of Realist theory.

This project began at Cornell University, where I had the great good fortune to study among a distinguished group of scholars. Peter Katzenstein was an ideal adviser. Peter was as generous with his incisive critiques as he was with his praise, and he seemed always to know precisely when I needed more of one than the other. It is only now, as I finish this book, that I fully realize just how much I learned from him. My other superb adviser, Jonathan Kirshner, more than anyone else, steered me away from all the bad ideas I had and then noticed first when I found a good one. Jonathan also reminded me what I was doing when I got lost, not infrequently, in the details. Valerie Bunce constantly amazed me with her support, ingenious insight, and apparently limitless knowledge of the history and politics of central and eastern Europe. I cannot overstate how important she was to the development of this book. Val understood the politics about which I was writing long before I did, and she patiently and thoughtfully guided me to a more informed appreciation of them. I was also very lucky that Matthew Evangelista arrived at Cornell after I had begun my research. I greatly appreciate his careful reading of my work and his suggestions for improving the presentation of my ideas. I am most grateful.

This project was supported financially by several fellowships, including a fellowship for East European Studies from the American Council of Learned Societies and a dissertation fellowship from the Institute for the Study of World Politics. I am grateful for their support. Cornell's Einaudi Center for International Studies and several of its programs helped fund my field research; I appreciate the support of the International Political Economy program and the Peace Studies program. I also appreciate the time that policy makers spent with me during my field research in Moscow, Kyiv, Minsk, and Vilnius. Because policy makers spoke with me on condition of anonymity, interviews are referred to by institution, number, location, and date. The Division of Research at Harvard Business School generously supported my research and writing as I completed the book. For research assistance, I am grateful to Kimberly Haddad, Lynsey Fitzpatrick, Victoria Kartashova, Gene Plotkin, and Irina Tratch. Chris Albanese cheerfully helped me manage countless details.

I am in debt to those who read and commented on portions of the manuscript as it developed. These readers identified and often corrected analytical and factual errors in successive drafts, each of which was, as a result of their efforts, better than the last. For their careful readings, I thank Peter Andreas, Katherine Burns, Tom Christensen, Terry Clark, James Clem, Alex Cooley, Keith Darden, Robert Gilpin, Eric Goldberg, Amy Gurowitz, Yoi Herrera, Meg Jacobs, Pål Kolstø, Beth Kier, Ulrich Krotz, David Moss, Forest Reinhardt, David Rivera, Julio Rotemberg, Matthew Rudolph, Andrew Schwartz, Oxana Shevel, Tim Snyder, Debora Spar, David Stasavage, Kevin Strompf, and David Yoffie. I am particularly grateful to Debora Spar, who gave me invaluable advice and read several successive drafts of key chapters during the delicate process of completing the book. I also appreciate the efforts of Roger Haydon, who offered insightful advice about both the prose and the argument and patiently guided me through the review process and final revisions.

Several people read and commented on entire drafts of the manuscript. For their scholarly generosity, I am grateful to Tim Colton, Paul D'Anieri, Tom McCraw, Adam Segal, Dick Vietor, Lou Wells, and three anonymous reviewers. My debt to Tom McCraw is particularly substantial because he read my manuscript with such care at a moment when I no longer knew how to improve it. The draft he returned to me included his suggestions for improving nearly every single line of prose, and I have followed his advice with great profit. Adam Segal was there from the beginning, listening to every idea I had during the rough transition from being exclusively a consumer of political science to being a producer, as well as reading nearly every word I have written over the past eight years.

My family's patience and generosity made this book possible. I am grateful for the support of my mother, Phyllis Kuehn, who encouraged me with apricot jam and kept the standard that my grandmother set; my father, Ahmed Abdelal, who reminded me that I could meet his high expectations; and my sister, Laila McClay. Jim, Martha, and Jeanine Battle seemed never to have doubts, and I sometimes borrowed their confidence.

Finally, my greatest debt is to my wife, Traci Battle, first for promising to catch me and then for the life that makes it all worthwhile.

RAWI ABDELAL

Boston, Massachusetts

CHAPTER ONE

Nation, State, and Economy

What societies want depends on who they think they are. For the past several centuries, societies have often thought—collectively—that they were nations and have constructed national identities for themselves. Various societal actors, including cultural elites, political parties, and governments, have sought to link those national identities to specific political and economic projects. That is *nationalism*: the attempt to link the idea of the nation to specific goals. Every nationalism is a proposal for the content of national identity—a society's collective interpretation of itself as a nation. There are almost always competing nationalist proposals within a society. All such nationalist proposals are debated, and every national identity is contested. Sometimes societies agree about who they think they are, but at other times or in other places they may not.

The outcomes of these societal debates are enormously consequential for the world's politics and economics. Nations are "imagined communities," to be sure.[1] But societies have powerful imaginations, which lead them to interpret similar material circumstances in very different ways. Because of their varying national identities, societies have contrasting understandings of the purposes of their statehood, even if it is only a statehood to which they aspire. Societies' collective identities lead them to their own in-

[1] The phrase is Benedict Anderson's. See his *Imagined Communities: Reflections on the Origin and Spread of Nationalism*, rev. ed. (London: Verso, 1991), now a classic interpretation of nationalism. For the most sophisticated and lucid explanation of the construction and institutionalization of national identities, see Rogers Brubaker, *Nationalism Reframed: Nationhood and the National Question in the New Europe* (Cambridge: Cambridge University Press, 1996).

terpretations of the purposes of economic activity, the legitimacy of certain economic institutions, and the meaning of their economic interdependence with others. Collective identities thus influence how societies and governments interpret their place in the world economy. This book offers a new way to think about the economic consequences of nationalism, especially the interactions among nationalisms, national identities, and the organization of economic activity in world politics.

The contemporary study of international relations (IR) and international political economy (IPE) lacks a theoretical framework to explain how, when, and why national identities and nationalisms affect the economic relations among states. This is a serious deficiency because it is impossible to make sense of fundamental patterns of interstate economic relations without understanding the influence of nationalism. Indeed, economic nationalism is one of the most widely misinterpreted phenomena of the modern world economy. Political scientists have tended to equate economic nationalism with mercantilism, or economic statism. Many economists have mistakenly assumed that nationalism always leads to protectionism and the pursuit of something close to autarky. Here I argue, in contrast, that economic nationalism and economic statism are concepts with distinct theoretical lineages as well as distinct empirical phenomena. And nationalism can create economic cooperation among some states even as it leads to discord among others.

Building on a neglected tradition in IR theory, I specify several necessary components of a framework that links nationalism to the world economy. In doing so, I outline a distinctively *Nationalist* perspective on IPE, that is, one defined here as explaining how nationalism and national identities affect cooperation and discord in the economic relations between particular states. The framework differs from the dominant theoretical perspectives in IPE: Realism, which focuses on the effects of statism and the international distribution of power; and Liberalism, which emphasizes the effects of economic incentives and international institutions.

Nationalism has four significant effects on governments' foreign economic policies. First, nationalism endows policy with fundamental social purpose, related to protecting and cultivating the nation. Nationalism also engenders the economic sacrifice necessary to achieve societal goals, to realize nationalists' vision of the future. Third, it lengthens the time horizons of society and government. Most significant, nationalism specifies a direction for foreign economic policy, away from the nation's "other" and often toward another, broader cultural space. Nationalisms lead governments to interpret their economic dependence on some states as a security threat but on other states as mutually beneficial exchange. The explanation of the directionality of economic nationalism I present here is a new contribution to the scholarly literatures on nationalism and IPE. I also synthesize the other three elements (social purpose, sacrifice, and lengthened time horizons), previously explored by other scholars of economic nationalism ranging from Friedrich List to E. H. Carr, into a revised and coherent *Nationalist* framework.

Applying the Nationalist perspective to an important puzzle of the post–cold war world economy, I illustrate the necessity of such an approach to IPE. This puzzle is the central question of the political economy of post-Soviet international relations: Why did the regional economy of post-Soviet Eurasia disintegrate among some states and reintegrate among others? After the Soviet Union collapsed in late 1991, its constituent fifteen republics became independent states, forming a distinct region commonly known as Eurasia. Russia was by far the most economically and militarily powerful, and its government openly sought to dominate politics in the former Soviet Union. The other fourteen post-Soviet states were economically dependent on Russia. Because they had just emerged from the same carefully planned and tightly integrated statewide economy, their mutual dependence at the start was pervasive (Table 1.1).

Post-Soviet governments interpreted their dependence on Russia in dramatically different ways. I show that the governments' diverse interpretations of dependence were closely linked to their contrasting preferences for the political-economic future of the region. Some post-Soviet governments, such as Belarus's, decided that dependence was a good reason for economic reintegration with Russia. A second group, typified by Lithuania, considered economic dependence on Russia a security threat and sought to reorient their economies to the West. Still a third group, exemplified by Ukraine, failed to choose a coherent economic strategy and remained oriented neither away from nor toward the Russian economy. These interpretations and preferences led post-Soviet governments to adopt divergent foreign economic strategies.

A crucial question is, What were the origins of post-Soviet governments' preferences? Scholars of IPE have put forward different approaches to the issue of preferences. Realists tend to assume the preferences of states and focus on power as the most important influence on state behavior. Liberals tend to deduce the preferences of societal actors from the structure of the economy and then aggregate them when analyzing the behavior of governments. A different approach is necessary to resolve the post-Soviet empirical puzzle and others like it. This approach explores the influence of a society's collective identity—especially its national identity—on the preferences of the government that acts on its behalf. Differences in the content and contestation of the national identities of post-Soviet societies led to varying government preferences for disintegration and reintegration.

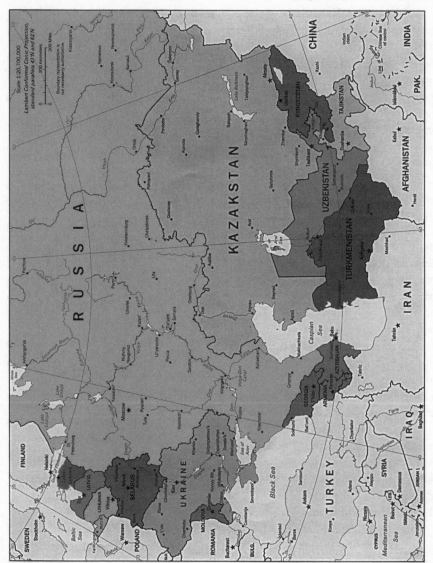

Post-Soviet Eurasia

Table 1.1 Power Indicators of Post-Soviet States, 1992

	Population (millions)	GDP (billions)	Armed Forces	Nuclear Weapons
Armenia	3.4	$2.1	32,700	No
Azerbaijan	7.5	$4.9	56,000	No
Belarus	10.5	$17.3	92,500	Yes
Estonia	1.6	$1.7	2,500	No
Georgia	5.7	$3.5	—	No
Kazakhstan	17.4	$20.2	40,000	Yes
Kyrgyzstan	4.7	$3.2	12,000	No
Latvia	2.6	$1.9	6,850	No
Lithuania	3.7	$3.4	8,900	No
Moldova	4.5	$4.2	11,100	No
Russia	148.9	$1,200.0	1,714,000	Yes
Tajikistan	5.9	$2.9	3,000	No
Turkmenistan	3.9	$3.9	28,000	No
Ukraine	52.2	$62.9	517,000	Yes
Uzebekistan	22.3	$14.0	45,000	No

Source: Adapted from International Institute for Strategic Studies, *The Military Balance, 1994–95* (London: Brassey's, 1994).

In other words, what post-Soviet societies wanted depended on who they thought they were.

A PUZZLE OF THE POST-SOVIET REGIONAL ECONOMY

There was no regionwide cooperation among all post-Soviet states during the 1990s even though, given their interdependence, collaboration seemed an obvious necessity. At least it seemed so to the International Monetary Fund (IMF) and World Bank. The IMF recommended that Soviet successor states maintain their monetary union and in 1992 even insisted that governments would not be entitled to IMF financing if they introduced their own currencies.[2] Nevertheless, some post-Soviet governments adopted new national currencies, the former currency union fell apart, and monetary relations became disorganized and chaotic. Following a similar logic, World Bank economists urged cooperation and preferential trading arrangements.[3] But trade relations became discordant, and

[2] Pavel Vanichkin, "Direktorat MVF sovetuiut nam sokhranit' edinoe torgovo-ekonomicheskoe prostranstvo" (Directorate of the IMF recommends that we preserve the single commercial-economic space), *Delovoi mir*, 30 September 1992. See also Brigitte Granville, "Farewell, Ruble Zone," in *Russian Economic Reform at Risk*, ed. Anders Åslund (London: Pinter, 1995).

[3] Constantine Michalopoulos and David G. Tarr, "Policy Recommendations," in *Trade in the New Independent States*, ed. Michalopoulos and Tarr (Washington, D.C.: World Bank, 1994), especially 261–62.

by the mid-1990s trade volume among post-Soviet states had declined to less than half its 1991 level. Of course, part of the breakdown of regional trade resulted from the creation of borders between these pieces of the collapsed Soviet state, as well as the economic decline that accompanied the transition from state-socialist to capitalist economic institutions. But leaders, mass publics, and organized economic actors throughout the former Soviet Union blamed political dissolution more than any other cause. They put the region's failed cooperation at the center of foreign economic policy debates.

Overall, the most striking aspect of the political economy of post-Soviet international relations was its variety, which was particularly evident in governments' policies toward regional monetary and trade arrangements.[4] Some governments sought regional economic reintegration. Armenia, Belarus, Kazakhstan, Kyrgyzstan, and Tajikistan, along with Russia, all promoted monetary and trade cooperation and the development of regional institutions, such as the Commonwealth of Independent States (CIS). The reintegrationists insisted on the rationality and reasonableness of their approach, which followed obvious material incentives—in contrast to what they called the "romanticism" and economic "naiveté" of nationalists throughout the region.

Another group of post-Soviet governments was ambivalent about economic reintegration. Azerbaijan, Georgia, Moldova, Turkmenistan, Ukraine, and Uzbekistan recognized the need for some cooperation with Russia and other CIS states. Their governments, however, rejected multilateral reintegration, primarily because they feared that the formal institutionalization of cooperation would strengthen Russia's regional hegemony.[5]

[4] In other words, the dependent variable for the post-Soviet cases in this book is the economic strategy of each state, particularly toward the ruble zone and regional trade arrangements. For a fuller discussion of the dependent variable, see chapter 3. On the variety of strategies, see Martha Brill Olcott, Anders Åslund, and Sherman Garnett, *Getting It Wrong: Regional Cooperation and the Commonwealth of Independent States* (Washington, D.C.: Carnegie Endowment for International Peace, 1999). For theoretical assessments of the variety of strategies among post-Soviet states, see Philip G. Roeder, "From Hierarchy to Hegemony: The Post-Soviet Security Complex," in *Regional Orders*, ed. David A. Lake and Patrick M. Morgan (University Park: Pennsylvania State University Press, 1997); and Hendrik Spruyt, "The Prospects for Neo-Imperial and Nonimperial Outcomes in the Former Soviet Space," in *The End of Empire? The Transformation of the USSR in Comparative Perspective*, ed. Karen Dawisha and Bruce Parrott (Armonk, N.Y.: M. E. Sharpe, 1997). On the influence of economic ideas on the international institutional choices of post-Soviet states, see Keith A. Darden, "Economic Ideas and Institutional Choice among the Post-Soviet States," paper presented at the annual meeting of the American Political Science Association, Washington, D.C., 31 August–3 September 2000.

[5] Some of these states' stances toward regional cooperation changed somewhat over time. Azerbaijan shifted its strategy several times with the rise (in June 1992) and subsequent decline (in June 1993) of the political influence of the nationalist Azerbaijani Popular Front under the leadership of President Abulfaz Elcibey. Moldova reversed its position after the

The three Baltic states—Lithuania, Latvia, and Estonia—composed a distinct third group of post-Soviet governments. They unambiguously rejected both economic reintegration and regional cooperation and remained outside the CIS. The Baltic governments also claimed that their policies, the opposite of the reintegrationists', were more rational because they followed long-term goals such as integration into the EU and economic reform even as they ignored short-term incentives to cooperate with Russia.

The experiences of Lithuania, Ukraine, and Belarus illustrate the variety of post-Soviet strategies. Because each typifies one of the patterns of post-Soviet political economy, together they cover the full range of the behavior I seek to explain in this book.

The specific differences in their governments' preferences and strategies are striking. During the 1990s the Lithuanian government interpreted economic dependence on Russia as a threat to state security and reoriented its economy toward the West.[6] Lithuania sought to reduce its dependence on Russia by diversifying its trade links and creating an independent currency.[7] The government's most important foreign policy goal was EU membership. The new Lithuanian constitution expressly prohibited the government from joining any political or economic unions on the territory of the former Soviet Union. The Lithuanian government negotiated a free trade agreement with the EU in 1994 but rejected free trade with Russia or the CIS. Economic relations with Russia were severely strained by Lithuania's Western foreign policy priorities. In 1995 Lithuania and Russia finally accorded each other most-favored-nation trade status, a minimal level of cooperation that characterizes most of the world's bilateral trade relations. Previously, Lithuania was one of only four countries in the world, including the two other Baltic states, not to have received most-favored-nation trade status from Russia, which sought to punish the Baltics for their reorientation. Lithua-

---

1994 election of the Agrarian Democratic Party, which opposed the Moldovan Popular Front's goal of reorienting toward the West and Romania. Over the course of the decade Armenia's commitment to the CIS increased, but primarily with regard to security cooperation. Meanwhile, by the end of the decade Turkmenistan and Uzbekistan had become less committed to the CIS, policy changes that were both reacting to and reinforcing the relative ineffectiveness of CIS institutions.

[6] Author's interviews nos. 1, 2, 3, 4, and 5, Ministry of Foreign Affairs of Lithuania, Vilnius, July and August 1998; author's interview, Administration of the President of Lithuania, Vilnius, July 1998. Also see Evaldas Nekrasas, "Is Lithuania a Northern or Central European Country?" *Lithuanian Foreign Policy Review* 1 (1998): 19–45; and Romunas Vilpisaukas, "Trade between Lithuania and the European Union," in *Lithuania's Integration into the European Union*, ed. Klaudijus Maniokas and Gediminas Vitkus (Vilnius: European Integration Studies Center, 1997).

[7] See Government of Lithuania, *Action Program of the Government of the Republic of Lithuania for 1997–2000* (Vilnius, 1997); Ministry of Foreign Affairs of Lithuania, *Lithuania's Foreign Policy* (Vilnius, 1997).

nia's monetary strategy also favored the EU, as the Bank of Lithuania intends ultimately to join the European monetary union.[8]

In contrast, the Belarusian government interpreted its economic dependence on Russia as mutually beneficial exchange, a reason for closer cooperation with Russia and the multilateral reintegration of the post-Soviet economic area.[9] Belarus therefore did not seek to reorient its economy either away from Russia or toward the West. Belarus's commitment to reintegration was strong enough to produce a string of agreements in 1997, 1998, and 1999 that symbolically united the Belarusian with the Russian state. Free trade and customs union agreements tightened the economic links between the two countries. The Belarusian government issued its own currency reluctantly and sought a new monetary union with Russia. Belarusian acquiescence paid handsome rewards, at least in the short run, since Russia subsidized Belarus's energy imports and regularly forgave its enormous energy debts.

Ukraine's foreign policy orientation was a middle course between that of Lithuania and Belarus, and between Russia and the West. Although the Ukrainian government sought close relationships with NATO and the EU, it did not apply for membership in either organization during the 1990s. The Ukrainian government interpreted economic dependence on Russia as a security threat, even if it did much less than Lithuania to achieve economic autonomy and reorient its economy Westward.[10] The government decided close cooperation with Russia was necessary but, unlike the Belarusian authorities, ruled out the possibility of multilateral reintegration. Ukraine adopted an independent currency in 1992, and the government made no plans for monetary unification with either Europe or Russia.[11]

Certain similarities among these three countries rule out some possible explanations for their divergent economic behavior. Therefore, comparing these cases as representatives of each of the three groups of post-Soviet states can reveal a great deal about the origins of patterns of cooperation and discord in the post-Soviet regional economy. Unlike in Latvia and Kazakhstan, for example, where large and vocal "ethnic Russian" minorities complicated domestic politics by claiming linguistic and cultural distinctiveness, Lithuanians, Ukrainians, and Belarusians considered them-

[8] Author's interview no. 1, Bank of Lithuania, Vilnius, July 1998. See also Bank of Lithuania, *Monetary Policy Program of the Bank of Lithuania for 1997–99* (Vilnius, 1997).

[9] See Karen Dawisha, "Constructing and Deconstructing Empire in the Post-Soviet Space," in *End of Empire?* ed. Dawisha and Parrott.

[10] Author's interview, Ministry of Foreign Affairs of Ukraine, Kyiv, June 1998; author's interview, Administration of the President of Ukraine, Kyiv, June 1998. For an overview, see Paul D'Anieri, *Economic Interdependence in Ukrainian-Russian Relations* (Albany: SUNY Press, 1999).

[11] Author's interview, National Bank of Ukraine, Kyiv, June 1998.

Table 1.2 Energy Dependence on Russia, 1992
(as percentage of total consumption)

	Oil	Gas
Lithuania	94	100
Ukraine	89	56
Belarus	91	100

Source: Adapted from Karen Dawisha and Bruce
Parrott, *Russia and the New States of Eurasia*
(Cambridge: Cambridge University Press, 1994).

selves to be majorities in their own states.[12] Unlike several Central Asian
and Caucasian republics—Tajikistan and Georgia, for example—none of
these three faced civil war or serious ethnic violence.

The economies these states inherited in 1991 were also similar. They were
all dependent on Russia, especially for oil and gas (Table 1.2). They had
few economic links with the West—in 1990 90 percent of Lithuania's total
commerce was with other post-Soviet states, as was 87 percent of Belarus's
and 82 percent of Ukraine's.[13] Even the structures of their economies were
similar (Table 1.3). Experts considered them to be among the most economically and technologically advanced republics of the Soviet Union and
ascribed to them the best prospects for economic independence.[14]

Finally, their politics shared a remarkable similarity, at least on the sur-
face: each of the three states was ruled directly by formerly Communist
elites and political parties during the 1990s. In 1992 Lithuania was the first
state in eastern Europe to return its former Communists to power through
parliamentary elections. Lithuanians also elected an important leader of
the Communist Party, Algirdas Brazauskas, as their first president. Similarly, Ukrainian and Belarusian governments and presidents also were
drawn from the ranks of former Communists. Yet these former Communists pursued divergent, even opposite goals. Being a former Communist
evidently meant very different things in different post-Soviet states.

Thus, little about their economics or politics preordained the choices
made by the Lithuanian, Ukrainian, and Belarusian governments in the early
1990s. Their dominant politicians might have learned the same lessons or
inherited the same material interests from the party membership they had
in common before the decade began. It was not because Belarus had more

[12] The best book on the Russian-speaking populations scattered across the former Soviet
Union is David D. Laitin, *Identity in Formation: The Russian-Speaking Populations in the Near Abroad*
(Ithaca: Cornell University Press, 1998).

[13] Constantine Michalopoulos and David G. Tarr, *Trade and Payments Arrangements for States
of the Former USSR* (Washington, D.C.: World Bank, 1992).

[14] See especially Gertrude Schroeder, "On the Economic Viability of New Nation-States,"
Journal of International Affairs 45, 2 (1992): 549–74; and Jürgen Corbet and Andreas Gim-
mich, *The Soviet Union at the Crossroads* (Frankfurt: Deutsche Bank, 1990).

Table 1.3 Share of Economy by Sector, 1990

	Agriculture	Industry	Construction	Transport	Other
Lithuania	33.4	34.1	13.4	5.9	13.3
Ukraine	30.3	41.3	9.7	6.0	19.4
Belarus	29.3	44.0	11.8	5.1	9.8

Source: World Bank, *Statistical Handbook: States of the Former Soviet Union* (Washington, D.C.: World Bank, 1992).

"ethnic Russians" or because its state was weaker or more threatened by the Russian military that its government acquiesced in Russian regional hegemony. Lithuania was no less dependent on Russia; it had no more economic links with the EU than the others; it was not somehow better prepared economically for autonomy from Russia. Neither their means nor their opportunities were significantly different. Yet they took different courses. Why?

NATIONAL IDENTITY AS THE EXPLANATION: AN APPLICATION OF THE NATIONALIST PERSPECTIVE

In Lithuania, Ukraine, and Belarus there were nationalists—people who invoked the nation in support of specific purposes and were motivated by those purposes. Each country's nationalists had mobilized during the late 1980s in opposition to Soviet authority. After 1991 Lithuanian, Ukrainian, and Belarusian nationalists continued to struggle against what they saw as the persistent "imperial" control of Russia throughout the region by economic means. These nationalists embodied the rise of nationalism in the region, and it is difficult to understand societal debates about the meaning of post-Soviet nationhood without an inquiry into these actors' goals and ideas. These nationalists set the terms of debate and framed the economic choices facing their governments.

If Lithuanian, Ukrainian, and Belarusian nationalists had had their way, their states' foreign economic strategies during the 1990s would have been the same. These nationalists strove to define the content of their societies' identities in similar ways. The most influential nationalists in these countries—Lithuania's Sajudis (later the Homeland Union), Ukraine's Rukh, and the Belarusian Popular Front—had remarkably similar ideologies and foreign policy goals.[15] For all three groups of nationalists, Russia was the most

[15] I interviewed leaders of the most important Lithuanian, Ukrainian, and Belarusian nationalist parties about their parties' goals as well as their similarities with one another. All agreed that they had substantively similar ideologies. Author's interviews nos. 1 and 2, Homeland Union, Vilnius, July 1998; author's interview, Rukh, Kyiv, July 1998; and author's interviews nos. 1 and 2, Belarusian Popular Front, Minsk, July 1998. These similarities are also

important "other," the state from which statehood had to be defended most of all. All three nationalist movements, which began as anti-Soviet, came to be oriented against Russia. These nationalists also argued that economic dependence on Russia was their states' primary security threat, even more serious than the unlikely arrival of invading Russian troops at their borders.

Most dramatic was the nationalists' commitment to the idea of their states' "return to Europe." These three nationalisms were not just anti-Russian; they were also pro-European. The nationalists wanted a reorientation of their states' economies, a change that required protectionism against Russia but free trade with the EU. The nationalists argued that the goal was worth the economic costs of reorientation and that autonomy from Russia would eventually bring its own rewards. In the long run, the nationalists argued, future generations of the nation would be European and rich. They demanded change at the expense of regional cooperation.

In opposition to the nationalists, other groups in all three countries demanded that the economic ties of the former Soviet Union be maintained and even strengthened. Invariably, among the groups that insisted on regional economic cooperation and reintegration were the industrialists and other organized business interests. They urged continuity and what they called "pragmatism," which became a code word for reintegration with Russia. These arguments forced post-Soviet societies and politicians to choose between reorientation and reintegration.

The political economy of post-Soviet international relations revolved around one central question: Did post-Soviet societies and politicians agree with their nationalists or not? As it turned out, the former Communists played a decisive role. During the first post-Soviet decade the defining political difference among the fourteen non-Russian states was the political and ideological relationship in each one between the formerly Communist elites and the nationalists—whether the former Communists marginalized the nationalists, arrested them, co-opted them, bargained with them, or even tried to become like them. These two groups both proposed

visible in their published programs. See Homeland Union, *Lithuania's Success* (Vilnius, 1996); Svetlana Chervonnaia, *Grazhdanskie dvizheniia v Litve* (Civic movements in Lithuania) (Moscow: TsIMO, 1993); Sajudis, *Obshchaia programma Litovskogo dvizheniia za perestroiku* (Overall program of the Lithuanian movement for perestroika) (Vilnius: Mintis, 1989); Rukh, *New Way for Ukraine* (Kyiv, 1998); Ivan Lozowy, *The Popular Movement of Ukraine Rukh 1994: Statehood, Democracy, Reforms* (Kyiv: International Relations Secretariat, Popular Movement of Ukraine Rukh, 1994); Rukh, *The Popular Movement for Restructuring Rukh: Program and Charter* (Baltimore: Smoloskyp Publishers, for the Ukrainian National Association, [1989] 1990); Belarusian Popular Front, "Belarus—To Europe! A Strategy of Defense of Independence," in *Documents of the Fifth Congress of the Belarusian Popular Front* (Minsk, 20–21 June 1997); and TsIMO, *Grazhdanskie dvizheniia v Belorussii: dokumenty i materialy, 1986–1991* (Civic movements in Belorussia: Documents and materials, 1986–1991) (Moscow: TsIMO, 1991).

and contested the meanings of each national identity. Their struggle to influence the content of national identity was contestation in action.

These different relationships revealed different degrees and kinds of societal consensus about national identity after Soviet rule; they are a useful measure of the content and contestation of national identity in the three societies. Lithuania's former Communists sided with its nationalists, Belarus's former Communists did not, and Ukraine's former Communists and nationalists were deadlocked. These outcomes indicated that the content of Lithuanian national identity was coherent and consensual; the content of Belarusian national identity was contested, fragmented, and ambiguous; and the content of Ukrainian national identity was contested regionally, as west and central Ukrainians largely accepted the arguments of the nationalists while east and south Ukrainians did not.

In other words, Lithuania's former Communists tried to become nationalists. Ukraine's former Communists bargained with and co-opted the nationalists. Meanwhile, in Belarus, the nationalists, ever unpopular, were beaten by police and arrested, all without much protest from the rest of Belarusian society. The axis of debate was the same in all three places, but the outcomes were different. The resolution of these debates, derived from collective interpretations of the purposes of the nation, shaped the broad outlines of each state's foreign economic policy.

Lithuanian national identity framed the society's political and economic debates, and Lithuania's foreign economic policy was coherent, purposive, and single-minded. Economic reintegration with Russia was an illegitimate option. Although Lithuania's former Communists and nationalists disagreed about many issues, and indeed rarely trusted each other, they shared a singular vision of the Lithuanian nation, a vision that gave both government and society the will to endure the economic sacrifice of reorienting toward Europe. The necessary sacrifices were obvious: the loss of Russian energy subsidies and, more broadly, Russia's favor in negotiating agreements on issues ranging from energy debts to trade. The central theme of Lithuania's economic policies was the victory of the long view over the short. These were policies motivated by national purpose, and they followed the direction of Lithuanian nationalism, both toward Europe and against Russia. This was Lithuania's economic nationalism.

In contrast, because Belarusian political elites and their fellow citizens did not share the Belarusian nationalists' interpretation of the content of national identity, they did not see the point of allowing the post-Soviet regional economy to continue to disintegrate. Not only did pursuing economic reorientation seem irrational; the costs of independent statehood itself seemed excessively high. Most Belarusians were not willing to bear the costs of economic autonomy from Russia because the goal was not widely shared. Without a coherent sense of national purpose or direction, the government therefore attempted only to reap short-term economic benefits from the state's relationship with Russia.

Ukraine's national identity was too contested and fragmented regionally for the government to make a decisive break from the CIS and toward Europe, so Ukraine could not choose a singular path. At the same time, Ukraine's nationalism was too well developed to be marginalized. Neither a purely pro-Western nor a purely pro-Eastern foreign policy was possible because it would have divided the country. The former entailed economic costs east Ukrainians were unwilling to bear, and the latter was unacceptable to west Ukrainians because of their interpretation of Ukrainian national identity. Domestic politics therefore undermined what might have been Ukraine's economic nationalism.

In sum, post-Soviet politics were full of ironies. Although the dominant *nationalisms* (specific proposals for the content of national identity) that emerged in these three states were similar, their *national identities* (the collective meanings ascribed to nations by societies) turned out to be quite different. What seemed rational in one sociopolitical context was sometimes the opposite of what seemed rational in another context. Some former Communists turned into nationalists; many nationalists espoused traditional political and economic liberalism. Other former Communists were conservative and avoided change but claimed to be liberal and rational because they cooperated with Russia, although those cooperative relations were based primarily on nonmarket transactions. These were curious politics at work.

COMPETING THEORETICAL EXPLANATIONS
DERIVED FROM LIBERALISM AND REALISM

The two most prominent theoretical traditions in IR and IPE are Realism and Liberalism, and they offer different basic views of how the world economy works. Theories derived in the Realist tradition describe a world economy composed of self-interested, rational states.[16] The lack of supranational authority—anarchy—means that states must ensure their own security from military and economic coercion. Realists tend to assume that states prefer economic autonomy, seek to maintain their relative position in the world economy, and as a result, struggle over the distribution of the

[16] See Jonathan Kirshner, "The Political Economy of Realism," in *Unipolar Politics: Realism and State Strategies after the Cold War*, ed. Ethan Kapstein and Michael Mastanduno (New York: Columbia University Press, 1999). For classic works of Realist political economy, see Stephen D. Krasner, *Defending the National Interest* (Princeton: Princeton University Press, 1978); and Robert Gilpin, *U.S. Power and the Multinational Corporation* (New York: Basic Books, 1975).

gains from economic cooperation. Cooperation therefore is elusive, an ephemeral outcome of material configurations. In the Realist tradition the distribution of material power among states is the most important influence on the politics, both cooperative and conflictual, of their trade and monetary relations.

In the Liberal tradition international cooperation is understood to be mutually beneficial exchange.[17] Economic incentives, rather than anarchy and power, affect prospects for cooperation and discord among states. The interests of individuals and firms play an important role in Liberal theories, which therefore focus on the variable material consequences of foreign economic policies. Where Realists emphasize means, Liberals focus on incentives.

Almost all accounts of economic cooperation and discord in the former Soviet Union have relied on the fundamental assumptions of either Realism or Liberalism, even if implicitly, in formulating their expectations for the behavior of post-Soviet governments. Several types of expectations were, or could have been, derived from these theoretical perspectives.

Two Liberal Approaches to Eurasia's Political Economy: Incentives and Institutions

Two specific variants of Liberal IR theory apply to the political economy of post-Soviet international relations. Both focus on material incentives. The first, more traditional version of Liberal political economy argues that domestic economic actors with different material interests shape foreign economic policies.[18] The second, neo-Liberal institutionalism, emphasizes that international institutions make cooperation easier to achieve by reducing transaction costs.[19] Both variants of Liberal political economy suggest that in the short and medium run, material interests would push post-Soviet states toward economic cooperation, possibly even reintegration. Post-Soviet states' interdependence would cause them to cooperate, domestic economic actors would lobby for regional reintegration, and CIS institutions would help organize the region's production and exchange. Both Liberal theories seem to fit the Belarusian case.[20]

[17] A classic work in the Liberal tradition of IPE is Robert O. Keohane and Joseph S. Nye, *Power and Interdependence*, 2d ed. (New York: HarperCollins, 1989). A recent reformulation of Liberal theory can be found in Andrew Moravcsik, *The Choice for Europe: Social Purpose and State Power from Messina to Maastricht* (Ithaca: Cornell University Press, 1998).

[18] See Jeffry A. Frieden and Ronald Rogowski, "The Impact of the International Economy on National Policies: An Analytical Overview," in *Internationalization and Domestic Politics*, ed. Robert O. Keohane and Helen V. Milner (Cambridge: Cambridge University Press, 1996).

[19] See Robert O. Keohane, *After Hegemony* (Princeton: Princeton University Press, 1984).

[20] Except, of course, for the fact that economic relations between Russia and Belarus were not primarily market-based, as described by classical Liberal theories of political

Many characteristics of post-Soviet political economy, however, are inconsistent with the behavior predicted by Liberal theories. Liberal theories cannot explain why numerous post-Soviet states politicized regional cooperation with concerns about autonomy and security from Russia rather than interpreted their economic relations as mutually beneficial exchange. This politicization led to a failure of CIS reintegration and multilateral economic cooperation. Neo-Liberal institutional theory cannot explain why all this occurred in one of the most densely institutionalized and economically interdependent regional systems in the world.

Moreover, material interests did not pull all the post-Soviet states back to Russia.[21] Contrary to traditional Liberal political economy, there was little variation in the preferences of domestic interest groups: nearly all organized economic actors, and especially the powerful industrial lobbies, throughout the former Soviet Union preferred regional cooperation and reintegration.[22] It is true that some suppliers of raw materials and metals preferred to sell their goods on world markets for higher prices. But no organized economic actors preferred a rapid and drastic reorientation of trade to the West and the disintegration of the post-Soviet regional economy. Post-Soviet states' manufactured goods were largely uncompetitive outside post-Soviet markets, as were most of their agricultural products, which faced the additional hurdle of agricultural protectionism in the EU and around the world. Thus, it was not the lobbying of distributional coalitions that led to the variety of post-Soviet foreign economic policies. Those coalitions actually wanted regional reintegration.

There were other material incentives to cooperate with Russia as well. At the time that Lithuania, Ukraine, and Belarus chose their economic strategies, Russia was still giving them enormous energy and raw materials subsidies, some 60 to 70 percent below world prices. As political scientist Matthew Evangelista concludes, "It is hard to argue that the policies of the republics in trying to break away from Moscow were driven strictly by pursuit of economic utility. Virtually all of them stood to lose."[23]

---

economy. The Belarusian economy was one of the least reformed in the region. Therefore, the consistency of Belarusian behavior with Liberalism is limited to Liberal approaches to IPE, which focus on economic relations among states rather than within them.

[21] On problems of applying sectoral and coalitional approaches to post-Soviet political economy, see Matthew Evangelista, "Stalin's Revenge: Institutional Barriers to Internationalization in the Soviet Union," in *Internationalization and Domestic Politics*, ed. Keohane and Milner; and Evangelista, "From Each According to Its Abilities: Competing Theoretical Approaches to the Post-Soviet Energy Sector," in *The Sources of Russian Foreign Policy after the Cold War*, ed. Celeste Wallander (Boulder, Colo.: Westview, 1996).

[22] On the preferences for reintegration of the organized economic actors and lobbies in each post-Soviet state, see the longer discussion in chapter 3 of this book.

[23] Evangelista, "Each According to Its Abilities," 183–84. See also Evangelista, "Stalin's Revenge," 175–85.

Two Realist Approaches to Eurasia's Political Economy:
Power Politics and International Opportunities

The Realist tradition of political economy also offers two ways to analyze the behavior of post-Soviet governments, and they have a common weakness: both are indeterminate. The most general Realist expectation for the post-Soviet regional economy was that some post-Soviet states would, at a minimum, seek economic autonomy from Russia. This pursuit of autonomy would likely lead to the following outcomes: cooperation would be difficult, regional reintegration would be impossible, and some states, alone or in concert, would balance against Russian power. In this Realist account post-Soviet states should have interpreted economic dependence on Russia as a security threat and acted accordingly. Not all post-Soviet governments interpreted economic dependence on Russia this way, however.

This observation leads to the second Realist expectation: instead of balancing against Russian hegemony and seeking autonomy, those post-Soviet states that either lacked available allies or sought to change the status quo might choose to bandwagon with Russia—in other words, to ally with Russia and acquiesce in its regional dominance.[24] Perhaps, this other Realist logic would suggest, Belarus allied closely with Russia because it was unsatisfied with the original post–cold war settlement in Eurasia or lacked alternate allies.

The indeterminacy of Realist approaches to post-Soviet political economy is demonstrated by comparing the experiences of Belarus and Lithuania. It is not merely that material variables cannot account for their differences; these variables projected completely different patterns of international relations. In late 1991, as both states emerged from the collapsed USSR, Belarus was larger than Lithuania, richer, stronger militarily, and even had nuclear weapons (Table 1.1). A pure power perspective would suggest that Belarus was in a better position to seek autonomy. Yet it was Belarus that acquiesced and reintegrated with Russia and the CIS.

Moreover, Belarus was not a revisionist state "bandwagoning for profit"[25] but the quintessential status quo state in Eurasia. Realist theories of bandwagoning suggest that vulnerable states might ally with threatening states out of necessity, even though, like all states, they would prefer autonomy. But the Belarusian government did not seem to want autonomy from Russia, for it did not interpret Russia as a threat. Belarusians did not pursue economic reintegration out of fear. The logic of Belarusian behavior thus is better described by Liberal theories of cooperation than by Realist theories of bandwagoning.

[24] Stephen M. Walt, *The Origins of Alliances* (Ithaca: Cornell University Press, 1987).

[25] Randall L. Schweller, "Bandwagoning for Profit: Bringing the Revisionist State Back In," *International Security* 19, 1 (1994): 72–107.

A second argument informed by Realist theory is that post-Soviet states chose their policies on the basis of the international opportunities available to them. But the availability of allies and alternate trade partners also did not determine these governments' foreign policy choices. In particular, support from the EU, or the West more broadly, did not lead Lithuania to break with Russia, nor did a lack of support force Belarus into reintegration. The EU's reactions to these new states were primarily a result of post-Soviet governments' policies, not their cause. Lithuanians announced their "return to Europe" immediately on independence. Belarusians committed their state and economy to Russia, the CIS, and "Eurasia" almost as quickly and insistently, and by 1995 the government had institutionalized economic reintegration with Russia. Belarus alienated the West, Lithuania alienated the East, and the results in retrospect take on a patina of inevitability. But they were not inevitable at all. The nationalists in each country proposed whole packages of policies (Western orientation, economic reform, and democratization) that were accepted or rejected in their entirety by their societies. Post-Soviet societies' and states' relative compatibility with European norms was a result of the historical and institutional forces that shaped their national identities, which in turn led to their different post-Soviet trajectories. Thus, these different international opportunities resulted from the historical differences that also led to their different domestic, national purposes.

The support of the West can hardly have caused Lithuania's reorientation because that support was not at all substantial. No one in the EU assured Lithuania of membership. Indeed, no one had by the year 2000. Formally, all Lithuania has to show for its efforts to reorient toward the EU is a free trade agreement and associate member status. Lithuania had no Western security guarantees that kept it outside Russia's sphere of influence, and NATO membership also seemed a long way off. More important, Lithuania's rejection of the CIS and the Eurasian economic space was not conditional on the acceptance of the West. There is probably nothing Western states could have done to dissuade Lithuanians from their attempt to achieve autonomy from Russia. And the EU could have done little to strengthen the position of the Belarusian nationalists within Belarusian society. No doubt a more accommodating EU policy would have altered Ukrainian and Belarusian political debates on the margins, and the interest that several EU states showed in Lithuania's future reinforced the government's Westward turn. But the opportunities presented by the EU clearly were not the decisive influences on the trajectories these countries chose in 1991. Their motives were much more important.

Realist theories have an even more difficult task explaining Ukraine, the regional power whose behavior should have conformed most to the expectations of Realist theory. A large state with significant military capabilities and economic potential, Ukraine was second only to Russia in material indicators of power in the region. Yet Ukraine did not balance against Russia. This fact means that no regional balance to Russian power emerged in the 1990s. Remarkably, the Ukrainian government, under pressure from the West but without receiving any external security guarantees, handed over its nuclear weapons to Russia, the only state in the region that it interpreted as a possible military threat, a move thought unlikely by Realist scholars.[26]

Ukraine, like Lithuania, initially pursued a policy of radical economic autonomy from Russia—what Realist theorists would have expected. But the Ukrainian government did not sustain its attempt to reorient the economy Westward.[27] Ukraine's nationalist movement and parties wanted to continue the policies of autonomy, but the rest of Ukraine's society did not. The government's grudging acceptance of close cooperation with Russia resulted from a significant reversal of Ukraine's foreign economic policy in 1992–93, a turnaround caused by divisions between the western and eastern halves of the country. In Realist logic, states do not have to respond to domestic divisions within society, but the Ukrainian government did.

In sum, Lithuania's policy of economic autonomy from Russia seemed to follow some Realist expectations, although its interpretation of the EU was consistent with Liberalism. Belarus's policy of economic reintegration with Russia seemed to follow all Liberal expectations. And Ukraine's incoherent middle course was an anomaly for both theoretical perspectives. Rather than assume state preferences, as Realist theories do, or deduce the preferences of individuals, firms, and states, as Liberal theories do, an alternate approach must explain why post-Soviet governments interpreted similar economic circumstances and prospects in such different ways.

A NATIONALIST PERSPECTIVE ON INTERNATIONAL POLITICAL ECONOMY

There can be little doubt that national identities affect the economic relations among states. A distinctively Nationalist perspective on IPE is useful to describe the influence on the world economy of national identities in general, especially their influence on the preferences and interpretations of governments. A Nationalist perspective shares with other perspectives on IPE the idea that the world economy is inherently political. But this is

[26] John J. Mearsheimer, "The Case for a Ukrainian Nuclear Deterrent," *Foreign Affairs* 72, 3 (1993): 50–66.

[27] Paul D'Anieri, "Dilemmas of Interdependence: Autonomy, Prosperity, and Sovereignty in Ukraine's Russia Policy," *Problems of Post-Communism* 44, 1 (1997): 16–26, at 21–22.

a certain kind of politicization of economic relations that is impossible to understand with Realist or Liberal theories of IPE: not Realist power, not Liberal institutions or material interests, but a specific kind of cultural identity based on the idea of the nation.[28] The economic relations among states are politicized by societies' debates about the meaning of their nations and the purposes of their states. The material facts of the world economy are important, of course, but they are only part of the story. The social facts of the world economy, national identities among them, are just as important for understanding the behavior of governments.

The articulation of a Nationalist perspective is not a simple theoretical task. A Nationalist perspective necessarily challenges the materialism of mainstream theories of IPE by emphasizing the causal power of constructed national identities. Such an approach deals with variables that are relatively difficult to study and observe. This makes it important to identify reliable indicators of the content and contestation of a national identity and to keep them separate from measurements of governments' preferences and strategies.[29]

A second challenge is presented by the history and existing terminology of IPE scholarship. The field already has something called the "Nationalist perspective," presented by political scientist Robert Gilpin in his *Political Economy of International Relations,* one of the most influential works of IPE of the past several decades.[30] What Gilpin calls the Nationalist perspective, however, is actually a thorough restatement of the Realist perspective. It emphasizes states motivated by their concerns for autonomy and power. In other words, there is no nationalism in it. Instead, there is statism—a description of the state as an actor with interests distinct from society's. Many Realist scholars, following Gilpin, have assumed that their tradition subsumes the Nationalist tradition and that nationalism's effects on economic relations are best understood as reasons of state rather than reasons of nation.

Nationalism is not the same as statism, however. In the study of IPE, economic nationalism and economic statism must be construed as distinct concepts, for they refer to distinct theoretical approaches and empirical phenomena. A putative nation is a population. A state is a set of political in-

---

[28] On the influence of cultural norms on international relations, see especially Peter J. Katzenstein, *Cultural Norms and National Security* (Ithaca: Cornell University Press, 1996); and Katzenstein, "Introduction: Alternative Perspectives on National Security," in *The Culture of National Security,* ed. Katzenstein (New York: Columbia University Press, 1996).

[29] In other words, it is necessary to keep the assessment of the explanatory variable (national identity) separate from assessments of the intervening and dependent variables (respectively, government preferences and government strategies). On this issue, see chapter 2 of this book.

[30] Robert Gilpin, *The Political Economy of International Relations* (Princeton: Princeton University Press, 1987), especially 31–34 and 41–54.

stitutions. Nationalism is an expression of a societal identity. Statism, as understood by Realists, is an expression of an autonomous state. In the Realist perspective there is no constituting "other," defined by identity; there is no domestic societal politics; no social purpose; and no historical memory. These crucial elements are essential characteristics of nationalism.

Ultimately, then, the main difference between the Realist and Nationalist traditions in IPE rests in two contrasting interpretations of the state. The Realist state is self-interested, but the Nationalist state is much more. Most important, it is purposive: nationalists do not merely aspire to statehood, and they do not seek to build state power for its own sake. Rather, nationalists have specific ideas about how and for whom the state should be governed. A government motivated by nationalism acts on behalf of its society, not on behalf of itself. Thus, as the historian E. H. Carr once suggested, economic nationalism and mercantilism are different: economic nationalism is social whereas mercantilism is statist.[31]

Building on the insight of Carr and the thought of Friedrich List, I distinguish the Nationalist from the Realist tradition in IPE, for which it has lately been mistaken. I go further than merely rehabilitating the Nationalist tradition, however. My broader goal is a more general theoretical perspective based on the ideas introduced in this chapter. National identities are social constructions that vary in their content and contestation. Nationalisms are proposals about purpose, sacrifice, the future, and the direction of policy—proposals that vary across time and political space.[32]

THE REST OF THE ARGUMENT IN BRIEF

In chapter 2 I take up this task and outline the Nationalist perspective more fully, comparing it with the Realist and Liberal perspectives and also with the Institutionalist perspective, an emerging constructivist approach to IPE that focuses on state identities, norms, and international society. One important conclusion emerges from the overlap between rationalist and constructivist accounts of economic policy making. In many cases it is not helpful to distinguish between ostensibly objective material interests and social identities as conceptual categories that necessarily compete for causal priority in social science. I do not argue that national identities trump material interests. Rather, national identities affect how governments interpret their material interests. The cultural contexts within which

---

[31] E. H. Carr, *Nationalism and After* (London: Macmillan, 1945), especially 5–6 and 22–23.
[32] See especially Valerie Bunce, *Subversive Institutions: The Design and Destruction of Socialism and the State* (Cambridge: Cambridge University Press, 1999), 12–13 and 147–51.

politicians are embedded define their best course of action; those cultural contexts vary; and therefore, variation in policies frequently results from cultural differences. In other words, the cultural contexts in which political elites sit affect the political positions where they stand. Thus, a Nationalist perspective on IPE applies even to states that do not seem very "nationalist." It applies to states such as Belarus because it explores the variety of national identities, including those that are ambiguous and contested, not just the coherent and consensual ones of the Lithuanian type.

In chapter 3 I offer a broad assessment of patterns of cooperation and discord in the post-Soviet regional economy, focusing on two key issues: money and trade. I explore the politics of the collapse of the so-called ruble zone and the failure of post-Soviet states to cooperate in their trade relations with one another. I also outline the theoretical issues at stake in explaining the variety of post-Soviet economic strategies.

Next I articulate the argument in detail for the three main case studies: Lithuania (chapter 4), Ukraine (chapter 5), and Belarus (chapter 6). These chapters are based on evidence about the content of societal debates drawn from newspapers and the platforms of dominant political parties, as well as from interviews with policy makers at these states' Ministries of Foreign Affairs, central banks, and presidential administrations and with politicians of their nationalist and formerly Communist political parties. These case studies illustrate that Lithuanian, Ukrainian, and Belarusian societies had contrasting understandings of their national identities, which influenced their interpretations of their foreign economic relations.

These chapters also demonstrate that many of the differences among post-Soviet national identities predated the fall of the Soviet Union and reflected divergent historical, institutional, and cultural experiences. It is not the case that Lithuanians have "always" hated the Russians or that Ukrainians and Belarusians have closer relations with Russia because they are all "Slavs." But it is true that their societal identities are both historical outcomes and ongoing processes, and constructivist theory offers us a way to analyze how the historical memories of these societies varied. It is important therefore to specify the moments in history when certain ideas of the nation became institutionalized and politically ascendant: nations, and their meanings, are not timeless.

The expansion of Russian and later Soviet authority across the territories of the Soviet Union varied along several dimensions. One dimension was time. Some territories, such as eastern Ukraine and most of Belarus, were incorporated into the tsarist empire centuries before others and became part of the Soviet Union. Some, such as the Baltic republics, had been part of tsarist Russia, then were independent states during the interwar years, and were later annexed by the Soviet Union. And still other territories, such as several western provinces of Ukraine, had never been part of any Russian empire until Soviet authorities incorporated them after World War II.[33]

The other important variable dimension of state authority was the pattern of control exercised on the Soviet Union's constituent societies. Political scientist David Laitin has demonstrated that three patterns of state control influenced the national identities of Soviet, and later post-Soviet, societies.[34] Although Laitin is primarily interested in explaining the integration of Russian-speaking populations into the societies of Soviet successor states, his distinction among types of elite incorporation also accounts for a wide range of variation in the timing and depth of nationalist mobilization before the collapse of the Soviet Union.[35] Thus, my empirical chapters trace the influence of these societies' divergent historical experiences on their identities and, ultimately, the economic choices they made much later.

After the case studies in chapters 4–6, in chapter 7 I apply the Nationalist framework to several other sets of historical experiences involving the reorganization of economic relations among successor states of empires: interwar east-central Europe after the collapse of the Habsburg empire, 1950s Indonesia after the collapse of the Dutch empire, and 1960s French West Africa after the collapse of the French empire. These historical comparisons generalize the theoretical arguments of the book for a better understanding of both economic nationalism and postimperial politics.

In the concluding chapter I address several broad theoretical and empirical issues, such as the conditions under which it is most useful to adopt a theoretical framework based on national identities. In IR it is common to hear scholars claim that the Realist and Liberal perspectives are necessarily in contest for theoretical superiority or analytical priority, and the conditions under which it is appropriate to adopt them are presumed to be universal. In contrast, as a theoretical perspective on IPE, the Nation-

---

[33] Roman Szporluk, "The Soviet West—or Far Eastern Europe?" *East European Politics and Societies* 5, 3 (1991): 466–82.

[34] Laitin, *Identity in Formation*, chaps. 2 and 3. For other historically informed typologies of post-Soviet national identities, see John A. Armstrong, "The Ethnic Scene in the Soviet Union," in *Ethnic Minorities in the Soviet Union*, ed. Erich Goldhagen (New York: Praeger, 1968); and Ronald Grigor Suny, "Provisional Stabilities: The Politics of Identities in Post-Soviet Eurasia," *International Security* 24, 3 (1999–2000): 139–78.

[35] The correlation is not perfect, however, and one of the case studies presented here, Belarus, is an exception. According to Laitin's model, Belarus and Ukraine should be more similar than they are. The politics of Belarusian and Ukrainian national identity are quite different: Ukrainian national identity is contested regionally whereas Belarusian identity is not. This reflects the fact that, as noted in Laitin, *Identity in Formation*, 65, western Ukraine was not ruled according to the "most-favored-lord" model but was incorporated more in the manner of the "integral" style applied by Soviet authorities to the Baltic republics. Although this regional variation is not crucial for the domestic political outcomes Laitin analyzes, it affected the foreign economic policies of Ukraine.

alist approach describes how one important variable—national identity—affects the economic relations among states.

National identities are underlying cultural factors in politics that, by framing societal debates, rule out certain foreign policy possibilities and privilege others. National identities always matter, even when they appear to be only the cultural backgrounds of politics that seem to be taken for granted. I do not conclude that a Nationalist perspective is necessary to answer all the important empirical questions of world politics. Although the appropriate domain is large, it is certainly not complete. National identity is only one among a number of other important influences on international political and economic outcomes.

Sometimes, however, national identities do matter most. There are contexts of world politics in which national identities are decisive influences on the economic relations among states. Postimperial politics are such a context. There is an inductive as well as deductive basis for this finding since nationalisms rise as empires fall and new states necessarily have fluid identities. This book provides abundant empirical evidence for the general deductive propositions.

I conclude with a reflection on the extent of applicability of the Nationalist perspective and suggest that national identities are likely to be most influential at other moments when state identities are in flux. These moments include, but are certainly not limited to, the postimperial moments that filled the twentieth century. The 1920s were a fundamental turning point in the history of central and eastern Europe, the 1950s for east and south Asia, the 1960s for Africa, and the 1990s for Eurasia. Nationalism was a central influence on the choices that governments in each of these regions had to make.

CHAPTER TWO

A Nationalist Perspective
on International Political Economy

How do national identities affect the economic relations among states? The answer to this question should be based on a theoretically sound and empirically useful conception of nations, nationalisms, and national identities. A rich scholarly literature on nationalism concludes that nations are modern and invented rather than timeless and primordial.[1] Nations are symbols, reifications of a society's collective identity. A nation is a cultural construct, with meanings ascribed to it by those who consider themselves members of a *national* community.[2]

National identities exist at two levels: the individual and the collective. At the level of the individual, national identities are *subjective* interpretations of membership in the nation. An individual's national identity is a matter of both choice and ascription. At the level of the collective, of a society, national identities are *shared* interpretations of the meaning of the nation. A society's national identity is a matter of social construction since

[1] See Karl W. Deutsch, *Nationalism and Social Communication*, 2d ed. (Cambridge: MIT Press, 1966); Ernest Gellner, *Nations and Nationalism* (Ithaca: Cornell University Press, 1981); E. J. Hobsbawm, *Nations and Nationalism since 1780*, 2d ed. (Cambridge: Cambridge University Press, 1992); and Benedict Anderson, *Imagined Communities: Reflections on the Origins and Spread of Nationalism*, rev. ed. (London: Verso, 1991).

[2] As Rogers Brubaker puts it, we should understand the nation "not as substance but as institutionalized form; not as collectivity but as practical category; not as entity but as contingent event." See his "Rethinking Nationhood: Nation as Institutionalized Form, Practical Category, Contingent Event," in his *Nationalism Reframed: Nationhood and the National Question in the New Europe* (Cambridge: Cambridge University Press, 1996). On the nation as symbol, see Katherine Verdery, "Whither 'Nation' and 'Nationalism'?" *Daedalus* 122, 3 (1993): 37–46.

almost everyone must be involved in determining collective meaning.[3] This makes national identities objective social facts that individuals cannot change by themselves. They are real in the sense that people often take nations as given, even if they sometimes refuse to take the meaning of their nations as given.

The fact that national identities are collectively interpreted creates the possibility that individuals will associate different meanings with the same national symbol. In this book I focus on the effects of national identities at the collective level, of societies' collective interpretations of their specifically national identities. Thus, national identity, as it is used here, is a collective identity shared among a population and defined by historical memory and cultural symbols, the most important of which is the "nation." Many national identities are also connected to language and religion. National identities, then, are social facts that achieve power because societies collectively believe them. When societies think they are nations, they are.

Nationalism is the use of the symbol of the nation for specific political, economic, and cultural purposes; it is the nation connected to a project. As Valerie Bunce argues, the projects and goals of different nationalists and, therefore, of different nationalisms vary quite dramatically across time and political space.[4] Nationalisms are proposals for what the content of national identity should be. In other words, nationalisms are attempts to ascribe political, economic, and cultural meanings to societies' understandings of themselves.

Nationalists, then, are societal actors who propose the nation's most important goals. They have fundamental goals for the states they seek to create or govern. They suggest who the members of the nation are and how they will be affected by different policies. Nationalists link the past to the future with arguments about historical destiny. Nationalists also identify the most likely threats to their goals.

THE CONTENT OF NATIONAL IDENTITIES

National identities vary—from society to society and over time—in two primary ways: in their content and contestation. National identity has content: self-understandings and goals that are cultural, political, and eco-

---

[3] On national identities at the levels of individuals and collectives, see David D. Laitin, *Identity in Formation* (Ithaca: Cornell University Press, 1998); and Verdery, "Whither 'Nation' and 'Nationalism'?" 40. Another common way to describe individual and collective identities is to say that the former are subjective whereas the latter are "intersubjective."

[4] Valerie Bunce, *Subversive Institutions: The Design and Destruction of Socialism and the State* (Cambridge: Cambridge University Press, 1999), 12–13 and 147–51. Verdery offers a

nomic.[5] The content of a national identity includes definitions of membership in the nation, the fundamental purposes of political authority, and the states that threaten those purposes.[6] This content thus specifies who the nation is, why the nation should be governed in a certain way, and who the nation is most emphatically not.

Many IR scholars have focused on the issue of membership, whether nationalisms propose ethnic or civic definitions of the nation and therefore whether national identities have ethnic or civic content.[7] In this common typology ethnic definitions of the nation focus on blood ties and ostensibly inherent attributes of individuals, whereas civic definitions focus on territory and place of birth. Arguably, the difference has implications for international politics: ethnic nationalisms are frequently thought to be more aggressive, more intractable, and therefore more problematic for peace and cooperation. In principle, this distinction and typology may be useful for understanding certain political problems caused by nationalism.

The ethnic-civic typology has serious limitations, however. A typology of nationalisms is not the same as a typology of national identities since the former are proposals for the content of the latter. A typology of national identities, therefore, would have to include the variability in the acceptance of particular nationalist ideas in a society, or the contestation of national identity (of which more later).[8]

The ethnic-civic typology of nationalisms is limited to two principles of membership. The content of national identities, however, is both more variable and more consequential than has generally been acknowledged in IR theory, because content includes specific national purposes and goals as well as threats. More than just membership is at stake in the construction and definition of national identities. A typology of national identities is not likely to be useful for explaining many political outcomes because

---

similar description of nationalism in "Whither 'Nation' and 'Nationalism'?" at 38, where she argues that nationalism is also the sentiment that leads people to respond to the use of the symbol of the nation.

[5] On the importance of the content of national identities, see Roman Szporluk, *Communism and Nationalism: Karl Marx versus Friedrich List* (New York: Oxford University Press, 1988), 164 and chap. 6; and Paul D'Anieri, "Nationalism and International Politics: Identity and Sovereignty in the Russian-Ukrainian Conflict," *Nationalism and Ethnic Politics* 3, 2 (1997): 1–28.

[6] See especially Ernst Haas, *The Rise and Decline of Nationalism* (Ithaca: Cornell University Press, 1997), 45.

[7] This is the most common typology. For thoughtful reviews of the typology and its relation to IR, see Charles A. Kupchan, "Introduction: Nationalism Resurgent," in *Nationalism and Nationalities in the New Europe*, ed. Kupchan (Ithaca: Cornell University Press, 1995); and Jack Snyder, "Nationalism and the Crisis of the Post-Soviet State," *Survival* 35, 1 (1993): 5–26.

[8] For another critique of typologies of nationalisms with similar reasoning, see Stanley Hoffman, "Nationalism and World Order," in his *World Disorders* (Lanham, Md.: Rowman and Littlefield, 1998), 203.

the content of a national identity is historically contingent, contextually specific, multifaceted, and contested.

The content of national identity is inherently relational because nationalist movements arise in interaction with (and frequently in opposition to) other nationalisms and states in the international system. The content of a national identity thus includes at least one direction, a state or nation against which identity is defined. Nations are frequently imagined to have at least one "other," external to the state, in addition to less significant "others" within and without. At the same time, however, the content of a national identity may include an affinity for another, broader cultural identity. Thus, there is often a two-way (anti- and pro-) direction of national identity.

THE CONTESTATION OF NATIONAL IDENTITIES

Who decides the content of national identity? Every society has nationalists who attempt to link the symbol of the nation to specific goals, to define the content of their society's collective identity. Not everyone in a society always agrees with how specific nationalists seek to construct their identity, however. Sometimes the nationalists cannot even agree among themselves, and there are competing nationalisms within a society. Nationalists can only offer proposals for the content of societal identity; they cannot dictate the content.

National identities also therefore vary in their contestation. Specific interpretations of the goals of the nation are sometimes widely shared in a society and sometimes less widely shared. The further apart the contending interpretations of national identity, the more that identity is fragmented into conflicting and potentially inconsistent understandings of what the goals of the nation should be.[9] Thus, the variable of contestation describes whether the rest of a society agrees (and how it disagrees) with its nationalists as well as whether the nationalists agree among themselves. The contestation of national identities is a social process, which also varies over time and across political space. Like content, the contestation variable is contextually specific, which means that it is more than a matter of degree. A useful description of contestation requires other adjectives, in addition to "high" or "low."

There are limits to what societal actors can claim to pursue in the name of the nation, and those limits exist in society itself. The symbol of the nation is not infinitely malleable in practice, even if it can potentially be linked to a wide variety of political, economic, and cultural projects. Na-

[9] In the language of Karl Deutsch, highly contested national identities reflect complete modernization but incomplete assimilation. See Deutsch, *Nationalism and Social Communication*; and Haas, *Rise and Decline of Nationalism*, 31–34.

tionalist policy proposals must seem plausible to the rest of society. They must fit with prevailing constructions of historical memory. In some societies and at some moments in history nationalists' specific ideas resonate, achieve widespread support, and are converted into policy. In other societies or at other times they do not. Political scientist Mark Beissinger's metaphor succinctly captures the contestation of national identity: many nationalisms bark, but only some bite.[10] Nationalists' ideas are powerless unless they are valorized.

NATIONALISMS, NATIONAL IDENTITIES, AND POLITICS

It is possible to draw several general conclusions about how nationalisms and national identities affect political outcomes. First, nationalisms can affect politics in two ways. A specific group of nationalists might itself simply make policies, if it is able to rule a state, either democratically or undemocratically. In this first instance it is not necessary to evaluate the collective identity of the society in order to understand how these nationalists pursue their political-economic goals. Rather, it is sufficient to evaluate the substantive ideology of the nationalists.

Alternately, nationalists may influence the politics of a state more indirectly by successfully proposing the content of their society's national identity. Their ideas might become popular and widespread even if the original nationalists themselves are not in charge. In this instance nationalisms frame policy debates, and the content of national identity can be described as coherent and consensual. Thus, sometimes societies enjoy consensus on the meaning and purpose of their nations.

When national identity is not consensual, it is important to describe both how much and how it is contested in order to understand the consequences for politics. For example, a national identity may be highly contested, in the sense that there are several competing nationalisms, none predominant, with the result that societal actors actively disagree among themselves about the content of national identity. Also, a national identity may be ambiguous if no nationalism becomes dominant and other cultural identities frame policy debates.[11] When the national identity of a society is highly contested or ambiguous, little sense of national purpose motivates the politics of a state. And in the absence of national purpose, governments are likely to fall back on what appear to be Liberal goals—the maximization of societal wealth and consumption. That is, governments may ascribe any number of purposes to

[10] Mark Beissinger, "Nationalisms That Bark and Nationalisms That Bite," in *The State of the Nation*, ed. John A. Hall (Cambridge: Cambridge University Press, 1998).

[11] These alternate identities can be broader or narrower than specifically national identities.

their societies' economic activity, as well as various meanings to their economic relations with other states. But when there are no agreed-on purposes or meanings, economic activity appears to be purely material rather than implicating social goals. Thus, in the absence of an externally defined threat to social purposes, governments generally interpret economic relations with other states as mutually beneficial exchange. Nationalists, of course, seek wealth and consumption, but those goals are linked, and sometimes subordinate, to the cultivation and protection of the nation.

NATIONALISMS, NATIONAL IDENTITIES, AND IR THEORY

These conclusions suggest two broad revisions to how IR scholarship treats nationalisms and national identities. First, IR theories that focus on the influence of nationalism should explicitly acknowledge the variability of nationalists' projects. IR scholars have focused primarily, and perhaps to a fault, on the problem of the intensity of nationalism. To wit, the consequences of "hypernationalism" in eastern Europe dominated an important debate about stability after the cold war.[12] The more "intense" a nationalism is, the bigger the problem for international stability, so the argument has generally been made.

A nationalism's intensity, as a conceptual variable, is ambiguous, however. There are three possible meanings. Intensity might mean the intensity of feeling among a population.[13] This idea is more easily understood by assessing the contestation of a national identity; it is a matter of societal agreement and disagreement. Or intensity might mean the extremity of the ideas in nationalism, and this is probably the most common interpretation of so-called hypernationalism. But such extremity is more simply understood as variability in nationalisms' goals in relation to other states. Third, scholars might mean intensity in the policy of a state. But that is what we are trying to explain in the first place, so this conception confuses the intensity of nationalist feelings among a population with the intensity of expression of nationalist ideas in the policy of a state.

Moreover, an emphasis on the amount of nationalism is not useful for understanding how the same nationalism can cause conflict with some states and cooperation with others. More broadly, some nationalisms are destabilizing for international politics, others are not, and it is impossible

---

[12] For contrasting interpretations, see John J. Mearsheimer, "Back to the Future: Instability in Europe after the Cold War," *International Security* 15, 1 (1990): 5–56; and Stephen van Evera, "Primed for Peace: Europe after the Cold War," *International Security* 15, 3 (1990–91): 7–57.

[13] This is how Kupchan describes the intensity of nationalism in his "Nationalism Resurgent."

to tell which is which without evaluating their specific proposals and their reception in society. In actual political and historical experience a nationalism's meaning has almost always been more consequential than its "intensity." This is contrary to the standard IR question about nationalism: How much? The more useful question to ask therefore is, What kind of nationalism? Or alternatively, Which nationalism?

This context-specific variability means that IR theories based on the concept of national identity (and, therefore, nationalism) should be constructivist simply because, as empirical phenomena, national identities are socially and politically constructed. Otherwise, with rationalist approaches to nationalism, too many of nationalism's effects on world politics go unobserved and unanalyzed. Nationalisms and national identities are ideas made powerful by people sharing them; they are social facts that societies take for granted but whose meaning varies from place to place and over time. As Katherine Verdery argues, many scholars have assumed that "just because something we call 'nationalism' occurs in many places, it is the same phenomenon in all of them—that similarity of form implies similarity of both content and cause. Social scientists often lump together 'nationalisms' that are quite different."[14]

Another revision to IR scholarship involves the expansion of constructivist theorizing to include domestically constructed societal identities and their consequences for economic policy. Constructivist IR theory has posed a challenge to the rationalist and materialist theories that dominate the field.[15] To date, however, it has focused more on international society and state identities than on domestic societies and national identities.[16] Although constructivists have generally sought to demonstrate the impor-

[14] Katherine Verdery, "Nationalism and National Sentiment in Post-Socialist Romania," *Slavic Review* 52, 2 (1993): 179–203, at 202.
[15] The IR literature informed by constructivism is quite rich. Good starting points are Peter J. Katzenstein, ed., *The Culture of National Security* (New York: Columbia University Press, 1996); and Alexander Wendt, *Social Theory of International Politics* (Cambridge: Cambridge University Press, 1999). For reviews, see Emanuel Adler, "Seizing the Middle Ground: Constructivism in World Politics," *European Journal of International Relations* 3, 3 (1997): 319–63; Ted Hopf, "The Promise of Constructivism in IR Theory," *International Security* 23, 1 (1998): 171–200; Jeffrey T. Checkel, "The Constructivist Turn in International Relations Theory," *World Politics* 50, 2 (1998): 324–48; and Richard M. Price and Christian Reus-Smit, "Dangerous Liaisons? Critical International Theory and Constructivism," *European Journal of International Relations* 4, 3 (1998): 259–94. For a philosophical discussion that is particularly clear, see John R. Searle, *The Construction of Social Reality* (New York: Free Press, 1995).
[16] Several prominent exceptions are Peter J. Katzenstein, *Cultural Norms and National Security* (Ithaca: Cornell University Press, 1996); and Elizabeth Kier, "Culture and French Military Doctrine before World War II"; Alastair Iain Johnston, "Cultural Realism and Strategy in Maoist China"; Thomas U. Berger, "Norms, Identity, and National Security in Germany and Japan"; and Michael N. Barnett, "Identity and Alliances in the Middle East," all in *Culture of National Security*, ed. Katzenstein.

tance of the identities of states, the long-standing academic consensus that national identities are social constructions has yet to be incorporated systematically into IR scholarship.

It is crucial to distinguish between national and state identities and their effects on world politics. States are political institutions. Putative nations refer to societies. State identities are informed by international norms, which specify how certain categories of states (for example, civilized states, European states, welfare states) are both regulated and constituted by the practical content of international society.[17] National identities are informed by domestic societies, whose identities refer to the population of a state rather than to the state itself. As Peter Katzenstein summarizes: "State identities are primarily external; they describe the actions of governments in a society of states. National identities are primarily internal; they describe the processes by which mass publics acquire, modify, and forget their collective identities."[18] As James Fearon puts it, state identities are role identities whereas national identities are type identities.[19] The study of how national identities affect world politics is therefore similar to the study of how domestic cultural norms affect politics: it is based on a historically informed inquiry into the causal and purposive beliefs embedded within a shared identity.[20]

NATIONALISMS, NATIONAL IDENTITIES, AND ECONOMICS

To sum up, it is clear that national identities have purposive content and that societies debate those purposes. Connected to those purposes is a society's interpretation of other states and putative nations, especially those that threaten the achievement of goals linked to the nation. Therefore, a key element of national identities, and nationalisms in general, is their directionality.

[17] See especially Alexander Wendt, "Collective Identity Formation and the International State," *American Political Science Review* 88, 2 (1994): 384–97. On international society and state identities and interests, see Martha Finnemore, *National Interests in International Society* (Ithaca: Cornell University Press, 1996). On international norms and state identities, see Audie Klotz, "Norms Reconstituting Interests: Global Racial Equality and U.S. Sanctions against South Africa," *International Organization* 49, 3 (1995): 451–78; Richard Price, "A Genealogy of the Chemical Weapons Taboo," *International Organization* 49, 1 (1995): 73–103; and Amy Gurowitz, "Mobilizing International Norms: Domestic Actors, Immigrants, and the Japanese State," *World Politics* 51, 3 (1999): 413–45.

[18] Peter J. Katzenstein, "United Germany in an Integrating Europe," in *Tamed Power: Germany in Europe*, ed. Katzenstein (Ithaca: Cornell University Press, 1997), 20.

[19] James Fearon, "What Is Identity (as We Now Use the Word)?" unpublished manuscript, Stanford University, November 1999.

[20] On cultures and cultural norms, see Katzenstein, *Cultural Norms and National Security*; Elizabeth Kier, *Imagining War: French and British Military Doctrines between the Wars* (Princeton:

Although nationalisms vary from society to society and over time, they consistently include proposals for certain styles of foreign economic policy. The directionality inherent in national identity engenders a direction for foreign economic policy. Nationalisms favor economic policies that emphasize separateness and autonomy from specific states in the international system; protectionism in trade is therefore a common consequence of nationalism.[21] But this "nationalist" protectionism usually has a direction, an orientation. Nationalism might lead to economic discord among states, as economists have long argued, but it is neither general nor random discord. Nationalism results in discord with *specific* states, and it may even lead to cooperation with other specific states.

A related issue is what societies are willing to do to achieve the goals proposed in their various nationalisms. A shared national identity makes a society more willing to bear the economic costs of pursuing the goals that compose the content of its identity. Thus, nationalism engenders sacrifices and lengthens the time horizons of a national community. These were insights of Friedrich List (1789–1846), the preeminent economic nationalist.[22]

In List's framework a shared national identity creates a national community—a nation.[23] The nation means much more than the collection of individual citizens of a state. The interests of the nation are "infinitely different" from the interests of individuals, if "each individual is to be regarded as existing for himself alone, and not in the character of the national community." The Adam Smith variety of Liberal political economy made the mistake, according to List, of assuming that individuals were "mere producers and consumers" who "do not concern themselves for the prosperity of future generations." The Liberals, List went on to say, assumed that individuals were forward-looking, but only for themselves, not for the nation. The individuals who populate the theories of Smith are decadent and selfish; "they trouble themselves little about the power, the honor, or

---

Princeton University Press, 1997); and Alastair Iain Johnston, *Cultural Realism: Strategic Culture and Grand Strategy in Chinese History* (Princeton: Princeton University Press, 1995).

[21] Similarly, nationalism tends to privilege monetary sovereignty.

[22] See Szporluk, *Communism and Nationalism*, especially chaps. 8, 9, and 10. Also see Keith Tribe, "*Die Vernunft des List*: National Economy and the Critique of Cosmopolitical Economy," in his *Strategies of Economic Order* (Cambridge: Cambridge University Press, 1995). In contrast to Szporluk and Tribe, a great deal of the secondary literature on List focuses on whether his, or other nationalists', or mercantilists' ideas about protectionism and economic development were correct or analytically coherent. This is beside the point, at least for the purposes of this book. The Nationalist tradition in IPE contains causal assumptions about economic development that may not be useful. I emphasize the descriptive and explanatory elements of the Nationalist tradition.

[23] Of course, List would be considered more primordialist (i.e., nations always exist) and essentialist (i.e., people are inherently members of their nations) in his conception of nations and national identities.

the glory of the nation." But according to List, members of a nation do not think it foolish to make present sacrifices for the benefit of future members of the nation. List's understanding of the state was also distinct from the traditional Liberal conception of the state's regulative role. The state was supposed to transform a mere "economy of the people" into a "national economy," to give the statewide economy national meaning.[24] The state, for List and other Nationalists, acts on behalf of the nation. The economic activity, production and commerce, that the state promotes is in the service of fundamental national purposes.

Following List's logic, nations—or societies with consensually shared national identities—can achieve these benefits of lengthened time horizons and political will for sacrifice. But contested and fragmented national identities do the opposite: they limit sacrifice, separate economic activity from national purpose, and shorten time horizons. The outcome is what List would criticize as a decadent society, lacking an unambiguous collective national purpose, its atomistic individuals intent only on short-term material gain. Both kinds of outcomes can fit within a theoretical framework that explicitly addresses the variability of content and contestation of national identities.

Economic nationalism, then, is economic policy that follows the national purpose and direction. It is a set of policies that results from a shared national identity, or from the predominance of a specific nationalism in the politics of a state. Economic nationalism is an economic policy outcome, a result of the politics of nationalism within a society. Thus, economic nationalism is not a policy of statist self-interest, in the Realist sense.[25]

REINTERPRETING ECONOMIC NATIONALISM

Economists and political scientists have tended to misinterpret economic nationalism as a theoretical concept and empirical phenomenon. Economists have usually equated economic nationalism with protectionism and the pursuit of autarky and argued that nationalism leads to a failure of cooperation among states.[26] Indeed, some economists, Frank Knight among

[24] Friedrich List, *The National System of Political Economy* (New York: Augustus M. Kelley, [1841] 1966), 172–73, 195, 167, and 199. Also see David Levi-Faur, "Friedrich List and the Political Economy of the Nation-State," *Review of International Political Economy* 4, 1 (1997): 154–78, at 169–70.

[25] The best critique of the Realist interpretation of economic nationalism as an expression of statism is George T. Crane, "Economic Nationalism: Bringing the Nation Back In," *Millennium* 27, 1 (1998): 55–75. For a similar assessment, see Peter J. Burnell, *Economic Nationalism in the Third World* (Boulder, Colo.: Westview, 1986).

[26] See, for example, Beth V. Yarborough and Robert M. Yarborough, *The World Economy: Trade and Finance*, 2d ed. (Chicago: Dryden, 1991), chap. 11; Mancur Olson, "Economic

them, argued that nationalism's influence on the world economy is even more pernicious than mere trade protection since economic nationalism leads also to collectivism and fascism.[27] Economists' negative characterizations of economic nationalism led one of the great historians of nationalism, Hugh Seton-Watson, to reject the expression *economic nationalism* as a misnomer.[28] Rather than dismiss it, I suggest that economic nationalism can be made a coherent concept by linking it to nationalism, the effects of which are much more variable and context-specific, and less destructive of international economic order, than economists have usually appreciated.

For the purposes of this book, the more difficult analytical issue arises in the relation of nationalism to theories of IPE. When Realist scholars have analyzed economic nationalism, they have tended to equate it with statism or mercantilism. In other words, Realists have frequently described economic nationalism as quintessentially realpolitik behavior. The basic tenet of statism in Realist theory, however, is that the state is an autonomous actor with its own interests, which are distinct from the interests of society or various societal actors. Statism, not nationalism, has driven the Realist tradition and theories derived within it.

Gilpin, in the most important example of this view, suggests that the Nationalist and Realist traditions of IPE are essentially identical. Economic nationalism, Gilpin argues, is conceptually equivalent to "mercantilism, statism, protectionism, the German Historical School, and, recently, New Protectionism." The "central idea" of economic nationalism is "that economic activities are and should be subordinate to the goals of state-building and the interests of the state." This argument, however, is a description of the statism that informs Realist theories of IPE. Gilpin concludes that "economic nationalism is based on the Realist doctrine of international relations." Together these arguments compose what Gilpin labels the "Nationalist perspective" on IPE.[29] Realist scholars have therefore tended to assume that their tradition subsumes the Nationalist tradition.[30]

Nationalism and Economic Progress," *World Economy* 10, 3 (1987): 241–64; Otto Hieronymi, ed., *The New Economic Nationalism* (New York: Praeger, 1980); and J. G. Hodgson, ed., *Economic Nationalism* (New York: H. W. Wilson, 1933).

[27] Frank H. Knight, "Economic Theory and Nationalism," in his *Ethics of Competition, and Other Essays* (London: Allen and Unwin, 1935). Also see William E. Rappard, "Economic Nationalism," in *Authority and the Individual* (Cambridge: Harvard University Press, 1937); and Michael Heilperin, *Studies in Economic Nationalism* (Geneva: Droz; Paris: Minard, 1960).

[28] Hugh Seton-Watson, *Nations and States: An Inquiry into the Origins of Nations and the Politics of Nationalism* (Boulder, Colo.: Westview, 1977), chap. 1.

[29] The first two quotations are in Robert Gilpin, *The Political Economy of International Relations* (Princeton: Princeton University Press, 1987), at 31, the third at 42. More generally, see 31–34 and 41–54.

[30] For a few examples of the conflation of economic nationalism and mercantilism, see Robert Gilpin, "Economic Interdependence and National Security in Historical Perspective,"

In contrast, I argue that the Nationalist tradition is distinct and that a Nationalist perspective on IPE (if it is to take nationalism seriously as a causal variable) should be separate from the Realist perspective. Nationalism and statism are not the same concepts. The economic policies that result from nationalism are different from the policies that result from statism in their direction, purpose, and causes.

DISTINGUISHING THE NATIONALIST PERSPECTIVE ON IPE

It is easiest to lay out the theoretical foundations of a Nationalist perspective on IPE by distinguishing them from those that underlie the Realist tradition, as well as those of both Liberal and Institutionalist approaches (Table 2.1).[31] These perspectives and approaches are rich and heterogeneous traditions within which specific theories have been derived.[32] This comparison does not imply an abstract contest among them: their relative usefulness for understanding world politics is an empirical question, not a matter of whether one or another grand perspective on IPE is more right. The purpose here is to show that the Nationalist tradition is different and that its distinctness has been underappreciated in IR and IPE scholarship.

Basic Assumptions

Theories derived within the Realist tradition of IPE are generally based on the assumption that states are rational, self-interested, unitary actors.[33] States strive for relative power and relative gain, thereby politicizing the economic relations among them. States guard their economic autonomy jealously and are loath to engage in cooperation that increases their de-

---

in *Economic Issues and National Security*, ed. Klaus Knorr and Frank N. Trager (Lawrence: Regents Press of Kansas, 1977), 39–42; Edward Mead Earle, "The New Mercantilism," *Political Science Quarterly* 40, 4 (1925): 594–600; J. B. Condliffe, "International Trade and Economic Nationalism," *International Conciliation* 476 (1951): 549–81, at 551–52; Condliffe, *The Commerce of Nations* (New York: W. W. Norton, 1950), 83–108 and 273–81; and Henrik Schmiegelow and Michele Schmiegelow, "The New Mercantilism in International Relations," *International Organization* 29, 2 (1975): 367–91.

[31] This comparison is not meant to imply that constructivist approaches to IPE are limited to those focused on national and state identities or that these four broad perspectives are the universe of possibilities. The Marxist tradition, for example, is neglected here, for reasons of space.

[32] For a discussion of the richness of the Realist and Liberal traditions in IR theory, see Michael W. Doyle, *Ways of War and Peace* (New York: W. W. Norton, 1997), parts 1 and 2.

[33] For an excellent review, see Jonathan Kirshner, "The Political Economy of Realism," in *Unipolar Politics: Realism and State Strategies after the Cold War*, ed. Ethan Kapstein and Michael Mastanduno (New York: Columbia University Press, 1999).

Table 2.1 A Comparison of Perspectives on International Political Economy

	Rationalist		Constructivist	
	Liberal	Realist	Institutionalist	Nationalist
Actors	Individuals, firms	States	Governments (or states)	Governments
Explanatory variable	Configuration of interests	Distribution of power	State identity	National identity
Sources of actor behavior	Economic incentives, institutions	Power, security	International norms and institutions	Purpose and direction of national identity
Conception of the state	Regulatory, pluralist	Self-interested, rational, unified	Purposive, linked to international and domestic society	Purposive, linked to society
Implications for foreign policy	State preferences are determined by domestic politics	State preferences are given by assumption	Government preferences are defined by state identity	Government preferences are defined by national identity
Internal goals of state authority	Maximization of domestic consumption	State building, extraction	Variable, dependent on norms and socialization	Distribution, national content of institutions
External goals of state authority	Development, growth	Relative development, autonomy	Variable, dependent on norms and socialization	Relative development, autonomy from specific states
Implications for IR	Cooperation is mutually beneficial exchange	Cooperation is politicized by relative power and relative gain	Cooperation is determined by norms and institutions	Cooperation is politicized by national identity

pendence, particularly on strategic goods or powerful states.[34] These features of international politics make cooperation among states difficult to achieve. Realist theories of cooperation suggest that changes in the international distribution of power determine the possibilities for cooperation, with powerful states, or hegemons, necessary to coordinate economic cooperation.[35] Alternatively, Realists have argued that the distribution of power, which underlies alliance patterns, affects whether the externalities of economic relations among states increase or decrease state security.[36] Realist theories tend to be both rationalist and materialist: states pursue exogenously given goals; states respond to material forces in world politics; they seek security and are influenced by power.

The Liberal tradition in IPE is more diffuse and includes both political scientists and economists. Individuals and firms are the key actors, both of which are assumed to follow economic incentives. With this logic the configuration of interests among these actors determines patterns of government policy. Institutions play an important role in Liberal theories. In neo-Liberal theories institutions organize cooperation, which is understood to be mutually beneficial exchange among states.[37] The more traditional Liberal theory, recently reformulated, holds that domestic institutions influence how societal preferences are aggregated into state preferences.[38] Like Realist theories, both neo-Liberal and traditional Liberal theories of IPE tend to be rationalist and materialist.

Constructivist approaches to IPE, including both the Institutionalist and Nationalist perspectives, rest on different theoretical foundations. Most important, they tend to be neither rationalist nor materialist. Contrasting constructivism with rationalism does not necessarily mean abandoning the idea that governments behave "rationally," in the sense that they have ordered preferences over outcomes, or interests they seek to achieve. Constructivism means studying the social processes that influence the formation of

[34] See Kenneth N. Waltz, *Theory of International Politics* (New York: McGraw-Hill, 1979), 104–7; Joseph M. Grieco, "Realist International Theory and the Study of World Politics," in *New Thinking in International Relations Theory*, ed. Michael W. Doyle and G. John Ikenberry (Boulder, Colo.: Westview, 1997), 168; and Krasner, *Defending the National Interest*, 37–39, 41.

[35] See Stephen D. Krasner, "State Power and the Structure of International Trade," *World Politics* 28, 3 (1976): 317–47; Robert Gilpin, *War and Change in World Politics* (Cambridge: Cambridge University Press, 1981); and Joseph M. Grieco, *Cooperation among Nations* (Ithaca: Cornell University Press, 1990).

[36] Joanne Gowa, *Allies, Adversaries, and International Trade* (Princeton: Princeton University Press, 1994).

[37] Robert O. Keohane, *After Hegemony* (Princeton: Princeton University Press, 1984); and David A. Baldwin, ed., *Neorealism and Neoliberalism* (New York: Columbia University Press, 1993).

[38] Andrew Moravcsik, "Taking Preferences Seriously: A Liberal Theory of International Politics," *International Organization* 51, 4 (1997): 513–53.

interests and preferences. Whereas rationalist approaches deduce or assume preferences in order to assess the influence of other variables, constructivist approaches endogenize preferences.

Departing from the materialism of mainstream IPE theories also does not mean that power and economic incentives are unimportant; the material facts of the world economy are still powerful in constructivist approaches. What is different is that these facts by themselves are indeterminate: norms, cultures, and identities give meaning to material facts so that governments can interpret and react to them. In addition, constructivist approaches assume that the world's economy consists of both material facts and social facts, such as collective understandings of appropriate behavior, cultural norms, and the identities of actors.

The Institutionalist perspective on IPE thus offers a way of understanding the influence of institutions that is different from the approach taken by neo-Liberalism. Whereas neo-Liberal theories assume that institutions solve information problems for states and can only constrain their behavior, Institutionalist IPE finds that institutions and international society can actually create and mold the identities of states and other social and economic actors. Institutionalist IPE thus emphasizes state identities and the international contexts that influence them.[39]

The Nationalist perspective, reformulated here, privileges the influence of domestic societies on governments' preferences. National identities influence how governments interpret the material reality of their economy and its relation to other states' economies. How a government interprets its economic dependence on other states is a good example. Those interpretations vary, but not just according to material variables such as power. Instead, the content of national identity helps give dependence meaning to a society and its government. Dependence on some powerful states can be interpreted as a security threat whereas dependence on other powerful

---

[39] On Institutionalist approaches to international political economy, see especially Peter J. Katzenstein, Robert O. Keohane, and Stephen D. Krasner, "*International Organization and the Study of World Politics*," *International Organization* 52, 4 (1998): 645–85, particularly 674–82; and Joseph Jupille and James A. Caporaso, "Institutionalism and the European Union," *Annual Review of Political Science* 2 (1999): 429–44. Also, for example, see Katzenstein, "United Germany"; John Gerard Ruggie, *Constructing the World Polity* (London: Routledge, 1998); Ruggie, *Winning the Peace* (New York: Columbia University Press, 1996); Ruggie, "Multilateralism: The Anatomy of an Institution," in *Multilateralism Matters*, ed. Ruggie (New York: Columbia University Press, 1993); Ruggie, "International Regimes, Transactions, and Change: Embedded Liberalism in the Postwar Economic Order," *International Organization* 36, 2 (1982): 379–415; Ruggie, "Embedded Liberalism Revisited: Institutions and Progress in Postwar International Economic Relations," in *Progress in Postwar International Relations*, ed. Emanuel Adler and Beverly Crawford (New York: Columbia University Press, 1991); and James A. Caporaso, "International Relations Theory and Multilateralism: The Search for Foundations," in *Multilateralism Matters*, ed. Ruggie.

states can be interpreted as mutually beneficial exchange. National identities thus affect how governments view the legitimacy of trading partners and currency arrangements. They affect how a government conceives of its economic role in relation to neighboring states and the necessity of autonomy from specific actors and states in the world economy.

Like other constructivist approaches to IPE, the Nationalist perspective begins with the assumption that the state is fundamentally purposive and connected to domestic society. Rather than describe states that are representative of societal interests or states that are distinct from society, the Nationalist perspective describes the state as a set of political and social relations, an institutional and spatial terrain within which governments act.[40]

Finally, it is important to clarify that an analytically coherent approach to national identities in IR and IPE must be based on constructivist theoretical logic because national identities are social constructions whose meanings to societies vary. In contrast, Moravcsik, in his astute reformulation of Liberal theory, suggests that national identities are part of the Liberal tradition. According to Moravcsik, there is a "set of fundamental societal preferences concerning the scope of the 'nation,' which in turn suggest the legitimate location of national borders and the allocation of citizenship rights."[41] This claim is problematic for several reasons. The "scope" of the nation is part of the content of national identity, and it is therefore constructed, contested, and variable over time. More broadly, if we believe the scholarly consensus that national identities are constructed, it is not useful to base our theoretical understanding of their role in world politics on Moravcsik's first core assumption: "that the fundamental actors in international politics are individuals and private groups, who are on the average rational and risk averse and who organize exchange and collective action to promote differential interests imposed by material scarcity, conflicting values, and variations in societal influence."[42] A society's collective identity is not the same as a collection of the interests or "values" of individuals. Clearly, not every domestic theory of government preferences fits within Liberal IR theory. Although both Realists and Liberals have recently claimed theoretical proprietorship of nationalism, it makes more sense to analyze it with constructivist approaches.

Internal Goals of Governments and States

In Liberal theories of political economy, states are usually understood not to have fundamental internal purposes other than promoting the wealth,

---

[40] For more on state theory, see Katzenstein, *Cultural Norms and National Security*, chap. 2.
[41] Moravcsik, "Taking Preferences Seriously," 526.
[42] Moravcsik, "Taking Preferences Seriously," 516–17.

development, and consumption of domestic society. Theories derived in the Realist tradition generally begin with the assumption that states are concerned principally with state building and the extraction of revenue from domestic society.[43] For Institutionalist approaches, the internal goals of states are influenced by international society's norms of appropriate behavior.

Unlike these other perspectives, the Nationalist perspective describes how governments are concerned with distributive issues in the domestic economy. Because the content of a national identity specifies membership in the nation, governments privilege the economic status of members of the nation. As a result, the distribution of income and wealth, patterns of employment, and ownership of capital are politicized along national lines.[44] Therefore, national identities influence the legitimacy of owners of property and capital within the domestic economy. Historically, this connection has been particularly true for land, a fundamental link between national identity and the national economy.[45]

In contrast to the Realist tradition, which focuses on the uniformity of statewide institutions, the Nationalist perspective emphasizes the efforts of governments to make state institutions more "national," more responsive

[43] This is the traditional business of the mercantilist state. State building is instrumental for the creation of centralized power and unified, statewide markets. Eli F. Heckscher, *Mercantilism* (London: Allen and Unwin, [1931] 1955), vol. 1, especially 22, 28, and chaps. 1, 2, 4, and 8. See also Jacob Viner, "English Theories of Foreign Trade before Adam Smith," in his *Studies in the Theory of International Trade* (New York: Harper, 1937); Viner, "Power versus Plenty as Objectives of Foreign Policy in the Seventeenth and Eighteenth Centuries," *World Politics* 1, 1 (1948): 1–29; and Gustav Schmoller, *The Mercantile System and Its Historical Significance* (New York: Macmillan, 1897). Of course, mercantilism and Realism are not identical even if contemporary Realist political economy is informed by the statism of mercantilist thought. See especially Kirshner, "Political Economy of Realism"; Stephan Haggard and Chung-in Moon, "The South Korean State in the International Economy: Liberal, Dependent, or Mercantile?" in *The Antinomies of Interdependence*, ed. John Gerard Ruggie (New York: Columbia University Press, 1983); and Richard J. Samuels and Eric Heginbotham, "Mercantile Realism and Japanese Foreign Policy," *International Security* 22, 4 (1998): 171–203, especially 190–94. On Realism and extraction from domestic society in the service of state power, see Michael Mastanduno, David A. Lake, and G. John Ikenberry, "Toward a Realist Theory of State Action," *International Studies Quarterly* 33, 4 (1989): 457–74; and Fareed Zakaria, *From Wealth to Power: The Unusual Origins of America's World Role* (Princeton: Princeton University Press, 1998), chap. 2.

[44] Frank H. Golay, Ralph Anspach, M. Ruth Pfanner, and Eliezer B. Ayal, *Underdevelopment and Economic Nationalism in Southeast Asia* (Ithaca: Cornell University Press, 1969), chap. 1; Bruno Dallago and Milica Uvalic, "The Distributive Consequences of Nationalism: The Case of Former Yugoslavia," *Europe-Asia Studies* 50, 1 (1998): 71–90; Albert Breton, "The Economics of Nationalism," *Journal of Political Economy* 72, 4 (1964): 376–86; and Harry G. Johnson, "A Theoretical Model of Economic Nationalism in New and Developing States," in *Economic Nationalism in Old and New States*, ed. Johnson (Chicago: University of Chicago Press, 1967).

[45] Colin Williams and Anthony D. Smith, "The National Construction of Social Space," *Progress in Human Geography* 7, 4 (1983): 502–18, especially 504–9.

to and protective of the nation, however defined.[46] In other words, the Nationalist perspective describes state building with a national purpose, as opposed to the Realist understanding of state building for its own sake.

External Goals of Governments and States

According to Realist theories, states are interested in issues of distribution in their foreign economic relations: states pursue the relative gains of cooperation, worry about the relative distribution of power and wealth in the international system, and fight over distribution at the "Pareto frontier" of mutually beneficial cooperation.[47] The state in Realist theory pursues autonomy from other states and market forces and understands economic dependence on other states, especially those more powerful, as a threat to state security. In contrast, Liberal theories tend to assume that states are concerned primarily with development and economic growth, though not necessarily in relative terms.[48] Institutionalist approaches to political economy are concerned with how governments behave consistently with norms of appropriate conduct in the economic relations among states and engage in economic practices that lead other governments to recognize specific state identities.

The Nationalist perspective shares with Realist theories their emphasis on relative development and economic autonomy. In general, nationalisms lead to competitive behavior by governments. Thus, economic nationalism includes the pursuit of relative economic development.[49] Economic nationalism can also be defined by the goal of economic autonomy.[50] But

---

[46] For this insight, see Rogers Brubaker, "Nationalizing States in the Old 'New Europe'—and the New," *Ethnic and Racial Studies* 19, 2 (1996): 411–37.

[47] See Grieco, *Cooperation among Nations*; and Stephen D. Krasner, "Global Communications and National Power—Life on the Pareto Frontier," *World Politics* 43, 3 (1991): 336–66.

[48] Robert O. Keohane and Joseph S. Nye, *Power and Interdependence*, 2d ed. (New York: HarperCollins, 1989), chaps. 2 and 3.

[49] Carlton J. H. Hayes, *The Historical Evolution of Modern Nationalism* (New York: Richard R. Smith, 1931), chap. 7, especially 232. Also see Liah Greenfeld, "The Worth of Nations: Some Economic Implications of Nationalism," *Critical Review* 10, 3 (1995): 555–84; Alexander Gerschenkron, "Economic Backwardness in Historical Perspective," in his *Economic Backwardness in Historical Perspective: A Book of Essays* (Cambridge: Harvard University Press, 1962), especially 24–25, a discussion of nationalism as a motivating force in late industrialization; and James E. Moffat, "Nationalism and Economic Theory," *Journal of Political Economy* 36, 4 (1928): 417–46, especially 443–44.

[50] See Dudley Seers, *The Political Economy of Nationalism* (New York: Oxford University Press, 1983); Jan Kofman, "Economic Nationalism in East-Central Europe in the Interwar Period," in *Economic Nationalism in East-Central Europe and South America, 1918–1939*, ed. Henryk Szlajfer, trans. Maria Chmielewska-Szlajfer and Piotr Goc (Geneva: Droz, 1990); T. E. Gregory, "Economic Nationalism," *International Affairs* 10, 3 (1931): 289–306; and Yoichi Itagaki, "The North-South Problem and Economic Nationalism," *Developing Economies* 9, 2 (1971): 111–32.

relative to and from which states? Competition and the pursuit of autonomy are not necessarily universal, with or from all states. On this question the causal mechanisms of the Nationalist perspective are distinct from those in Realist theories. The content of national identity helps determine the states against which relative success is measured and from which autonomy is pursued. Material facts are important, but national identities, and the historical memories embedded in them, lead governments to varying interpretations of them. The directionality of economic nationalism tends to be specific.

Therefore, a Nationalist perspective would expect trade protection against some states and trade cooperation with others. Statism and nationalism are not equivalent to protectionism, but they can be competing explanations of it.[51] Similarly, monetary cooperation, even monetary union, with some states could be consistent with a society's understanding of its identity whereas close monetary relations with the nation's most significant "other" might be avoided. National identities frame societal debates about trade and monetary relations, especially fundamental choices about trade and monetary integration with other states. The Nationalist perspective is not necessarily less pessimistic than the Realist perspective; it is pessimistic for different reasons.

ISSUES OF APPLICATION AND METHOD

Applying the Nationalist perspective to a specific empirical problem requires several steps of analysis, necessary to avoid tautological reasoning and ensure falsifiable research. Three crucial variables—national identity, government preferences, and government strategies—must be kept analytically and empirically distinct. Although it is important to contextualize national identities in order to understand and describe their influence on political outcomes, the same kind of social scientific analysis can be used to organize research on each specific national identity. Therefore, the approach offered here is general because it describes how to relate any national identity to political economy. But it also demands specific knowledge about the situations to which it is applied since the differences among national identities are more consequential than their commonalities. A research agenda informed by a constructivist view of national identities is necessarily historical and cultural.

---

[51] See Burnell, *Economic Nationalism*, 77–78; and James Mayall, "Reflections on the 'New' Economic Nationalism," *Review of International Studies* 10, 4 (1984): 313–21. Also see Mayall, *Nationalism and International Society* (Cambridge: Cambridge University Press, 1990).

The first step is to assess the content and contestation of national identity. One analytical difficulty is that content and contestation are not separate variables since contestation is the social process by which content is defined. We cannot study the content of a society's collective identity without assessing how that society agrees and disagrees about it. The most straightforward way to approach the issue is to describe various nationalist proposals for the content of identity so that it is clear at least what a society's nationalists want that content to be. The platforms and publications of nationalist political parties are an appropriate place to begin.

Then the question of contestation: How do other societal actors accept or reject the nationalists' vision of the national interest? Researching how policy debates, both public and parliamentary, connect the nation to various political issues and goals can help answer this question. It is also possible simply to evaluate the platforms and publications of other political parties. If all political parties share the foreign policy goals of the nationalists, it is a reliable indicator that a consensual, shared national identity frames policy debates and influences the preferences of the government. If other political parties contest the goals of the nationalists, or even the meanings and purposes attributed to the nation, national identity is more contested. It is important also to describe how it is contested: the distance between contending versions of national identity, the acrimony of the debate, and variations by age, class, or region within the populace, for example.

Research into content and contestation can thus be kept separate from government preferences and government strategies, which require their own independent measurements. Interviews with political elites and policy makers and government white papers can help specify government preferences. These preferences cannot be inferred from strategies themselves, which are the outcomes IR theories are supposed to explain.[52]

Finally, there are some data to which scholars do not have access, even in principle: whether political elites and policy makers themselves share the dominant interpretation of their society's national identity, or whether they are simply rational actors who instrumentally advance that interpretation to get elected or maintain their power. In other words, do political elites really believe in the cultural values they represent? It is possible to turn this empirical difficulty into an analytical strength, however. The Nationalist perspective is most fundamentally about the cultural contexts of decision making about economic strategy. The cultural contexts within which political elites and policy makers are embedded helps define their interests and their best course of action. Because those cultural contexts

---

[52] In the language of rationalist theory, this means we cannot assume that policies "reveal" preferences.

vary, we can attribute variation in policies to variation in contexts, regardless of whether political elites were instrumental or true believers in national purposes defined by society.

This way of thinking about the analytical problem is similar to the argument, made by Peter Katzenstein, Robert Keohane, and Stephen Krasner, that there is a point of complementarity between rationalist and constructivist approaches to politics on the issue of common knowledge—the shared information of actors in a given social context.[53] The approach to national identity presented here promises similar productive overlaps between rationalist and constructivist theories. In principle, the analysis of collective identities' influence on politics can accommodate several different behavioral assumptions about the goals of elites and policy makers even if a historical, inductive, constructivist approach to nationalisms and national identities serves as the general analytical orientation.

[53] Katzenstein, Keohane, and Krasner, "*International Organization*," 680–82.

CHAPTER THREE

Economic Relations among Post-Soviet States

Russia and the other fourteen post-Soviet states inherited a currency union based on the Soviet ruble and thus composed the so-called *rublevaia zona*, or ruble zone. Having been part of the Soviet economy, which was designed to achieve economies of scale through an extraordinary degree of enterprise and regional specialization, post-Soviet states also inherited an unusual degree *and* kind of economic interdependence. This was more than just a lot of commercial exchange. Almost all post-Soviet manufacturers relied on links to other manufacturers, many of them monopolies, in their production chains, many of which were now divided by new state borders. Additionally, the relatively poor quality of Soviet manufactured goods was legendary by the time the Union collapsed. Not only did post-Soviet manufacturers need one another; they also needed post-Soviet markets, the few in the world in which their products could be sold. Post-Soviet societies faced difficult choices about how to reorganize the economic relations among them. Their industries needed to cooperate with one another. So did their governments, if those industries were then to have a large captive market.

These economic imperatives, material facts of the post-Soviet regional economy, ensured that seeking economic autonomy from Russia, or the post-Soviet region as a whole, would be costly in the short run. Post-Soviet trade relations were the most consequential for long-run patterns of economic relations among the new states, and the range of strategies available to governments with regard to commercial cooperation was wide. Beyond exchanging most-favored-nation trade status, post-Soviet states could have entered preferential trading arrangements with one another and even created a free trade area, customs union, or common market. In contrast, monetary relations offered starker trade-offs between reintegration and autonomy during the first years after the Soviet collapse. Money, it turned out, was a more decisive economic issue. When it came to the ruble zone, post-Soviet governments had to choose to remain or to introduce a new national currency.

MONETARY RELATIONS

Russia itself finally destroyed the ruble zone in the summer of 1993, despite the fact that it had been trying to hold the currency union together since the autumn of 1991.[1] Before Russia's policies changed, however, five states had already exited (Table 3.1).

Early Exit: The Baltic Republics

Estonia, Latvia, and Lithuania exited the ruble zone as quickly as they could.[2] Estonia was first out, in June 1992. Estonians had been discussing an independent currency since 1987. Virtually all Estonian political elites agreed on the necessity of an independent currency, and so they created one. Thus, in the summer after the Soviet collapse, the Bank of Estonia introduced the kroon.

The material incentives to remain in the ruble zone were irrelevant to Estonia's decision: the Russians could not have paid Estonians enough to remain in the ruble zone. No one could have—even the IMF and European Community warned Estonia of the dire consequences of exiting the currency union.[3] Nevertheless, Estonians, who used to say they would live off potato peels if that were the cost of independence, celebrated their new currency. On 22 June 1992, at the Viljandi "Ugala" Theater in Tallinn, they held the Kroon Ball to honor the symbol of their monetary sovereignty.

---

[1] This section draws from Rawi Abdelal, "National Strategy and National Money: Politics and the End of the Ruble Zone, 1991–1994," Harvard Business School Working Paper 01-022, October 2000. For the best account of monetary politics within Russia, complementary to these developments in Russia's monetary relations with other post-Soviet states, see David Woodruff, *Money Unmade: Barter and the Fate of Russian Capitalism* (Ithaca: Cornell University Press, 1999).

[2] See Saulius Girnius, "Establishing Currencies in the Baltic States," *RFE / RL Research Report* 2, 22 (1993): 35–39. Also see Erik Whitlock, "Introducing National Currencies: Causes and Consequences," *RFE / RL Research Report* 1, 30 (1992): 49–52.

[3] See Ardo Hansson and Jeffrey Sachs, "Crowning the Estonian Kroon," *Transition* 9 (1992): 1–2. Also see Daniel Michaels, "Focus on Estonia—Baltic Success: Estonia Defies Advice in Creating Currency That Boosts Economy," *Wall Street Journal Europe*, 30 August 1993; and Philippe Legrain, "Estonia Proudly Wears Its Kroon of Thorns: The First Ex-Soviet Republic to Dump the Ruble and Beat Inflation—But at a Price," *Financial Times*, 23 June 1993.

Table 3.1 Exits from the Ruble Zone

Estonia	June 1992
Latvia	August 1992
Lithuania	October 1992
Ukraine	November 1992
Kyrgyzstan	May 1993
Azerbaijan	July 1993
Georgia	August 1993
Armenia	November 1993
Belarus	November 1993
Kazakhstan	November 1993
Moldova	November 1993
Turkmenistan	November 1993
Uzbekistan	November 1993
Tajikistan	May 1995

Source: Adapted from Patrick Conway, *Currency Proliferation: The Monetary Legacy of the Soviet Union,* Princeton Essays in International Finance, no. 197 (1995).

Many Estonians bought new wallets to hold their kroons. After the currency changeover the government, amid much fanfare, put Estonia's stock of rubles on a train to Moscow.[4]

The next piece of Estonia's monetary strategy seemed to many observers to be paradoxical. The first thing the government did with its newly established monetary autonomy from the Central Bank of Russia (CBR) was to give it away to the Germans: Estonia pegged its currency to the deutsche mark. Thus, Estonians politically linked their autonomy from Russia to their shared understanding of the purposes of their statehood; exiting the Russian sphere of influence served one of these purposes, the "return to Europe." As Siim Kallas, the governor of the Bank of Estonia, argued: "In 1992, the Bank of Estonia was accused of knowingly attempting to destroy the current traditional economic relationship with the East. To some extent we did."[5] The plan, in other words, was to "break the dominant position of trade with the East."[6]

The analysis of Estonia's first president, Lennart Meri, is even clearer. Estonia, President Meri argued, was rejecting "the last colonial empire in the world." Estonia's money was symbolic: "The kroon is not a piece of

[4] See Philippe Legrain, "Real Money," "Last Days of the Ruble in Estonia," and "Estonians Wait and Then Celebrate the New Money's Coming," all in *Baltic Independent,* 26 June 1992. Also see Lisa Trei, "The Cost of Independence Runs High in the Baltic Countries," *Dallas Morning News,* 18 June 1992; and "The Ruble: Helter Skelter," *The Economist,* 27 June 1992.

[5] Siim Kallas, "Pros and Cons of the Reintroduction of the Estonian Kroon," in *Conference on the Reintroduction of the Estonian Kroon* (Tallinn: Bank of Estonia, 1993), 9. Also see Mart Sorg, "Estonian Strategies in the Reconstruction of Its Monetary System," in *The Competitiveness of Financial Institutions and Centers in Europe,* ed. Donald E. Fair and Robert Raymond (Dordrecht: Kluwer, 1994).

[6] Siim Kallas and Mart Sorg, "Currency Reform," in *Transforming the Estonian Economy* (Tallinn: Institute of Economics, Estonian Academy of Sciences, 1995), especially sec. 5.

paper; the kroon is the flag of Estonian economic and political independence." Of course, the introduction of the kroon was costly since leaving the ruble zone cut the "umbilical cord" of subsidized Russian energy supplies. But Meri rejected this short-term thinking, deriding "those who would like to be rich today at the expense of our children and grandchildren." He concluded, "Money is politics, and politics is money."[7]

Latvia and Lithuania followed Estonia's path out of the ruble zone, largely for the same reason—to achieve autonomy from Russia—and at approximately the same time, during the summer and early autumn of 1992. Also like Estonia, Lithuania and Latvia had been planning their new currencies for several years. In the spring and summer of 1989 the Supreme Soviets of all three states adopted similar economic autonomy plans, each of which outlined their intentions to create an independent currency.[8] Then, on 2 March 1990, the Latvian parliament adopted a resolution, "On the Bank of Latvia," that created a central bank independent of the Soviet Gosbank, two days before Latvians adopted their declaration of independence. In July 1990 the Latvian parliament passed a resolution titled "On the Program to Create the Republic of Latvia's Monetary System," with specific plans to introduce a national currency as soon as possible. Then, in May 1992, the Latvian central bank introduced the Latvian ruble, a temporary currency that was separate from Russian monetary authority and sole legal tender by August.[9]

Similarly, in May 1992 the Bank of Lithuania issued the talonas, a currency supplementary to Soviet rubles currently circulating. In October the bank issued the talonas as a provisional currency and withdrew rubles from circulation. Thus October 1992 marks Lithuania's official departure from the ruble zone.[10] By 1997 the Bank of Lithuania and the government began

[7] Lennart Meri, "Estonia Has More Gold than Europe," in *Conference on the Reintroduction of the Estonian Kroon*, quotations at 6 and 7.

[8] Kalev Kukk, "Five Years in the Monetary Development of the Baltic States: Differences and Similarities," *Bank of Estonia Bulletin* 5 (1997); and Seija Lainela and Pekka Sutela, "Escaping from the Ruble: Estonia and Latvia Compared," in *Integration and Disintegration in European Economies*, ed. Bruno Dallago and Giovanni Pegoretti (Aldershot: Dartmouth, 1995), 229, 239.

[9] On Latvia, see Philippe Legrain, Anthony Robinson, and John Lloyd, "Latvia Issues Parallel Ruble," *Financial Times*, 15 May 1992; and Legrain, "Kroon Prompts Latvian Move," *Baltic Independent*, 10 July 1992. The Latvian lat was not officially introduced until 1993. See "Latvia Finally Ditches Temporary Money," *Baltic Independent*, 22 October 1993.

[10] In June 1993 the bank introduced the litas, the permanent currency. See Andrius Uzkalnis and Peter Morris, "Litas to Replace the Talonas," *Baltic Independent*, 25 June 1993; Andrius Uzkalnis and Tarmu Tammerk, "Litas Arrives Backed Only by Central Bank's Word," *Baltic Independent*, 2 July 1993; Gitanas Nauseda, "Development of the Lithuanian Monetary System and the European Union," in *Lithuania's Integration into the European Union*, ed. Klaudijus Maniokas and Gediminas Vitkus (Vilnius: European Integration Studies Center, 1997); and Bank of Lithuania, *Annual Report 1995* (Vilnius, 1996).

making longer-term plans to peg the Lithuanian currency to the euro and, eventually, to join the European monetary union.[11]

Despite these similar policies, there were some differences among the three Baltic states' approaches to new national currencies. For example, Latvia did not choose an external, European anchor for its new currency, the lat, whereas Lithuania chose to tie its currency, the litas, to the dollar, and Estonians pegged their kroon to the German mark. But in all three Baltic republics political elites nearly unanimously supported new currencies, at whatever economic cost, and rejected the "occupation ruble."[12] There was never any doubt that they would reject the post-Soviet monetary union.

Out Just in Time: Ukraine and Kyrgyzstan

Ukraine exited the ruble zone in November 1992, but less decisively than the Baltic states. Ukraine's first government had originally planned to do exactly what the Baltic governments did: introduce an independent currency and reorient the economy away from Russia and toward the West. In March 1992 President Leonid Kravchuk outlined a plan to achieve economic autonomy from Russia, and a new currency was a central component.[13] Internal dissension about the necessity of economic autonomy and an independent currency, however, including the strenuous opposition of Ukrainian industrialists, delayed Ukraine's exit from the ruble zone until November 1992, when the government introduced the karbovanets as a transitional currency.

The hyperinflation of the karbovanets after its introduction undermined the credibility of the new currency immediately, and many Ukrainians called for the state's return to the ruble zone. President Kravchuk rejected the possibility of ruble-zone membership. He complained: "A single

[11] See Bank of Lithuania, *Monetary Policy Program of the Bank of Lithuania for 1997–99* (Vilnius, 1997), 2, 12, and 15–16. Also see Bank of Lithuania, *Annual Report 1997* (Vilnius, 1998), 6, 32–33, and 76–77.

[12] See "Kroons, Lats, Litas," *The Economist*, 3 July 1993. The industrial lobbies in the three states, however, staunchly opposed leaving the ruble zone. See, for example, Anatol Lieven, *The Baltic Revolution: Estonia, Latvia, and Lithuania and the Path to Independence* (New Haven: Yale University Press, 1993), 356–57.

[13] The plan was reprinted in "Kravchuk's Report Had the Effect of an Exploding Bomb," *Komsomol'skaia pravda*, 26 March 1992, in *Current Digest of the Post-Soviet Press* 44, 12 (1992): 15–16. Also see Sergei Tsikora, "Iz SNG Ukraina ne vykhodit, no ekonomicheskii kurs—meniaet" (Ukraine is not leaving the CIS, but its economic course is changing), *Izvestiia*, 25 March 1992; Chrystia Freeland, "Ukraine Plans to Sever Russian Economic Links," *Financial Times*, 24 March 1992; Alex Shprintsen, "Ukraine Will Speed Up Breakaway from Russia," *Los Angeles Times*, 25 March 1992; Serge Schmemann, "Ukraine's Parliament Votes to Replace the Ruble," *New York Times*, 26 March 1992; and "Ukraine's Parliament Approves Plan That Could End Nation's Use of the Ruble," *Wall Street Journal*, 25 March 1992.

ruble—the same for all states? That is not a ruble zone, but a ruble state."[14] The Ukrainian currency, Kravchuk argued, was a fundamental component of Ukrainian sovereignty. He insisted, "Those who assert that Ukraine should enter a common banking, financial, and monetary system are actually against Ukraine's independence."[15] In the end, President Kravchuk significantly scaled back the plans for economic autonomy from Russia, primarily because there was not nearly as much public support for breaking ties with Russia as there was in the Baltic states.[16]

Kyrgyzstan also left the ruble zone before Russia destroyed it, but its policy reflected a different influence. Rather than popular nationalist support for an independent currency or autonomy from Russia, the creation of the Kyrgyzstani som, a process led by President Askar Akaev, was part of a sweeping economic reform package designed by the IMF to integrate the country into the world economy. It was a directionless policy, in the sense that it was oriented neither toward the West, symbolized by Europe, nor toward the East, symbolized by the Commonwealth of Independent States. It was also top-down, as Akaev was convinced by IMF officials of the need for an independent money for low inflation and stabilization. Thus, the IMF had dramatically changed its approach to the ruble zone and by 1993 was urging independent currencies on all post-Soviet states as a way to end the hyperinflation of the ruble zone.[17] The IMF's flip-flop on the ruble zone undermined its credibility among many post-Soviet leaders, and it was able to convince only Kyrgyzstan to introduce a new currency as part of a liberalization and reform strategy. The reaction of Kyrgyzstani society to the new currency reflected differences in their interpretation of the Kyrgyz national idea. More than 80 percent of ethnic Kyrgyz approved of the new currency whereas 61 percent of the ethnic Russian minority and 50 percent of the ethnic Kazakh minority believed it was a mistake. Most annoyed with the new currency were the Kyrgyzstani industrialists,

[14] Quoted in Stanislav Prokupchuk, "Leonid Kravchuk: 'Davaite schitat'sia s segodniashnimi realiiami'" (Leonid Kravchuk: "Let's take into account today's realities"), *Trud,* 19 January 1994.

[15] Quoted in Vladimir Skachko, "'Kto khochet v rublevuiu zonu—tot protiv nezavisimosti'" ("He who wants to join the ruble zone is against independence"), *Nezavisimaia gazeta,* 25 March 1994.

[16] Paul D'Anieri, "Dilemmas of Interdependence: Autonomy, Prosperity, and Sovereignty in Ukraine's Russia Policy," *Problems of Post-Communism* 44, 1 (1997): 16–26. Ukraine introduced its permanent currency, the hryvnia, in September 1996. See Tony Barber, "Money Marks Ukraine's Identity," *The Independent,* 3 September 1996; and Matthew Kaminski, "Kiev Looks West as Turnaround Begins," *Financial Times,* 27 September 1996.

[17] Patrick Conway, *Currency Proliferation: The Monetary Legacy of the Soviet Union,* Princeton Essays in International Finance, no. 197 (1995), 40.

who argued that exit from the ruble zone was a disaster for their production and market ties with Russia and the rest of the former Soviet Union.[18]

Russia Breaks What's Left of the Ruble Zone

By July 1993 nine post-Soviet states (Armenia, Azerbaijan, Belarus, Georgia, Kazakhstan, Moldova, Tajikistan, Turkmenistan, and Uzbekistan) remained in the ruble zone with Russia. None could print rubles, but for several years all had been quite generous in issuing noncash credit to firms within their borders.[19] Price liberalization and Russian stinginess with new notes caused cash shortages that led most states to introduce ruble supplements, but these coupons were merely temporary measures to create enough money for their economies to function.

Beginning in mid-1992, Russia had attempted to lead the coordination of monetary policies within the ruble zone in an effort to restrain the profligate credit emission of the other members. The failure of these attempts was an increasing source of frustration for the CBR and many government officials, a fact that created political tension between Russia and the other members.[20]

It is easy to understand why. After Soviet dissolution all fifteen of the region's central banks could loan noncash rubles to their local banks, which could in turn lend to local companies, which then could use the rubles to purchase imports from Russia. Because Russia had a trade surplus with all fourteen of the other post-Soviet states during 1992, the other fourteen could finance their trade deficits with rubles they created themselves.

This arrangement was quite a good deal for the other post-Soviet states. Russian business enterprises also benefited, as did businesses throughout the region. The costs of excessive credit were spread across all the states. Although the only real losers in the deal were the Russian economy as a whole and the Russian government, they were big losers. The total bill for

[18] See Eugene Huskey, "Kyrgyzstan Leaves the Ruble Zone," *RFE / RL Research Report* 2, 35 (1993): 38–43, at 41–42. For more on the Kyrgyzstani currency reform, see Claudia Rosett, "Kyrgyzstan Is Out from Under the Ruble," *Wall Street Journal*, 18 May 1993; Rosett, "Changing Money: New Kyrgyz Currency May Show Escape Path from Ruble Zone," *Wall Street Journal Europe*, 19 May 1993; and John Lloyd, "IMF Watches as Kyrgyzstan Fights the Battle of the Som," *Financial Times*, 21 May 1993. On the opposition of organized economic interests, particularly the industrial lobby, see also "The Battle of the Som," *The Economist*, 29 May 1993.

[19] In the Soviet monetary system there were two circuits for money: cash and credit. Cash (*nalichnye*) rubles were used to pay wages and in retail stores. Noncash (*beznalichnye*) rubles were used for credit allocations from Gosbank and transactions between enterprises. This distinction, an institutional legacy of the Soviet economic system, carried over into the post-Soviet period and complicated the monetary transformations of Russia and the other republics.

[20] See, for example, Elisabeth Rubenfien, "An Unhappy Interdependence," *Wall Street Journal Europe*, 21 December 1992.

cheap credits and subsidized energy and raw materials was, by some estimates, $15 billion per year.[21]

The Russian government was willing to pay for some of the bill, such as the subsidized energy, because those subsidies were under its control and it could use them to attempt to extract political concessions from other post-Soviet states.[22] But the government and CBR considered the credit creation of the other central banks a serious problem. Moreover, there were significant internal differences among Russian political elites about whether Russia should expend resources to maintain its sphere of influence or get its own house in order and shed the economic burdens of empire.[23]

The first Russian attempt to restrain the largesse of the other ruble-zone states came in the summer of 1992. On 21 June 1992 President Yeltsin warned ruble-zone states that they would have to accept CBR control over their credit emissions and issued a decree that the Soviet-era ruble was now Russian.[24] This move was partially a response to the Ukrainian government's announcement on 12 June that its central bank would double the country's money supply by issuing new credits.

Then, on 1 July 1992, the CBR restrained the power of the post-Soviet central banks to create ruble credit and began keeping separate ruble accounts for each state.[25] This meant that the central banks of other post-Soviet states could still issue credit but the CBR would keep track, bilaterally, of which banks issued how much and where it ended up. In other words, the credit that non-Russian central banks issued, though it was still denominated ostensibly in rubles, was no longer identical to the credit that the CBR issued. So, for example, the CBR would no longer accept "Ukrainian" or "Belarusian" rubles as if they were equivalent to its own credit. Almost immediately, implicit exchange rates developed between the different types of rubles that were still circulating in the accounts of enterprises, commercial banks, and central banks. Some rubles were discounted more heavily than others, based in part on their relative inflation.

---

[21] See John Lloyd and Steve Levine, "West Sees Danger in End of Ruble Zone," *Financial Times*, 12 November 1993.

[22] See Daniel Drezner, *The Sanctions Paradox* (Cambridge: Cambridge University Press, 1999), part 2.

[23] These perspectives were epitomized by the political and ideological struggle between Yegor Gaidar, a liberal reformer who argued that the ruble zone complicated Russia's economic reform and stabilization, and Viktor Chernomyrdin, an empire-saver of sorts who sought to keep the ruble zone together in order to institutionalize Russian regional hegemony and its influence in the near abroad.

[24] "O merakh po zashchite denezhnoi sistemy Rossii" (On measures for the defense of the monetary system of Russia), Presidential Decree no. 636, 21 June 1992.

[25] See John Lloyd and Dmitri Volkov, "Russia Cracks the Whip over the Ruble Zone," *Financial Times*, 31 July 1992; and Anders Åslund, *How Russia Became a Market Economy* (Washington, D.C.: Brookings, 1995), 125.

Nevertheless, a number of post-Soviet states remained committed to the ruble zone. As of July 1992 none of the five Central Asian republics was planning to introduce an independent currency. As Nazar Shaparov, president of the State Central Bank of Turkmenistan, explained of his country's approach to the ruble zone, "We plan to stay in for some time." Bisenchaly Tadjiiakov, deputy governor of the National Bank of Kazakhstan, insisted, "If we are forced to leave, we will be the last to do so."[26]

Then, in August 1992, the Russian government announced that other post-Soviet states could trade directly with Russian exporters through commercial banks rather than through their respective central banks. This meant that importers of Russian goods needed credit issued by the CBR. After this announcement, credit created by the other central banks was useful only within the state whose bank created it. In other words, each state had its own version of the same currency circulating in banks, though all states had exactly the same currency circulating as cash. Finally, in May 1993, the CBR suspended other central banks' power to create credit altogether.[27]

The beginning of the end of the ruble zone came in July 1993, when Russia attempted to force the exit of the remaining nine members, whose governments had seemed content to remain. During the first half of 1993, as the CBR was wrangling with the other central banks about credit emission, it was also issuing new ruble notes without the traditional picture of Lenin and the fifteen languages of the constituent republics. The new rubles were distinctly Russian, not Soviet, and the CBR refused to include the new notes in their ruble shipments to the other members of the currency area. Then, on 24 July, CBR chairman Viktor Gerashchenko announced that all pre-1993 rubles would no longer be legal tender in Russia as of 26 July and that they could be exchanged at a set rate within Russia.[28] Since only Russia had the new notes, the other ruble-zone states were using cash rubles—2.2 trillion of them—that were now worthless in Russia.[29] All the printing presses were in Russia. Thus, only a year and a half after the collapse of Soviet authority, a number of important Russian

[26] Shaparov and Tadjiiakov are quoted in Lloyd and Volkov, "Russia Cracks the Whip."

[27] See, for example, "The Ruble Zone: Behind the Façade," *The Economist*, 19 September 1992; and "The Ruble: Twilight Zone," *The Economist*, 22 May 1993.

[28] "Soobshchenie Tsentral'nogo banka Rossiiskoi Federatsii" (Announcement of the Central Bank of the Russian Federation), *Rossiiskaia gazeta*, July 27, 1993. See Mikhail Leontiev, "Rossiia vvela natsional'nuiu valiutu, prikryv eie telom Gerashchenko" (Russia introduces a new currency, covering it with the body of Gerashchenko), *Segodnia*, 27 July 1993; Vitaly Marsov, "Skhvatka politicheskikh bul'dogov" (Clash of political bulldogs), *Nezavisimaia gazeta*, 27 July 1993; and Oleg Polukeev, "Finansovye manevry pravitel'stva" (Financial maneuvers of the government), *Nezavisimaia gazeta*, 27 July 1993.

[29] Sergei Modestov, "Urok sosediam po byvshemu SSSR" (Lesson for neighbors of the former USSR), *Nezavisimaia gazeta*, 27 July 1993. See also Åslund, *How Russia Became a Market Economy*, 129.

officials, including some in the administration of President Boris Yeltsin and in the CBR, had obviously changed their minds about the political and economic desirability of the ruble zone.[30] Their message to the other ruble-zone states was quite clear. "Russia appears to have achieved the main objective of its currency reform," the *Financial Times*'s John Lloyd reported on 28 July. "Mr. Viktor Gerashchenko, the central bank governor, said yesterday that the forced exchange of pre-1993 rubles had compelled former Soviet republics still using the Russian currency to opt in or out of the ruble zone."[31]

Enough Is Enough: Azerbaijan, Georgia, Moldova, Turkmenistan

Azerbaijan, Georgia, Moldova, and Turkmenistan reacted to Russia's surprise currency reform by introducing independent currencies.[32] In Azerbaijan powerful political forces had favored breaking with Russia and creating a new currency immediately after the dissolution. But Azerbaijan left the ruble zone much later, in July 1993, just after Russia attempted to eject it and the remaining members from the currency union. The lateness of Azerbaijan's currency introduction reflected the ambivalence of its internal debate about the political meaning and importance of a national money. Azerbaijan's government made no plans to introduce a currency until June 1992, when Abulfaz Elcibey, head of the Azerbaijani Popular Front, by then a political party that emerged from the nationalist movement, was elected president. President Elcibey withdrew the country from the CIS and proposed ambitious plans to turn the state's economy away from Russia and toward Turkey and the West. Elcibey's campaign message was nationalist: "Azerbaijan needs to establish an independent state with its own currency and army."[33] Toward this end, Elcibey created a ruble supplement, the manat, in August 1992. The country was to switch completely to the manat on 15 June 1993, by

---

[30] Yegor Gaidar, however, interpreted the currency exchange as an attempt by conservative forces in the administration to undermine popular support for the economic reform process—despite the fact that the dominant purpose was to finish off the ruble zone, whose existence Gaidar had found troubling from the beginning.

[31] John Lloyd, "Currency Change Puts Pressure on Republics," *Financial Times*, 28 July 1993. See also John Lloyd, "Ruble Reform Splits Cabinet: Finance Chief Wants Central Bank Measure Overturned," *Financial Times*, 28 July 1993; Steven Erlanger, "Wrestling for Rubles," *New York Times*, 28 July 1993; James Rupert, "Invalidation of 'Old' Ruble Notes Shakes Russians," *Washington Post*, 26 July 1993; and James Rupert, "Yeltsin under Fire over Money Move," *Washington Post*, 28 July 1993.

[32] See "How the Republics View the Ruble Purge," *Associated Press*, 26 July 1993.

[33] Quoted in "Nationalist Elected President in Azerbaijan," *New York Times*, 9 June 1992.

presidential decree, but on 13 June rebels overthrew Elcibey's government and returned the former Communist chief Heidar Aliev to power. Aliev, who remained in power throughout the 1990s, delayed the currency change until late July 1993, when Russia itself was trying to eject Azerbaijan, and all others, from the ruble zone. The change in Azerbaijan's approach to its currency reflected a broader rapprochement with Russia, as Aliev, to the dismay of the nationalists, returned Azerbaijan to the CIS.[34]

Georgia had introduced a supplemental currency, the menati, priced at par with the ruble, in April 1992 as a way to deal with cash shortages. The Georgian government had a very difficult time convincing Georgians that the menati would remain at par with the ruble, however, and an informal exchange rate arose. The menati implicitly lost value relative to the ruble throughout the end of 1992 and the first half of 1993. When the Russian currency reform of July 1993 left Georgia with the suddenly worthless rubles, the government announced that on 2 August the menati would be the sole legal tender.[35] As in Azerbaijan, Georgian nationalists had supported exiting the ruble zone much earlier and remaining outside the CIS, but state weakness and civil war kept the state well within the Russian sphere of influence.

Turkmenistan reacted to the Russian monetary exchange by announcing that it would leave the ruble zone as soon as possible, and it rejected the possibility of monetary reintegration.[36] Russia's surprise currency reform was a crucial moment in the making of Turkmenistani foreign economic policy because the way member states were forced from the ruble zone made it clear that Russia was essentially an unreliable economic partner. Turkmenistan introduced its currency, the manat, on 1 November 1993.

Moldova had already introduced a supplemental currency in July 1992 as a way to deal with cash shortages. The government did not adopt a new, independent currency until November 1993, well after the July 1993 currency reform.[37] The Moldovan Popular Front, after coming to power in

[34] See Justin Burke, "Commonwealth Leaders Hold Off Russian Ruble's Collapse," *Christian Science Monitor*, 29 June 1992; "New Money," *Financial Times*, 10 August 1992; Colin Barraclough, "Azerbaijan Democrats on Verge of Losing Power," *Christian Science Monitor*, 18 June 1993; and Leyla Boulton, "Azerbaijan Turns to Old Guard," *Financial Times*, 14 June 1993. Also see Tadeusz Swietochowski, *Russia and Azerbaijan: A Borderland in Transition* (New York: Columbia University Press, 1995), 221–27.

[35] See Conway, *Currency Proliferation*, 50–54. However, the hyperinflation of the mena i led to the de facto dominance of other currencies, notably the old rubles, in most commercial transactions.

[36] "New Currency for Turkmenistan," *Financial Times*, 20 August 1993; "Turkmenistan Sets New Currency," *Wall Street Journal*, 20 August 1993.

[37] "Moldova Sets Currency," *New York Times*, 25 November 1993.

parliamentary elections in 1990, had planned to introduce a Moldovan national currency in January 1992,[38] but various technical matters and the lack of domestic political consensus on the issue delayed the country's exit from the ruble zone. When the Moldovan Popular Front lost power, the plans for a new currency were postponed. By the time the Moldovans finally introduced their currency, the leu, only Armenia and Tajikistan were still using the old ruble notes.

The "Ruble Zone of a New Type":
Armenia, Belarus, Kazakhstan, Tajikistan, and Uzbekistan

Armenia, Belarus, Kazakhstan, Tajikistan, and Uzbekistan reacted to the July currency reform in Russia by insisting that they would continue to use the ruble even though they had no way of receiving the new ruble notes.[39] For example, the Kazakhstani policy position in the ruble zone was consistent between December 1991 and July 1993: President Nursultan Nazarbaev favored both the currency union and an interstate bank to regulate credit emission among member states and cash distribution from the Russian ruble printing presses.[40] Still, in early 1992 Nazarbaev's administration had prepared a contingency plan to create an independent currency if necessary and had contracted a British company to print it. But the Kazakhstani government remained committed to the ruble zone because of its substantial material benefits.[41]

Belarus was likewise committed to ruble-zone membership. In 1991 and again in 1992 the Belarusian government introduced the Belarusian ruble, nicknamed the *zaichik*, or bunny, after the image on its face, as a supplement to the Russian ruble to deal with persistent cash shortages. The government and central bank frequently insisted, however, that the *zaichik* was not meant to become a new national currency. Uzbekistan also remained committed to the ruble zone. And Tajikistan, mired in civil war, was making no plans for an independent currency.

---

[38] See "Moldova to Issue New Currency," *Wall Street Journal*, 24 January 1992; and "Ukrainians, Rich in Rubles, Hunt Bargains Next Door," *New York Times*, 29 January 1992.

[39] See John Lloyd, "Some Rubles Are More Equal than Others," *Financial Times*, 28 July 1993. See also Chrystia Freeland, "Survey of Armenia," *Financial Times*, 7 June 1995.

[40] See, for example, Mikhail Alexandrov, *Uneasy Alliance: Relations between Russia and Kazakhstan in the Post-Soviet Era, 1992–1997* (Westport, Conn.: Greenwood, 1999), 65, 67, 156–57. At least part of the logic for Nazarbaev's commitment to a better-organized monetary union was to increase other CIS states' influence over the distribution of cash rubles, which Russia had been keeping largely for itself. This is similar to France's commitment to European monetary union as a way to increase its influence over the conduct of monetary policy in a European macroeconomy dominated by the German Bundesbank. See Joseph Grieco, "The Maastricht Treaty, Economic and Monetary Union, and the Neorealist Research Program," *Review of International Studies* 21, 1 (1995): 21–40.

[41] Alexandrov, *Uneasy Alliance*, 157–58.

In August and September 1993 these five states, along with Russia, agreed to create a *rublevaia zona novogo tipa*, a "ruble zone of a new type." On 7 August 1993 Russian president Yeltsin met with Kazakhstani president Nazarbaev and Uzbekistani president Islam Karimov in Moscow, agreed in principle to create a common monetary system, and invited other CIS states to participate.[42] On 20 August Nazarbaev made another trip to Moscow to reiterate Kazakhstan's commitment to remain in the ruble zone. Then, on 7 September, Armenia, Belarus, Kazakhstan, Russia, Tajikistan, and Uzbekistan met in Moscow and agreed to use the "Russian Federation ruble" as their common currency, signing an agreement called "On Practical Measures to Establish a New-Type Ruble Zone."[43] On 8 September Belarus and Russia signed a bilateral monetary integration agreement. Then, during September, Armenia, Belarus, Kazakhstan, Tajikistan, and Uzbekistan each signed another, bilateral agreement with Russia to unify their monetary systems.

The old ruble zone was chaotic and decentralized; the new-type ruble zone was to be orderly and centralized. Russia proposed to solve the problem of cooperation that had plagued the old ruble zone with a very simple institutional design: all authority would reside in Moscow at the CBR.

In exchange for the material benefits of a currency union with Russia, then, these five states agreed to let the CBR make monetary policy for them all. At a speech in August 1993, for example, Kazakhstani president Nazarbaev explained that his state was "technically prepared to leave the ruble zone, but that he believed it would be more profitable to stay in it."[44]

The price of ruble-zone membership soon seemed to be as inflationary as the ruble itself, however. It was not enough anymore simply to submit to Russian monetary authority in exchange for the new Russian ruble notes. In November 1993 Russia clarified the terms for membership: the cash rubles would be given to ruble-zone members as state credit. In other words, the central banks of the five other states would be obligated to pay interest to the CBR for the rubles as if the ruble notes were a loan. Furthermore, Russia insisted that the ruble-zone states deposit at the CBR hard currency or gold worth 50 percent of the value of the ruble "loan." These conditions would hold for a trial period of six months, after which time, if Russia deemed the ruble-zone states acceptable partners in the

---

[42] See Åslund, *How Russia Became a Market Economy*, 131.

[43] See Elena Kolokol'tseva, "Rublevaia zona novogo tipa: chetkii kontrol' za peredvizheniem i strogii nachal'nik" (Ruble zone of a new type: Tight control on movement and a strict boss), *Segodnia*, 9 September 1993; Mikhail Leontiev, "Rublevaia zona v reanimatsii" (Ruble zone in resuscitation), *Segodnia*, 9 September 1993. The agreement was "Soglashenie o prakticheskikh merakh po sozdaniiu rublevoi zony novogo tipa" (Agreement on practical measures for the creation of a ruble zone of a new type), Moscow, 7 September 1993.

[44] See Alexandrov, *Uneasy Alliance*, 169.

monetary union, the hard-currency collateral and interest would be returned and the ruble notes would no longer be treated as a loan. In addition, the member states could exchange their old ruble notes for the new, but at a confiscatory rate of approximately three for one. Finally, the members were required not to introduce an independent currency for a period of five years.[45]

These Russian conditions obviously destroyed any chance for the new-type ruble zone to succeed. Russia had changed from a generous leader of post-Soviet monetary cooperation seeking to pay post-Soviet republics for their political acquiescence to a self-interested hegemon intent on either profiting from the ruble zone or destroying it.[46] Armenia, Belarus, Kazakhstan, and Uzbekistan introduced independent currencies in November 1993, complaining all the way out of the ruble zone.[47] For example, Kazakhstan's deputy prime minister Sembaev protested that the Russian conditions were "purposefully designed to be unacceptable" and that Kazakhstan was being "pushed out of the ruble zone."[48] As President Nazarbaev explained to the Kazakhstani parliament, "We made all possible concessions, but now Moscow has asked us to do the impossible—hand over billions of dollars."[49] In the end, the monetary situation of these four states was rather ridiculous. For more than three months, they had been using rubles that were worthless in Russia, and they could not afford to pay Russia what it wanted for new rubles. They were forced to introduce independent currencies. Only Tajikistan, in the chaos of its civil war, continued until May 1995 to use the old Soviet-era ruble.[50]

[45] See Viktor Kiianitsa, "Proshchanie s rublem" (Bidding the ruble farewell), *Moskovskie novosti*, 21 November 1993; Andrei Illarionov, "Vyigraiut vse" (Everybody will win), *Delovoi mir*, 13 December 1993; Yuri Petrov, "Natsional'nye valiuty" (National currencies), *Delovoi mir*, 13 December 1993; and Alexandrov, *Uneasy Alliance*, 172.

[46] In the language of the theory of monetary dependence, in late 1993 Russia sought to extract wealth from member states or expel them; previously it had sought to entrap them by making membership attractive. See Jonathan Kirshner, *Currency and Coercion: The Political Economy of International Monetary Power* (Princeton: Princeton University Press, 1995), chap. 4.

[47] See Gregory L. White, "Russian Talks over Ruble Zone Hit Roadblock," *Wall Street Journal Europe*, 2 November 1993; and Geoff Winestock and Sander Thoenes, "Russia: Ruble Zone Fails after Only Two Months," *Inter Press*, 3 November 1993.

[48] Quoted in Alexandrov, *Uneasy Alliance*, 172. See also White, "Russian Talks"; and Wendy Sloane, "Two Former Republics Drop Soviet-Era Ruble; Moscow's Conditions for Joining Ruble Zone Called Too Stringent," *Christian Science Monitor*, 17 November 1993. For more on Kazakhstan's relationship to the ruble zone, see Peter Rutland and Timur R. Isataev, "Kazakhstan," in *First Steps toward Economic Independence: New States of the Postcommunist World*, ed. Michael L. Wyzan (Westport, Conn.: Praeger, 1995), 97–100.

[49] Quoted in Steve Levine, Gillian Tett, and John Lloyd, "Turkmenistan Leads New Ruble Refugees," *Financial Times*, 2 November 1993.

[50] See "Tajik Ruble Substitute for Russian Ruble," *New York Times*, 15 May 1995. Russia eventually distributed the new ruble notes to Tajikistan for "humanitarian" reasons.

Despite having introduced an independent currency, Belarus began to negotiate its return to Russian monetary authority throughout the end of 1993 and beginning of 1994, even as the other members of the ruble zone's hard core had given up on regional monetary union. In January and February 1994 Russian and Belarusian officials made public their intentions to unify the two states' monetary systems, including the significant detail that Belarus would continue to receive Russian energy supplies at the subsidized prices Russian consumers and industrialists received on the domestic market.[51] In April 1994 Viacheslav Kebich and Viktor Chernomyrdin, Belarus's and Russia's respective prime ministers, signed a treaty to unify the Belarusian and Russian economies and monetary systems.[52] As Kebich explained, it was utterly rational for Belarus to agree to Russia's terms because of his country's economic dependence on its large neighbor.[53] In the end, however, the monetary union agreement was just paper. Russia and Belarus continued throughout the 1990s to negotiate monetary union on the occasion of each of their political integration agreements in 1996, 1997, 1998, and 1999. Their bilateral monetary unification did not take place, however, and at the end of the first post-Soviet decade only Russia still used its ruble. The ruble zone seems gone for good.

TRADE RELATIONS

The commercial relations among post-Soviet states, as well as the production networks they shared, were politicized. As with their currencies, post-Soviet governments had contrasting interpretations of their trade with Russia and one another. There were several attempts to create regionwide

---

[51] See Mikhail Berger, "Belorussiia obmeniala chast′ svoego suvereniteta na rossiiskie rubli" (Belarus exchanged part of its sovereignty for Russian rubles), *Izvestiia*, 14 April 1994. Also see Lee Hockstader, "Belarus Slowly Drifts toward Moscow Orbit," *Washington Post*, 28 January 1994; Valery Zhdanko, "Bunny Is Ready to Compromise—Russian and Belarusian Experts Discuss Details of the Two Monetary Systems," *Segodnia*, 3 February 1994, in *Current Digest of the Post-Soviet Press* 46, 5 (1994): 24; and Yelena Kolokoltseva, "Belarus Insists on Cheap Gas from Russia—Talks on Merging 'Bunny' and Ruble Are Stalled," *Segodnia*, 26 February 1994, in *Current Digest of the Post-Soviet Press* 46, 8 (1994): 26.

[52] See Ustina Markus, "The Russian-Belarusian Monetary Union," *RFE / RL Research Report* 3, 20 (1994): 28–32; and "Russia, Belarus Agree on Monetary Union," *Financial Times*, 13 April 1994.

[53] Viacheslav Kebich, "Videt′ istinu: K dogovoru ob 'edinenii denezhnykh sistem Belorussii i Rossii'" (See the truth: Toward the treaty of "unification of the monetary systems of Belarus and Russia"), *Belaruskaia niva*, 27 April 1994.

trade cooperation among all fifteen states and to construct a new institutional foundation for their commercial relations. None succeeded. The post-Soviet regional economy, once it had divided into fifteen independent economies, did not reintegrate.

Early Attempts to Institutionalize Soviet and Post-Soviet Trade

In October 1991, two months before the Soviet Union completely fell apart in December, the leaders of eight union republics—Armenia, Belarus, Kazakhstan, Kyrgyzstan, Russia, Turkmenistan, Tajikistan, and Uzbekistan—agreed to create the Economic Union, which was supposed to be both a free trade area and currency union. Lithuania, Latvia, and Estonia had already exited the Soviet Union in August 1991, so their governments did not attend the October meeting. Another four republics, still part of the USSR, refused to attend the meeting and rejected the idea of an economic union. These four—Azerbaijan, Georgia, Moldova, and Ukraine—expressed ambivalence about their economic relations with the other republics, an ambivalence that characterized their societies' interpretations of the regional economy throughout the rest of the decade.

In December 1991 Boris Yeltsin, Leonid Kravchuk, and Stanislav Shushkevich, representing the governments of Russia, Ukraine, and Belarus, respectively, dissolved the 1922 treaty that had formally organized the Soviet Union. Later that month eleven Soviet republics agreed to create the CIS, which was supposed to ensure close economic cooperation among members, among other goals.[54]

Lithuania, Latvia, and Estonia did not join the CIS, of course. One remaining Soviet republic, Georgia, refused to join the CIS until October 1993, when the imminent collapse of the state forced Georgian president Eduard Shevardnadze into closer relations with Russia in exchange for military support. And Azerbaijan was outside the CIS for approximately one year, between October 1992, when President Elcibey led the state out of the commonwealth, and October 1993, after Elcibey's fall from power. By the end of 1993 the question of CIS membership was settled: the three Baltic states were out, the other twelve post-Soviet states were in.

[54] For recent assessments of the CIS, see Martha Brill Olcott, Anders Åslund, and Sherman W. Garnett, *Getting It Wrong: Regional Cooperation and the Commonwealth of Independent States* (Washington, D.C.: Carnegie Endowment for International Peace, 1999); Paul Kubicek, "End of the Line for the Commonwealth of Independent States," *Problems of Post-Communism* 46, 2 (1999): 15–24; Richard Sakwa and Mark Webber, "The Commonwealth of Independent States, 1991–1998: Stagnation and Survival," *Europe-Asia Studies* 51, 3 (1999): 379–415; and Abraham S. Becker, "Russia and Economic Integration in the CIS," *Survival* 38, 4 (1996–97): 117–36.

Economic Institutions of the CIS

Between late December 1991 and January 2000 the leaders of CIS mem ber states held twenty-three multilateral meetings and signed hundreds agreements dealing with both security and economic issues. Despite pro nouncements about the importance of maintaining a "single economi space" within the CIS, trade among CIS states declined rapidly during 199 which was the first full year their economic relations were *inter*state rathe than *intra*state. To deal with the deterioration in their trade relations, a s rious problem in the estimation of many post-Soviet leaders, represent tives of CIS states created the Economic Court in July 1992 to interpret an enforce CIS economic agreements. The court's rulings, of which there wei only a handful during the 1990s, did not appear to be binding, howeve Rather, they were "recommendations" to member states, which frequent and openly refused to comply. By the end of the decade the Economic Cou had still not become an important institution for economic reintegration Indeed, a number of CIS states rejected its authority altogether.[55]

In May 1993 CIS states agreed to establish a new "Economic Unio among themselves. By this point post-Soviet leaders no longer spoke "maintaining" the common economic space. Instead, many began to spe of "reintegrating" their economies, and regional reintegration became dominant theme of post-Soviet political economy. In September 1993 th CIS states made the Economic Union official. The Treaty of Economi Union proposed the successive creation of a free trade area, a custom union, a common market, and ultimately a monetary union. Then, in O tober 1994, officials of CIS states created the Interstate Economic Com mittee, which was to be the decision-making authority within the Economi Union. In principle, the Economic Committee was to become a truly supr national authority to promote cooperation among CIS states, the Eurasia analog of the European Commission.

The Reintegrationists

For a subset of CIS states, these CIS institutions fostered cooperation The governments of several post-Soviet states sought to use the CIS as a institutional framework for economic reintegration. Although the CIS wa nearly universally derided as ineffectual by outside observers, Belarus, Ka zakhstan, and Russia consistently supported the CIS institutions that pro moted trade cooperation. For these three states, which provided much o the impetus toward regional reintegration, trade cooperation was quit

---

[55] Gennady M. Danilenko, "The Economic Court of the Commonwealth of Independen States," *New York University Journal of International Law and Politics* 31 (1999): 893–918.

successful during the 1990s. Belarus, Kazakhstan, and Russia pushed forward the agenda of the Economic Union and later the creation of the Interstate Economic Committee.[56]

Then, in 1995, economic reintegration in the CIS became, in the parlance of west European integration, "multispeed." The three most committed reintegrationist states, Belarus, Kazakhstan, and Russia, established a Customs Union within the context of CIS institutions but without the agreement of other CIS states.[57] They did, however, invite all other CIS states to join their so-called customs union, which Kyrgyzstan did in 1996 and Tajikistan in 1999.[58] The integration agreements tightened commercial ties within this subset of post-Soviet states. Toward these continuing efforts to reintegrate the post-Soviet economic space, Belarus, Russia, Kazakhstan, Kyrgyzstan, and Tajikistan established, at least nominally, a Common Market.[59] Ultimately, however, their "free trade," "customs union," and "common market" were incomplete since Russia did not harmonize its own trade policies.[60] Still, trade among these states did not collapse, as it did at the regionwide level.

By the end of the decade Russia and Belarus had become even more economically interdependent than they were in 1992. Russian-Belarusian economic and political integration was itself a project embraced by the leaders of the two states. Beginning in April 1994, when the two states agreed

[56] On their support for the Economic Union, see Aleksander Bekker, "Economic Union Rests on Political Underpinnings," *Segodnia*, 28 September 1993, in *Current Digest of the Post-Soviet Press* 45, 39 (1993): 27–28.

[57] Matthew Kaminski and Sander Thoenes, "Not Very Common, Not Much Market," *Financial Times*, 15 August 1996.

[58] A customs union is a free trade area with a common external tariff. Of course, by this point post-Soviet states had neither free trade nor a common external tariff, though a number of them had agreed to both and had created institutions with these technical names. See Constantine Michalopoulos and David G. Tarr, "The Economics of Customs Unions in the Commonwealth of Independent States," *Post-Soviet Geography and Economics* 38, 3 (1997): 125–43. Also see Grigory Selianinov and Marat Salimov, "Troistvennyi tamozhennyi soiuz: v SNG rodilsia vse-taki tamozhennyi soiuz, a ne rublevaia zona" (Three-way customs union: In the end the CIS has given birth to a customs union, not a ruble zone), *Kommersant'*, 31 January 1995; Mikhail Globachev, "Belorussiia, Kazakhstan, Kirgiziia i Rossiia sozdali nechto bol'shee, chem SNG, no ne imeiushchee nazvaniia" (Belarus, Kazakhstan, Kyrgyzstan, and Russia create something that is more than the CIS but lacks a name), *Nezavisimaia gazeta*, 30 March 1996; and Aleksei Chichkin, "Tamozhnia schitaet do piati" (Customs can count to five), *Rossiiskaia gazeta*, 27 February 1999.

[59] Svetlana Karpekova and Gaiaz Alimov, "Obshchii rynok dlia chetverykh" (Common market for four), *Izvestiia*, 22 January 1998; and "Prezidenty RF, Belorussii, Kazakhstana, i Kirgizii ne vozrazhaiut protiv prisodeniia Tajikistana k tamozhennomu soiuzu 'chetverki,' zaiavlaiut v Dushanbe" (Presidents of Russian Federation, Belarus, Kazakhstan, and Kyrgyzstan do not object to the addition of Tajikistan to the customs union of "four," they announce in Dushanbe), *Interfax*, 3 April 1998.

[60] Yuri Chubchenko, "Soiuznaia nedogovorennost'" (Union disagreement), *Kommersant'*, 24 May 2000.

to form a monetary and customs union, Russia and Belarus engaged in bilateral economic cooperation that grew more comprehensive each year.[61]

Throughout the decade Belarus reiterated its agreements in political-economic relations with Russia, agreements that produced real economic integration and vague, largely unimplemented plans for political integration.[62] Thus, in April 1997, Belarus and Russia signed a treaty of "Closer Union" that was proclaimed by Minsk to have been very "profitable." Valentin Velichko, Belarus's minister of CIS affairs, lauded the increase in commercial exchange that resulted. At the time the agreements were signed, the Russian government forgave Belarus's energy debt, which had reached almost $1.2 billion.[63] Then, in December 1998, Belarus and Russia announced their plans for a common policy on economic and military issues as well as a common currency and single budget.[64] Still another union treaty, to form a confederation, was signed by Belarus and Russia on 8 December 1999, the third integration agreement in as many years.[65]

Contrary to the view that the collapse of trade among CIS states was inevitable, Belarus, Kazakhstan, Kyrgyzstan, Russia, and Tajikistan demonstrated that it was practically possible to achieve the levels of interdependence they shared in 1992. Apparently, all post-Soviet governments had to do was accept economic dependence on Russia as a simple material fact, neither good nor bad and certainly not to be avoided.

In general, Armenia supported the CIS and economic institutions in addition to its close bilateral relations with Russia. Armenia was more enthusiastic about military cooperation, however. Although the Armenian

[61] See Geoff Winestock, "Russia, Belarus Sign Agreement to Form Customs Union," *Journal of Commerce*, 21 April 1994; Milan Ruzicka, "Russia-Belarus Customs Union Takes Effect," *Journal of Commerce*, 18 July 1995; and Matthew Kaminski, "Belarus Heads Back to the Russian Fold," *Financial Times*, 16 May 1995.

[62] In fact, Belarus has been more eager to give up elements of its sovereignty than Russia has been to take it. See "Slavic Symbolism," *The Economist*, 5 April 1997; Alessandra Stanley, "Russia Dilutes a Treaty with Belarus, then Signs," *New York Times*, 3 April 1997; and Lee Hockstader, "Belarus, Russia Move toward a New Union; Proposal Exposes Split in Yeltsin Camp over Integration," *Washington Post*, 3 April 1997.

[63] "V Minske schitaiut, chto sozdannyi god nazad soiuz Rossii i Belorussii vygoden oboim gosudarstvam" (In Minsk they perceive that the union of Russia and Belarus created a year ago was profitable for both states), *Interfax*, 1 April 1998. For similar assessments by the Belarusian government about the economic advantages of union with Russia, see Svetlana Karpekova and Boris Vinogradov, "Belorussiia prazdnuet den' edineniia s Rossiei" (Belarus celebrates day of union with Russia), *Izvestiia*, 2 April 1998.

[64] See Michael Wines, "Russia and Belarus Move toward Economic Integration," *New York Times*, 26 December 1998; Wines, "Belarus's Chief Pursues Dream to Revive the Soviet Union," *New York Times*, 27 December 1998; and "Russia and Belarus: Hello Minsk, Farewell Kazan?" *The Economist*, 9 January 1999.

[65] Michael Wines, "Russia and Belarus Agree to Join in a Confederation," *New York Times*, 9 December 1999; and Charles Clover, "Russia and Belarus in New Treaty on Reunification," *Financial Times*, 9 December 1999.

government supported the Economic Court, the Economic Union, and the Interstate Economic Committee, it did not join the Customs Union or Common Market created by the other reintegrationist states.[66]

Ambivalent States

The governments of Azerbaijan, Georgia, Moldova, Turkmenistan, Uzbekistan, and Ukraine did not fully support the economic institutions of the CIS and in some instances refused even to sign, much less implement, CIS economic agreements. Among these six, five states—Georgia, Uzbekistan, Ukraine, Azerbaijan, and Moldova—attempted to establish a more unified voice in CIS military affairs by creating their own organization, known by an acronym, GUUAM, formed from their initial letters.[67] GUUAM's importance in the region increased steadily during the last few years of the decade.

Azerbaijan, Georgia, and Moldova, all reluctant members of the CIS, were ambivalent about economic reintegration over the course of the decade. Their foreign economic policies were internally inconsistent over time. At various moments during the 1990s each of these three states was ruled by nationalists who sought to reorient their trade. Then in all three states anti-Russian nationalists lost elections or were forced from power, and their political successors adopted more accommodating trade policies with regard to CIS institutions. These erratic commercial policies reflected serious domestic political struggles over the proper orientation of the state.

Turkmenistan generally opposed efforts to reintegrate the post-Soviet commercial space and favored bilateral ties with its economic partners, although the government had expressed some support for CIS economic institutions when it signed the Economic Union treaty in December 1993, several months after other CIS states. Uzbekistan, initially ambivalent about economic reintegration, by the end of the decade also generally opposed it, though President Karimov embraced GUUAM and other, specifically Central Asian regional alternatives.

Finally, Ukraine, the most geopolitically important of these states, shifted its commercial policy during the early 1990s in one of the more dramatic policy turnarounds of the decade. President Kravchuk's plan to achieve economic autonomy from Russia included the reorientation of Ukraine's trade toward Europe.[68] As part of this strategy, Ukraine's leaders refused

[66] See Olcott, Åslund, and Garnett, *Getting It Wrong*, 25 and 172.

[67] Originally it was GUAM; Uzbekistan joined in April 1999. See Taras Kuzio, "Promoting Geopolitical Pluralism in the CIS—GUUAM and Western Foreign Policy," *Problems of Post-Communism* 47, 3 (2000): 25–35; and Olcott, Åslund, and Garnett, *Getting It Wrong*, 166–69.

[68] D'Anieri, *Economic Interdependence*.

to sign major CIS cooperation agreements. For example, Ukraine became an "associate" of the Economic Union in 1993, the only CIS state with such an ambiguous status.

By the end of 1992 Ukraine's economy was already mired in crisis.[69] The Ukrainian economy had collapsed, in part because of the rupturing of economic ties among the former Soviet republics. Fuel shortages, the closure of foreign markets that had only a year earlier been part of a single economy, and the weak Western demand for Ukrainian products led a number of Ukrainians, especially the industrialists, to question the autonomy policy. As the economic crisis unfolded, Ukrainian politics divided on the issue of economic autonomy and the importance of reorientation.

Under enormous political pressure, President Kravchuk publicly reassessed Ukraine's economic relationship with Russia at the second congress of the Ukrainian Union of Industrialists and Entrepreneurs, which had been among the most influential critics of the autonomy policies. Kravchuk admitted, "We obviously overestimated the potential of our economy."[70]

In 1993 the Ukrainian government changed course and ended the autonomy policies. As political scientist Paul D'Anieri argues, "The policy of cutting ties with Russia has now been reversed as the price of economic independence has proved too high."[71] In May and June 1993 Ukraine cut import and export quotas, and in August it eliminated the value-added tax on trade with Russia and other CIS members. The government thus began to cultivate a new economic relationship with Russia.

Ukraine trod a fine line after the reversal of its economic autonomy policies. The government recognized the need to cooperate with Russia, but this cooperation was not to be economic reintegration. As the Ukrainian Ministry of Foreign Affairs explained in a 1994 memorandum, Ukraine acknowledged "the general need for the coordination of foreign economic activity within the CIS," but "such coordination must not contravene its national interests, especially the development of its own economy and its movement toward integration in different geographic directions."[72] This logic led Ukraine to reject the Customs Union as well.[73]

---

[69] See Ihor Burakovsky, "The Economic Situation in Ukraine," *Politychna Dumka* 1 (1993): 166–68.

[70] *Interfax*, 6 March 1993, in FBIS-SOV-93-044, 9 March 1993, 36.

[71] D'Anieri, "Dilemmas of Interdependence," 21–22.

[72] Ministry of Foreign Affairs of Ukraine, "Ukraine's Position on CIS Membership," 21 October 1994, Kyiv, reprinted in *Ukrainian Quarterly* 50, 4 (1994): 410–11. The memorandum went on to assert, "Ukraine independently determines the objectives of its own political activity within the CIS framework, and can also alter its form of participation within the CIS, or terminate it entirely."

[73] Taras Kuzio, *Ukraine under Kuchma: Political Reform, Economic Transformation, and Security Policy in Independent Ukraine* (New York: St. Martin's, 1997), 187 and 210. See also Boris

Lithuania, Latvia, and Estonia: Outside the CIS

The three Baltic states also adopted plans to reorient their trade. Unlike Ukraine, they followed through. Lithuania, Latvia, and Estonia rejected multilateral trade deals that included post-Soviet or CIS states and ruled out bilateral free trade agreements with Russia as well. Their commercial relations with Russia had been acrimonious even before the Soviet Union collapsed in late 1991. In Lithuania, demands for autonomy and the rise of a mass nationalist movement led Soviet leader Mikhail Gorbachev to impose a ten-week embargo on oil and gas supplies. Lithuanian authorities did not capitulate.[74]

Lithuania and the other two Baltic states also sought normal, most-favored-nation (MFN) trade status with Russia even as they rejected the CIS and its economic institutions. The Russian government refused, however, apparently to demonstrate its dissatisfaction with the Baltic states' turn toward the West. Russia finally offered Lithuania MFN status in November 1993. The agreement, signed when Russian prime minister Chernomyrdin traveled to Vilnius to meet Lithuanian president Brazauskas, would have cut the Russian customs duties faced by Lithuanian exporters by half. But the agreement foundered in the Russian Duma, where parliamentarians demanded that the Lithuanian government be more cooperative on issues of economics and security, including transit across Lithuania to the Kaliningrad region of Russia. Instead of MFN, the Duma imposed its highest agricultural duties on imports from all three Baltic republics.[75] The Duma did not ratify the Lithuanian MFN agreement until 1995, and commercial relations between the two states were politicized throughout the decade, as they were for the other two Baltic states.

SUMMARY: VARIATION IN SUPPORT
FOR MONETARY AND TRADE COOPERATION

The sources of Russian behavior with regard to the CIS and the post-Soviet economic space in general are not explored at length here. But it is

---

Vinogradov, "Leonid Kuchma sokhraniaet skepsis po otnosheniiu k SNG" (Leonid Kuchma maintains skepticism about relationship with CIS), *Izvestiia*, 16 October 1997.

[74] However, they called a moratorium on Lithuania's independence declaration before entering negotiations with Moscow. See Alfred Erich Senn, *Gorbachev's Failure in Lithuania* (New York: St. Martin's, 1995); and Martha Brill Olcott, "The Lithuanian Crisis," *Foreign Affairs* 69, 3 (1990): 30–46.

[75] See Saulius Girnius, "Relations between the Baltic States and Russia," *RFE / RL Research Report* 33, 33 (1994): 29–33. See also Andrius Uzkalnis, "Lithuania-Russia Meeting Resolves

clear that Russia did not coherently or consistently promote economic reintegration among post-Soviet states, although it frequently took steps to en-
courage regional cooperation that increased its own power relative to other
states. When monetary cooperation appeared to be too costly and when
trade cooperation contradicted powerful Russian economic interests, the
Russian government sacrificed the interests of its CIS neighbors.

What of the other fourteen post-Soviet states? Three were decisive in
their orientation toward Europe and away from the post-Soviet economic
space. Lithuania, Latvia, and Estonia were the first out of the ruble zone
and rejected CIS membership and economic institutions.

Then there were six states that played either ambivalent or contradictory roles in the post-Soviet economy. Ukraine's exit from the ruble zone
was relatively early, but the Ukrainian government compromised its pursuit of trade autonomy. Azerbaijan, Georgia, Moldova, and Turkmenistan
all left the ruble zone when it became clear that Russia was an unreliable
monetary leader. All four also changed their economic strategies during
the 1990s as new governments rose and fell from power and as CIS economic institutions were shown increasingly to be ineffective. Uzbekistan's
monetary and commercial strategies seemed to contradict each other
somewhat, since the Uzbekistani government had been willing to be a
member of the new-type ruble zone but came to oppose regional trade
integration.

Finally, five reintegrationist states were decisive in their orientation toward Russia and the CIS. Armenia, Belarus, Kazakhstan, and Tajikistan all
promoted monetary union and commercial reintegration. Kyrgyzstan also
supported CIS economic institutions, despite the fact that it exited the
ruble zone earlier than the other reintegrationists.

Alternate Rationalist Explanations

As we saw in chapter 1, Liberal and Realist theories of IPE cannot account for the variation in post-Soviet monetary and commercial policies.
Several other explanations, related to traditional Liberal theories, focus on
economic variables. Each provides insight into some aspect of the politics
of post-Soviet economic relations, but none accounts for the wide variety
of strategies adopted by governments in the region.

Little," *Baltic Independent,* 12 November 1993; and Kornelija Jurgatiene and Ole Wæver,
"Lithuania," in *European Integration and National Adaptations,* ed. Hans Mouritzen, Ole Wæver,
and Hakan Wiberg (Commack, N.Y.: Nova Science, 1996), 203.

The Design of the Ruble Zone

There was a striking institutional flaw underlying the ruble zone.[76] All post-Soviet states shared a single currency. The Russian central bank had control of all the printing presses, so it alone could create cash rubles. Before 1991 the Soviet state bank, Gosbank, had local branches in each of the fifteen republics. After Soviet dissolution those local branches of Gosbank became the central banks of the newly independent republics and could create noncash rubles by emitting credit. Therefore, at the beginning of 1992 the ruble zone was a currency union with fifteen independent monetary authorities. It was thus a hyperinflationary disaster waiting to happen because every central bank could issue credit and spread the costs of the inflation across the entire currency union.[77]

There were two reasons post-Soviet central banks created large amounts of ruble credit. The first was seigniorage—the real value of resources transferred to a government through money growth, which includes both the resource transfer from increased private holdings of money and the so-called inflation tax. One might think that the need for seigniorage would induce post-Soviet states to exit the ruble zone. As economist Stanley Fischer argues, seigniorage is usually a reason to leave a currency union, not to remain in one, because a currency union's constituent governments must share seigniorage.[78] If Russia, for example, were keeping seigniorage revenues for itself, then post-Soviet governments might have left the ruble zone. This would have been a particularly powerful incentive between 1991 and 1993 because seigniorage tends to be more important in countries that are politically unstable and have inefficient tax collection systems— the situation facing nearly all post-Soviet governments.[79] Thus, the desire

[76] This is a separate issue from whether the ruble zone was an optimum currency area. I show elsewhere that optimum currency area theory adds little to our understanding of the causes of the collapse of the ruble zone. See Abdelal, "National Strategy and National Money."

[77] On this design flaw as the primary cause of the ruble zone's instability and ultimate collapse, see Jeffrey Sachs and David Lipton, "Remaining Steps to a Market-Based Monetary System in Russia," in *Changing the Economic System in Russia*, ed. Anders Åslund and Richard Layard (London: Pinter, 1993); Carsten Hefeker, *Interest Groups and Monetary Integration* (Boulder, Colo.: Westview, 1997), chap. 7; Marek Dabrowski, "From the Soviet Ruble to National Rubles and Independent Currencies: The Evolution of the Ruble Area in 1991–1993," in *Integration and Disintegration in European Economies*, ed. Dallago and Pegoretti; Orlowski, "Disintegration of the Ruble Zone"; and King Banain and Eugene Zhukov, "The Collapse of the Ruble Zone, 1991–93," in *Establishing Monetary Stability in Emerging Market Economies*, ed. Thomas D. Willett, Richard C. K. Burdekin, Richard J. Sweeney, and Clas Wihlborg (Boulder, Colo.: Westview, 1995).

[78] Stanley Fischer, "Seigniorage and the Case for a National Money," *Journal of Political Economy* 90, 2 (1982): 295–313.

[79] See Alex Cukierman, Sebastian Edwards, and Guido Tabellini, "Seigniorage and Political Instability," *American Economic Review* 82, 3 (1992): 537–55.

for seigniorage among post-Soviet states might have been a reason for the ruble zone's collapse.

In fact, however, the incentives associated with seigniorage were quite the opposite. Most post-Soviet states had an incentive to remain in the ruble zone to get the gains from seigniorage and push the costs onto other states. Seigniorage revenues have inherent limits since there are costs to high levels of inflation. In a currency union, however, the costs of inflation are shared by all member states.

Because all fifteen central banks in the ruble zone could emit credit, the institutional structure of the union led to a competition for seigniorage whereby each bank sought to create more credit than other banks in the union.[80] As long as these governments were relatively indifferent to the resulting inflation (and most acted as though they were during 1992 and 1993), they faced an incentive to remain in the ruble zone and create as much credit as they could at the expense of the other members. Many of them, therefore, did. Thus, during late 1991 and early 1992 the need for seigniorage may have been holding the ruble zone together at the same time that it caused the ruble zone to be inflationary.

The second reason the central banks of the successor states created large amounts of ruble credit was that it was possible to finance trade deficits with other states, and with Russia in particular, simply by issuing credit to local commercial banks, which could extend it to local importers, with the resulting (decreasingly valuable) ruble credit balances ending up in the accounts of other central banks.[81] Thus, governments could orchestrate the transfer of real resources from other post-Soviet republics, and especially Russia, to firms and citizens within their borders simply by emitting more credit.

No doubt this institutional flaw ultimately would have been fatal to the ruble zone, at least as it was organized between December 1991 and July 1993. But this problem does not explain how, when, or why the ruble zone actually collapsed. Most important, four post-Soviet states—Estonia, Latvia, Lithuania, and Ukraine—introduced currencies while these seigniorage revenues were most available to them and when they could have transferred real resources from Russia to their economies by emitting more credit. Moreover, the currency reform programs of the three Baltic states emphasized macroeconomic stabilization and, if necessary, deflation. Lithuania, Latvia, and Estonia created the most disciplined and least inflationary monetary regimes of the former Soviet Union, through a combination of political will, independent central banks, and external nominal anchors. Clearly, seigniorage is not what they were after by exiting the ruble zone.

[80] For an excellent discussion, see Conway, *Currency Proliferation.*
[81] See Benjamin J. Cohen, *The Geography of Money* (Ithaca: Cornell University Press, 1998), 78–80.

Further, the other ruble-zone members were indifferent to the hyper-inflation that resulted from the institutional flaw, or at least indifferent enough not to change their policies and leave the ruble zone in favor of monetary stabilization. Even when Russia reasserted control over the ruble zone, first in June 1992 and then, decisively, in July 1993, at least five post-Soviet states—Armenia, Belarus, Kazakhstan, Tajikistan, and Uzbekistan—were still willing to participate in a currency union in which seigniorage would accrue only to Russia and in which they could no longer finance their trade deficits with Russia by issuing credit.

This institutional flaw is most useful for understanding why the Russian government and central bank ultimately became dissatisfied with the ruble-zone members' taking advantage of the currency union and why they eventually decided to force members to choose either to subordinate their monetary policies to Russia's or to leave the ruble zone. But the flaw offers little insight into the variety of the other post-Soviet states' monetary strategies. That variety must have resulted from something else.

Preferences for Monetary and Commercial Policy
Deduced from Economic Sectors

Post-Soviet states' energy trade was linked directly to monetary politics. After the collapse of Soviet institutions Russia continued to subsidize production in the other successor states with hugely discounted energy and raw materials, by some estimates at 60 to 70 percent below world prices. In principle, Russia could have offered these subsidies to the other post-Soviet states regardless of whether or not they stayed in the ruble zone, but Russia sought to link ruble-zone membership, and political-economic acquiescence in Russian regional hegemony more generally, to the continuation of subsidies. Therefore, in the early 1990s post-Soviet governments interpreted monetary sovereignty and continued Russian energy subsidies as a trade-off. The choice was obvious to post-Soviet states, particularly after Russia made examples of the Baltic states, whose societies saw their energy and raw materials prices rise from approximately 30 percent of world levels all the way up to world levels in a matter of months after they introduced independent currencies in 1992.[82] Until Georgia entered the CIS in 1993 and while Azerbaijan was out of the CIS between 1992 and 1993, they too paid higher prices for the energy they imported from Russia.

So one possible explanation for the timing and motivation of exits from the ruble zone is the distribution of costs and benefits from the subsidies

---

[82] See John M. Kramer, "'Energy Shock' from Russia Jolts Baltic States," *RFE / RL Research Report* 2, 17 (1993): 41–49. Also see Olcott, Åslund, and Garnett, *Getting It Wrong*, 44–45.

Table 3.2 Impact on the Terms of Trade
of Changing to World Prices

Russia	+79
Turkmenistan	+50
Kazakhstan	+19
Kyrgyzstan	+1
Uzbekistan	−3
Tajikistan	−7
Azerbaijan	−7
Ukraine	−18
Belarus	−20
Georgia	−21
Armenia	−24
Latvia	−24
Lithuania	−31
Estonia	−32
Moldova	−38

Source: Adapted from David G. Tarr, "The
Terms-of-Trade Effects of Moving to World
Prices on Countries of the Former Soviet
Union," *Journal of Comparative Economics* 18,
1 (1994): 1–24.

implicit in post-Soviet states' trade with one another. Thus, an evaluation
of the terms-of-trade effects of moving to world prices is a useful way to assess post-Soviet states' economic dependence on Russia and the Eurasian
region (Tables 3.2 and 3.3). Besides Russia, as economist David Tarr
showed, only Kazakhstan and Turkmenistan, because they were not dependent on energy imports from Russia, faced potentially large incentives
to move to world prices and to leave the ruble zone.[83] Most of the twelve
other post-Soviet states faced large terms-of-trade losses from independent
currencies that would have, as Russia made clear, eliminated Russian energy subsidies.[84]

The economic consequences of introducing independent currencies in
the former Soviet Union were substantial and varied from state to state. As
a result, there were clear predictions about ruble-zone participation to be
made from an analysis of the costs and benefits of membership. Economists
Linda Goldberg, Barry Ickes, and Randi Ryterman tallied these costs and
benefits and offered a "balance sheet" that included both seigniorage and
terms-of-trade effects. In the early 1990s, according to this analysis, Kazakhstan and Turkmenistan faced large incentives to leave the ruble zone
and raise their energy prices to world levels and, at the same time, would

[83] Note, however, that Kazakhstan's refining facilities were quite limited and many of its oil
pipelines (and train tracks) ran into and through Russia. The analysis of these incentives is
based solely on the imports and exports of energy and raw materials.

[84] See David G. Tarr, "The Terms-of-Trade Effects of Moving to World Prices on the Countries of the Former Soviet Union," *Journal of Comparative Economics* 18, 1 (1994): 1–24.

Table 3.3 Intraregional Share of Soviet
Republics' Total Commerce, 1990

Turkmenistan	93
Estonia	92
Armenia	90
Lithuania	90
Latvia	89
Kazakhstan	89
Uzbekistan	89
Moldova	88
Azerbaijan	88
Tajikistan	87
Belarus	87
Georgia	86
Kyrgyzstan	86
Ukraine	82
Russia	61

Source: Constantine Michalopoulos and
David Tarr, *Trade and Payments Arrangements
for States of the Former USSR* (Washington,
D.C.: World Bank, 1992).

have incurred small income or output costs associated with a new currency. The three Baltic states "were expected to experience very large immediate income losses" that were "unlikely to be compensated by the net gains from the seigniorage revenues" that would accrue from national currencies. Thus, the economists concluded, "if there is any prediction to be made from the analysis of the short-term costs and benefits of leaving the ruble zone, it is that [the Baltic states] would try to remain in the ruble zone, while [Kazakhstan and Turkmenistan] would opt for a new currency."[85]

That is not what happened. Kazakhstan and Turkmenistan—the biggest potential winners from currency separation, according to this logic—did not leave the ruble zone in 1992. Lithuania, Latvia, and Estonia—among the biggest potential losers from currency separation—did. So the problem is not merely that the broadest and most powerful economistic prediction and explanation of the evolution of the ruble zone is incorrect. As Goldberg, Ickes, and Ryterman summarize, an "analysis of the costs and benefits of independent currencies is yielding opposite predictions from events." Therefore, they conclude, "Politics matter."[86] Post-Soviet govern-

[85] Linda S. Goldberg, Barry W. Ickes, and Randi Ryterman, "Departures from the Ruble Zone: Implications of Adopting Independent Currencies," *World Economy* 17, 3 (1994): 293–322, at 318–19 and 313.

[86] Goldberg, Ickes, and Ryterman, "Departures from the Ruble Zone," 320. For more on the trade-off between national currencies and continued subsidies, see Grant Spencer and Adrienne Cheasty, "The Ruble Area: A Breaking of Old Ties?" *Finance and Development* 30, 2 (1993): 2–10.

Table 3.4 Share of Economy by Sector, 1990

	Agriculture	Industry	Construction	Transport	Other
Armenia	17.3	45.4	25.4	4.1	7.8
Azerbaijan	37.6	34.8	11.7	5.2	10.8
Belarus	29.3	44.0	11.8	5.1	9.8
Estonia	20.3	50.5	10.5	7.2	11.5
Georgia	37.2	35.0	11.0	4.9	11.9
Kazakhstan	39.9	27.6	15.3	9.3	7.9
Kyrgyzstan	43.1	31.8	11.9	3.8	9.2
Latvia	21.8	51.2	8.1	7.5	11.3
Lithuania	33.4	34.1	13.4	5.9	13.3
Moldova	41.7	34.4	9.0	4.8	10.1
Russia	19.9	42.2	12.7	6.9	18.3
Tajikistan	38.3	28.6	14.7	4.2	14.3
Turkmenistan	47.9	15.7	17.9	8.5	10.1
Ukraine	30.3	41.3	9.7	6.0	19.4
Uzbekistan	44.0	23.8	14.9	5.7	11.4

Source: World Bank, *Statistical Handbook: States of the Former Soviet Union* (Washington, D.C.: World Bank, 1992).

ments' monetary strategies cannot be derived from the economic costs and benefits associated with ruble-zone membership.

There is also the possibility that former Soviet states' commercial policies reflected divergent economic structures or their places in the regional or world economy. Perhaps, for example, heavily industrialized republics were more likely to seek economic reintegration since their economies were more tightly linked to specific regional industries and more dependent on post-Soviet markets. Table 3.4 provides some evidence against this view, however. The most heavily industrialized republics did not necessarily seek reintegration.

Alternatively, perhaps energy-rich republics were more likely to reorient their economies since it was easier and more lucrative to sell oil and gas on world markets. Political scientist Matthew Evangelista evaluated these kinds of approaches to the post-Soviet energy sector and found that they could not explain why some governments sought autonomy because such approaches did not take into account how institutions affected the interpretation of economic incentives.[87] The most energy-rich did not necessarily attempt to reorient their economies, as the earlier discussion of the ruble zone indicated. Thus, like the incentives for ruble-zone membership

[87] Matthew Evangelista, "From Each According to Its Abilities: Competing Theoretical Approaches to the Post-Soviet Energy Sector," in *The Sources of Russian Foreign Policy after the Cold War*, ed. Celeste A. Wallander (Boulder, Colo.: Westview, 1996); and Evangelista, "Stalin's Revenge: Institutional Barriers to Internationalization in the Soviet Union," in *Internationalization and Domestic Politics*, ed. Robert O. Keohane and Helen V. Milner (Cambridge: Cambridge University Press, 1996).

associated with energy prices, the incentives associated with trade were not by themselves the decisive influence on trade strategies.

Of course, there is a wide range of theories that can be used to deduce the preferences of economic actors, and I do not definitively reject their usefulness for the post-Soviet region.[88] Nevertheless, there are good reasons to conclude that these rationalist accounts of political economy will be unable to tell the whole post-Soviet story.

First, to explain the variation in policies, it appears necessary to find variation in the preferences of economic actors. In other words, for a purely rationalist logic to hold, there must be some lobby in Lithuania, Latvia, and Estonia that convinced the government to reorient the economy, just as there must have been some lobby in Belarus and Kazakhstan that urged regional reintegration. The latter is true, but the former is not. Virtually all organized economic actors, especially the powerful industrial lobbies throughout the former Soviet Union, pressed for regional trade, at least, and reintegration, at most. There was no group of economic actors in any post-Soviet state that lobbied for the drastic reorientation of their state's trade away from Russia and the CIS and toward the West.[89] Obviously, the post-Soviet governments that sought to

---

[88] See Jeffry A. Frieden and Ronald Rogowski, "The Impact of the International Economy on National Policies: An Analytical Overview," in *Internationalization*, ed. Keohane and Milner; and Helen V. Milner, *Interests, Institutions, and Information: Domestic Politics and International Relations* (Princeton: Princeton University Press, 1997).

[89] For example, all fifteen post-Soviet states had some version of a statewide union of industrialists, in most called something like the Confederation of Industrialists and Entrepreneurs. In February 1992 these fifteen associations created the regionwide International Congress of Industrialists and Entrepreneurs to lobby for regional economic cooperation and reintegration. In addition, the state-level associations frequently met bilaterally and in smaller multilateral groups to promote economic ties among specific post-Soviet states. Interestingly, these industrial lobbies were themselves institutional holdovers since their organization depended on features of the Soviet economy. See the text of their founding document in "Soglashenie o sozdanii mezhdunarodnogo kongressa promyshlennikov i predprinimatelei" (Agreement on the creation of the International Congress of Industrialists and Entrepreneurs), *Delovaia Ukraina*, 6 October 1992. See also Yuri Galimov, "Tropa k integratsii" (The path to integration), *Delovoi mir*, 28 January 1994. The International Congress continued to lobby for regional cooperation and reintegration throughout the decade. See also, for example, the results of their fourth assembly, "Kurs na ekonomicheskoe sotrudnichestvo" (Course toward economic cooperation), in their *Vestnik delovoi zhizni* 13 (August 1997). On the preferences of Lithuanian industrialists, see "Lithuanian Producers Want Free Trade with Ukraine, Russia, Poland," *Baltic News Service*, 9 October 1997; "Agreement between Russian and Lithuanian Manufacturers Will Stimulate Economic Ties, Russian Manufacturer Believes," *Baltic News Service*, 12 September 1996; and Tamara Nikolaeva, "Litovskii i rossiiskii prem'ery sdelali to, chto ne uspeli sdelat' presidenty?" (Did the Lithuanian and Russian prime ministers do what the presidents did not manage to do?), *Nezavisimaia gazeta*, 20 November 1993. On the preferences of Ukrainian industrialists, see Vladimir Kulagin, "Predprinimateli Rossii

reorient their trade cannot have been convinced by some economic lobby, for none existed.

A second, even more powerful critique of a rationalist and economistic interpretation is fundamentally political: the *potential* domestic distributional struggles that can be deduced using rationalist theories simply did not exist in the former Soviet Union. The actual struggles over monetary and commercial policy in post-Soviet states were of a different kind. Economic actors, such as industrial lobbies, producer associations, and farmers, did not contest the economic orientation of their states among themselves because they essentially agreed on the necessity of reintegration. Thus, there were two kinds of policy outcomes: those in which governments and lobbies agreed and those in which governments rejected reintegrationist lobbies.

Although it may eventually be possible to construct a deductive logic based on economic characteristics of post-Soviet states and the regional economy of which they were a part to account for the variety of their economic strategies, that does not mean that the political sources of those strategies will then be explained. It is more useful to contextualize the politics of foreign economic policy making in the former Soviet Union with an account of the actual, not potential, politics that led some governments to choose reorientation and some to choose reintegration. The central lesson of this chapter's analysis is that although the material facts of the regional economy are important, by themselves they are of little use to the analysis of post-Soviet IPE because post-Soviet governments attached contrasting meanings to the economic incentives and disincentives facing them. In order to explain why they pursued such different policies, it is necessary to understand how they interpreted their currencies and commerce.

---

i Ukrainy vystupaiut protiv razrusheniia edinogo ekonomicheskogo prostranstva" (Entrepreneurs of Russia and Ukraine come out against destruction of the single economic space), *Izvestiia*, 21 October 1992; and Maksim Pavlov, "Rossiiskii i Ukrainskii soiuzy promyshlennikov—protiv granits" (Russian and Ukrainian unions of industrialists are against borders), *Kommersant'*, 21 October 1992. On the preferences of Belarusian industrialists, see Igor Siniakevich, "U 'promyshlennikov' teper' svoia partiia" ("Industrialists" now have their own party), *Nezavisimaia gazeta*, 9 October 1992; Liudmila Masliukova, "Direktorskii korpus podderzhivaet prem'erov" (Directors' body supports premiers), *Sovetskaia Belorussiia*, 20 March 1993; Viktor Bondarev, "Slaviane vyiasniaiut otnosheniia" (Slavs clarify relationship), *Kuranty*, 16 April 1994; "Otkrytoe pis'mo" (Open letter), *Sovetskaia Belorussiia*, 30 March 1993; and Olga Zagorul'skaya, "The System of Interest Representation in the Republic of Belarus," in *Emerging Social Actors*, vol. 3 of *Post-Soviet Puzzles: Mapping the Political Economy of the Former Soviet Union*, ed. Klaus Segbers and Stephan De Spiegeleire (Baden-Baden: Nomos Verlagsgesellschaft, 1995). I am grateful to Keith Darden for several helpful discussions on this point.

NATIONALISM AND IPE IN THE FORMER SOVIET UNION

To contextualize politics in the former Soviet Union with an understanding of the cultural frames and national identities that influenced political-economic outcomes is not an easy task, despite the fact that the Nationalist perspective on IPE offers clear suggestions for where to begin. In chapters 4, 5, and 6 I explore the interaction between national identity and political economy in Lithuania, Ukraine, and Belarus in detail. Here I offer a preliminary assessment of the usefulness of a Nationalist interpretation of the policies of the other eleven states.[90]

National Identities of Post-Soviet Societies

Nationalist movements arose as the Soviet Union began to come apart in the late 1980s and early 1990s,[91] but the levels of nationalist mobilization among Soviet republics were uneven. As powerful, mass-based nationalist movements in the Baltic republics demanded economic autonomy first, then political autonomy, and ultimately independent statehood, the societies of several other Soviet republics simply watched. Indeed, Soviet disintegration seemed to catch the Central Asian republics quite by surprise. Among these eleven other states, six (Armenia, Azerbaijan, Estonia, Georgia, Latvia, and Moldova) experienced significant nationalist mobilization before 1991 and five (Kazakhstan, Kyrgyzstan, Tajikistan, Turkmenistan, and Uzbekistan) did not. In Latvia and Estonia the nationalists' authority and fundamental goals were relatively uncontested during the 1990s, although large Russian-speaking populations in both states affected their domestic politics.[92] The stories of the other nine are more complicated.

---

[90] They are Armenia, Azerbaijan, Estonia, Georgia, Kazakhstan, Kyrgyzstan, Latvia, Moldova, Tajikistan, Turkmenistan, and Uzbekistan. For my original argument, see Rawi Abdelal, "Economic Nationalism after Empire: A Comparative Perspective on Nation, Economy, and Security in Post-Soviet Eurasia" (Ph.D. diss., Cornell University, 1999). For a somewhat different interpretation, see Andrei P. Tsygankov, "Defining State Interests after Imperial Disintegration: National Identity, Domestic Structures, and Foreign Trade Policies of Latvia and Belarus," *Review of International Political Economy* 7, no. 1 (2000): 101–37.

[91] The literature on Soviet and post-Soviet nationalisms is quite rich. See especially Ronald Grigor Suny, *Revenge of the Past: Nationalism, Revolution, and the Collapse of the Soviet Union* (Stanford: Stanford University Press, 1993); and Suny, "Provisional Stabilities: The Politics of Identities in Post-Soviet Eurasia," *International Security* 24, 3 (1999–2000): 139–78. See also Ian Bremmer and Ray Taras, eds., *New States, New Politics: Building the Post-Soviet Nations* (Cambridge: Cambridge University Press, 1997).

[92] See Graham Smith, "The Resurgence of Nationalism," in *The Baltic States: The National Self-Determination of Estonia, Latvia, and Lithuania*, ed. Smith (New York: St. Martin's, 1994);

Kazakhstan, Kyrgyzstan, Tajikistan, Turkmenistan, and Uzbekistan. As a preliminary indicator of the content and contestation of national identity, the absence of nationalist mobilization against Soviet authorities suggests that there was no specifically anti-Soviet or anti-Russian content within the national identities of the five Central Asian societies. Furthermore, the nationalist movements and parties that emerged in Central Asia after Soviet dissolution were marginalized politically. Many of them proposed anti-Russian and anti-CIS content for their societies' identities. Had they been able to acquire power, the Central Asian nationalists would have attempted to reorient their states' economies.

They were unsuccessful, however, primarily because those ideas and policy proposals were unpopular among both political elites and mass publics. In Kazakhstan, for example, nationalist movements and parties, including Zheltoqsan, Azat, and Alash, sought to reorient the economy toward China, Turkey, and Iran but failed to garner significant mass support and were opposed by the dominant People's Unity Party (later renamed National Unity Party), organized by President Nursultan Nazarbaev. In Kyrgyzstan the Asaba Party of National Revival and Ata-Meken (Motherland) Party convinced neither the majority of Kyrgyzstani society nor President Askar Akaev that rejecting the economic institutions of the CIS was necessary for the consolidation of statehood. In Tajikistan the Islamic Renaissance Party, secular democrats linked to the Rastokhez cultural revival movement, which replaced the Communists after the Soviet collapse, were overthrown in December 1992 by former Communists who sought to maintain close economic and political relations with Russia. Tajikistan's National Revival Movement, established in 1996 in opposition to the government, never became influential. The most prominent Turkmenistani nationalists, Agzybyrlik, were outlawed, along with other nationalist parties, while President Sapamurat Niazov maintained tight control over the political process. Similarly, Uzbekistan's nationalists, including the Unity Popular Movement Birlik, its offshoot Erk, and the Islamic Renaissance Party, were marginalized, suppressed, and eventually banned by President Islam Karimov. Thus, nationalist movements were not politically influential in Central Asian states during the 1990s.

Former Communists, frequently high-ranking officials such as Kazakhstan's Nazarbaev and Uzbekistan's Karimov, ruled these states relatively autocratically and actively sought to prevent the nationalist opposition from taking power. Central Asia's former Communists and formerly Soviet Communist parties (Kazakhstan's National Unity Party,

---

Rein Taagepera, *Estonia: Return to Independence* (Boulder, Colo.: Westview, 1993); and Toivo U. Raun, *Estonia and the Estonians*, 2d ed. (Stanford: Hoover Institution Press, 1991), 222–42.

Kyrgyzstan's Communist Party, Tajikistan's Communist Party, Turk-menistan's Democratic Party, and Uzbekistan's People's Democratic Party) did not turn into nationalists, and the most prominent political parties in the area opposed the nationalists' main goals.[93]

Azerbaijan, Georgia, and Moldova. Azerbaijan, Georgia and Moldova had some significant similarities. In all three, nationalist parties, such as the Azer-baijani Popular Front, the Moldovan Popular Front (renamed the Chris-tian-Democratic Popular Front in 1992), and the Georgian Popular Front and the Round Table coalition, enjoyed significant influence and power over their states' politics. Indeed, in each of these states nationalists directly controlled the government for some period of time after 1991 and sought to reorient their economies. Azerbaijan's nationalists proposed to orient the economy toward Turkey, Georgia's nationalists emphasized a general "West-ern" direction, and Moldovan nationalists sought a specifically pro-Roma-nian and generally pro-Western strategy. Most important, all three groups of nationalists interpreted Russia as their most important "other," against which to define their nation and from which to ensure independence and economic autonomy. They were emphatically anti-Soviet and anti-CIS.

The nationalists in these three states either lost power or were forced to compromise in the face of two serious challenges to their authority. First, other powerful political forces, including most former Communists and

[93] The best overview of Central Asia's political economy is Alexander Cooley, "Transition-ing Backwards: Concepts and Comparison in the Study of Central Asia's Political Economy," *Harriman Review* 11, 1–2 (1998): 1–11. On Central Asia in general, see Gregory Gleason: *The Central Asian States: Discovering Independence* (Boulder, Colo.: Westview, 1997); and Martha Brill Olcott, *Central Asia's New States: Independence, Foreign Policy, and Regional Security* (Washington, D.C.: United States Institute of Peace Press, 1996). On Kazakhstan, see Alexandrov, *Uneasy Alliance*, chaps. 4–5; Martha Brill Olcott, *The Kazakhs*, 2d ed. (Stanford: Hoover Institution Press, 1995); and Olcott, "Kazakhstan: Pushing for Eurasia," in *New States, New Politics*, ed. Bremmer and Taras. On Kyrgyzstan, see Eugene Huskey, "Kyrgyzstan: The Politics of Demo-graphic and Economic Frustration," in *New States, New Politics*, ed. Bremmer and Taras. On Tajikistan, see Barnett R. Rubin, "Russian Hegemony and State Breakdown in the Periphery: Causes and Consequences of the Civil War in Tajikistan," in *Post-Soviet Political Order*, ed. Bar-nett R. Rubin and Jack Snyder (London: Routledge, 1998); and Muriel Atkin, "Tajikistan: Re-form, Reaction, and Civil War," in *New States, New Politics*, ed. Bremmer and Taras. On Uzbeki-stan, see Gregory Gleason, "Uzbekistan: The Politics of National Independence," in *New States, New Politics*, ed. Bremmer and Taras; William Fierman, "The Communist Party, 'Erk,' and the Changing Uzbek Political Environment," *Central Asian Survey* 10, 3 (1991): 55–72; Shahram Akbarzadeh, "Nation-Building in Uzbekistan," *Central Asian Survey* 15, 1 (1996): 23–32; and Edward A. Allworth, *The Modern Uzbeks* (Stanford: Hoover Institution Press, 1990), 309–31. On Turkmenistan, see David Nissman, "Turkmenistan: Just Like Old Times," in *New States, New Politics*, ed. Bremmer and Taras; Shahram Akbarzadeh, "National Identity and Political Legitimacy in Turkmenistan," *Nationalities Papers* 27, 2 (1999): 271–90; and Alexander Cooley, "The Faltering Oil State," in *Holding the Course: Annual Survey of Eastern Europe and the Former Soviet Union*, ed. Peter Rutland (Armonk, N.Y.: M. E. Sharpe, 1999).

their successor political parties (Azerbaijan's Communist Party, Georgia's United Communist and Communist Parties, and Moldova's Agrarian Democratic and Socialist Parties), opposed the nationalists and their goals, primarily because they disagreed with the nationalists' interpretations of their respective nations. Perhaps even more problematic was the fact that various nationalist movements within these states competed with one another more than they cooperated.

As in Ukraine, there was significant regional variation in the contestation of national identity within the states. Reflecting divergent political, cultural, and institutional histories, serious differences existed in several regions of Azerbaijan, including Karabakh; among Abkhazia, South Ossetia, and the rest of Georgia; and between western and eastern Moldova, divided by the Dniestr River. These societies' dominant nationalist movements and parties did not achieve the political success that Baltic nationalists achieved; neither they nor their goals were as popular.

Foreign relations were a critical axis of debate between the nationalists and former Communists. When formerly Communist political elites retook power, as did Haidar Aliev in Azerbaijan in 1993, Eduard Shevardnadze in Georgia in 1992, and the Agrarian Democrats and Socialists in Moldova in 1994, they reestablished close economic and political ties with Russia. And in 1993 Azerbaijan rejoined the CIS, and Georgia joined for the first time, thus also linking their states to regional institutions.

The other significant challenge was the susceptibility of these states to Russian influence in their domestic security politics. Secessionist movements, and sometimes outright civil war, in Azerbaijan's Karabakh, Georgia's Abkhazia, and Moldova's Trans-Dniestr opened the door for Russia either to promote internal threats to political leadership as leverage or to offer military and economic support as a bargaining chip for closer political-economic ties.[94]

These two challenges were related. In none of these three states were the nationalists' visions of the state's future uncontested. And the very fact of their contestation, not least by the secessionist movements themselves, allowed increased Russian influence on their domestic politics and ultimately their foreign economic policies as well.[95]

---

[94] See Philip G. Roeder, "From Hierarchy to Hegemony: The Post-Soviet Security Complex," in *Regional Orders*, ed. David A. Lake and Patrick M. Morgan (University Park: Pennsylvania State University Press, 1997).

[95] On Azerbaijan, see Swietochowski, *Russia and Azerbaijan*, especially 221–28; and Shireen Hunter, "Azerbaijan: Searching for New Neighbors," in *New States, New Politics*, ed. Bremmer and Taras. On Moldova, see Charles King, *The Moldovans: Romania, Russia, and the Politics of Culture* (Stanford: Hoover Institution Press, 2000); and William Crowther, "Moldova: Caught between Nation and Empire," in *New States, New Politics*, ed. Bremmer and Taras; and on the

Armenia. Armenia's most influential nationalist movements and political parties, such as the Pan-Armenian National Movement, held a unique position in the former Soviet Union: they were not coherently anti-Russian.[96] Instead of Russia as the most important "other" in Armenian national identity, Turkey and Azerbaijan played more significant threatening roles in Armenians' historical memory and collective identity. In some prominent interpretations of Armenian history and its current politics, Russia was seen as a defender of Armenian culture and identity from neighboring Muslim states.[97]

Armenian national identity was coherent and its content widely shared. The Armenian nationalist movement enjoyed popular support and a relatively uncontested agenda. As in the Baltic states, many former Communists self-consciously became nationalists, adopting the goals and symbols of the nationalist movement. Indeed, the Armenian Communist Party had cooperated with the nationalist movement and in 1990 surrendered power to the nationalists without a struggle.

Summary Comparison

This sketch of the national identities of post-Soviet societies suggests some specific expectations for the economic relations among them. Most straightforwardly, when nationalist movements and political parties were able to hold power and implement their agenda, post-Soviet governments, with one exception, sought to reorient their economies—away from Russia, almost invariably understood as the most important "other" and most significant threat to economic, political, and cultural autonomy. The exception, Armenia, shows that not all post-Soviet nationalists were anti-Russian or inter-

---

goals of Moldovan political parties, see Vladimir Socor, "Moldova's Political Landscape: Profiles of the Parties," *RFE / RL Research Report* 3, 10 (1994): 6–14. On Georgia, see Ronald Grigor Suny, *The Making of the Georgian Nation*, 2d ed. (Bloomington: Indiana University Press, 1994), 317–36; and Stephen Jones, "Georgia: The Trauma of Statehood," in *New States, New Politics*, ed. Bremmer and Taras; and for a comparison of the policy positions of the nationalists and Communists in early Georgian elections, see Lynn D. Nelson and Paata Amonashvili, "Voting and Political Attitudes in Soviet Georgia," *Soviet Studies* 44, 4 (1992): 687–97.

[96] A few Armenian nationalist parties were oriented against Russia and the CIS, among them the Free Armenia Mission, but the most influential Armenian nationalists proposed traditional anti-Turkic content for their society's collective identity. Explicit anti-Russianism, even among nationalists who sought more autonomy from Russia, was rare. See Suny, "Provisional Stabilities," 156–59.

[97] See Nora Dudwick, "Armenia: Paradise Lost?" in *New States, New Politics*, ed. Bremmer and Taras; and Ronald Grigor Suny, *Looking toward Ararat: Armenia in Modern History* (Bloomington: Indiana University Press, 1993).

preted Russia as their most significant threat. In Armenia nationalists and former Communists largely agreed on the importance of close economic and political ties with Russia and within the framework of the CIS.

The broader issue is how national identities themselves—as underlying cultural frames—influenced the economic relations among post-Soviet states. First, there are those societies with national identities whose content, proposed by nationalist movements and parties, was widely shared and therefore relatively uncontested. In Latvia and Estonia the nationalists came to power and influenced societal debates about economic strategy so that the entire political spectrum, including most former Communists, embraced the nationalist agenda of economic reorientation. In contrast, Armenian national identity, also coherent and widely shared, led the state to cooperate closely with Russia.

Then there were those societies in which the nationalists' proposals for the content of their national identities was heavily contested, sometimes with significant regional variation in mass publics' interpretation of their collective identities. Azerbaijan, Georgia, and Moldova fall into this category, and they demonstrate also how the preferences of the first post-Soviet governments after 1991 were insufficient to achieve their goals. This was true, first, because of a failure of societal resolve, since the goals of the governments were not as widely shared as in other societies, for example, in the Baltic. Also, internal state weakness allowed Russia to influence their domestic politics and affect military and economic outcomes. It was not that the governments of these states necessarily preferred their ambivalent economic strategies. Rather, their erratic and often contradictory strategies were outcomes of the interaction among government preferences, the ambivalence of their societies' collective identities, and the capabilities of their states to resist Russian influence.

Finally, there were societies whose collective interpretation of their national identities was ambiguous, incoherent, fragmented, or highly contested: Kazakhstan, Kyrgyzstan, Tajikistan, Turkmenistan, and Uzbekistan. In these states anti-Soviet, anti-Russian, and anti-CIS policies proposed by nationalist groups were largely rejected by most other societal actors. In Kazakhstan, Kyrgyzstan, and Tajikistan the marginalization of the nationalists and the ambiguity of national identity led their post-Soviet governments not to interpret economic dependence on Russia as a significant threat to state security or economic autonomy. They promoted economic cooperation within the framework of CIS institutions because their leaders believed this strategy was at least a partial solution to their economic woes. Economic reintegration, regionwide and with Russia specifically, for these governments, seemed natural.

Two Possible Exceptions

The economic strategies of Turkmenistan and Uzbekistan do not seem to be comprehensible in Nationalist terms. Although both began independent statehood with ambivalent economic strategies, even supportive of regional trade agreements and the ruble zone, the governments of both increasingly sought economic autonomy during the decade. Turkmenistan's economic orientation seemed almost paradoxical. Among Central Asian states its government most vehemently rejected regional economic reintegration within the framework of the CIS, but at the same time, it maintained the closest and least strained bilateral economic relations with Russia.[98] Although Turkmenistan's close economic relations with Russia were consistent with the ambiguity and contestedness of Turkmenistani society's national identity, the government's rejection of the CIS must have resulted from some other cultural frame of political economy.

Thus, these evolving orientations—from acquiescence to the rejection of regional institutions—did not result from the ascendance of nationalist political parties. Nor did they derive from an increasingly coherent or more widely shared national identity among Turkmenistanis and Uzbekistanis, although the governments of both states, despite being composed of essentially the same elites who ruled before 1991, embarked on nation-making projects. The governments of Uzbekistan and Turkmenistan thus co-opted some of the goals of the very nationalists they repressed. Although their foreign economic policies certainly are related to their nation-making and state-building goals, there is little in this book's analytical framework that can explain why they alone, of the five Central Asian republics, eventually chose such a path.

The Promise of a Nationalist Explanation

Even so, an approach based on the content and contestation of the national identities of post-Soviet societies is more useful for understanding the region's economic reorganization than standard Realist or Liberal approaches to IPE and the economistic interpretations reviewed in this chapter. Applying the Nationalist perspective explains a great deal of the variation among post-Soviet states. And it also has the advantage of explaining many of the actual political struggles and debates that oc-

[98] See Rainer Freitag-Wirminghaus, "Turkmenistan's Place in Central Asia and the World," in *Post-Soviet Central Asia*, ed. Touraj Atabaki and John O'Kane (London: Tauris, 1998).

curred in the twelve post-Soviet states whose politics and policies were consistent with the Nationalist perspective.[99]

Tracing the processes of policy making in post-Soviet states demonstrates that the variables emphasized by the Nationalist perspective were decisive influences on governments' choices. In the next three chapters I explore the foreign economic policies of Lithuania, whose government sought to reorient its economy Westward; Ukraine, where the government compromised its effort to reorient and maintained close economic ties within the CIS; and Belarus, whose government sought reintegration with Russia and the post-Soviet region as a whole. In all three states the collective identities of their societies were crucial influences on the direction their politics and economics took.

[99] This is twelve of fourteen, with Turkmenistan and Uzbekistan the exceptions. Russia is not included in this list.

CHAPTER FOUR

Lithuania: Toward Europe and the West

Lithuanians' interpretation of Europe was central to their interpretation of their nation during the 1990s. The most important meaning Lithuanians attached to Europe was its cultural, religious, and historical separateness from Russia and from the post-Soviet space, or "Eurasia." Almost everyone agreed that Lithuania, having regained independence, would "return to Europe," with the European Union (EU) Europe's most prominent symbol and EU membership the ultimate recognition of having a European state. For many Lithuanians, the tasks of orienting their state toward Europe and away from Russia were equivalent. In an interview with historian Timothy Garten Ash a member of the Lithuanian parliament, the Seimas, articulated this definition: "Europe is . . . not-Russia!"[1]

Drawing a mental map of Europe that excluded Russia involved some creativity, however, because Lithuanians also commemorated their state's location in the "center" of Europe rather than its "east." Just north of Vilnius, the capital, is the Europas Parkas, "Open-Air Museum of the Center

[1] See Timothy Garten Ash, "Journey to the Post-Communist East," *New York Review of Books*, 23 June 1994. For this citation and further discussion of east-central European societies' conceptions of Europe and Russia, see Valerie Bunce, "The Visegrad Group: Regional Cooperation and European Integration in Post-Communist Europe," in *Mitteleuropa: Between Europe and Germany*, ed. Peter J. Katzenstein (Providence: Berghahn, 1997). On the importance of various conceptions of Europe to Lithuanian national identity, see also Evaldas Nekrasas, "Is Lithuania a Northern or Central European Country?" *Lithuanian Foreign Policy Review* 1 (1998): 19–45, especially 21–22; and Kornelija Jurgatiene and Ole Wæver, "Lithuania," in *European Integration and National Adaptations*, ed. Hans Mouritzen, Ole Wæver, and Hakan Wiberg (Commack, N.Y.: Nova Science, 1996).

of Europe." Founded in 1991, the Europe Park is located at the geographical center of Europe, at least as it was determined by the French National Geographic Institute in 1989. Lithuania is thus supposed to be central to Europe even literally. The park can be at the center of Europe, however, only if Europe extends all the way to the Ural Mountains in Russia, a traditional but no less problematic dividing line between Europe and Asia some eight hundred miles east of Moscow.

Despite the inconsistency, both meanings of Europe—Russia's exclusion and Lithuania's centrality—were important to Lithuanians' national identity during the 1990s. This way of understanding the proper orientation and identity of the Lithuanian nation, and therefore the state that acts on its behalf, influenced the government's approach to external economic relations. Trade with the EU was to be welcomed whereas trade with Russia was a threat to state security and political autonomy. The government sought to join Europe's monetary union but refused membership in the ruble zone. "Integration" into the EU, NATO, and other institutions of the Western, "trans-Atlantic community" was the government's most important strategic goal. But the government rejected all post-Soviet institutions, the Commonwealth of Independent States (CIS) included, and any efforts toward the "reintegration" of the Eurasian economic space. Indeed, Lithuania's potential participation in post-Soviet regional institutions was pronounced unconstitutional. In June 1992 the Lithuanian parliament adopted the Constitutional Act on Nonalignment of the Republic of Lithuania to Post-Soviet Eastern Alliances, which specified that the state would "never and in no way join any new political, military, economic or any other state alliances or commonwealths formed on the basis of the former USSR."[2]

The government's attempt to reorient the Lithuanian economy exacerbated the country's economic crisis during the first few years of economic transition. Russia offered subsidies and favorable trade agreements to reintegrationist states such as Belarus, thus easing the costs of Soviet economic dissolution. In contrast, it charged world prices for energy and raw materials exports to Lithuania. Russia also withheld most-favored-nation trade status as punishment for Lithuania's rejection of the CIS and unwillingness to compromise on issues important to the Russian government, such as military transit across Lithuania to the Kaliningrad region of Russia.[3]

Almost all Lithuanians believed that the government's foreign economic policies were partially responsible for the economy's sorry state. But there

---

[2] Supreme Council of the Republic of Lithuania, "Constitutional Act on Nonalignment of the Republic of Lithuania to Post-Soviet Eastern Alliances," No. I-2622, 8 June 1992.

[3] Kaliningrad, which borders Poland and Lithuania and is on the Baltic Sea, is separated from the rest of the territory of the Russian state by Latvia and Lithuania.

were two contrasting interpretations of the costs of the pro-Western policy. Some powerful organized economic actors in Lithuania, such as the Lithuanian Confederation of Industrialists, demanded closer economic cooperation with post-Soviet states to redress the problem. Theirs was the minority position, however. Many other Lithuanians justified the costs of reorientation. Lithuanian nationalists, especially, exhorted sacrifice for the nation's sake. Autonomy from Russia and the country's return to Europe were worth some short-term economic pain. In the long run, future generations of the Lithuanian nation would prosper from the choice for Europe, so the argument went.

Thus, Lithuanians' shared interpretation of national purpose legitimated their sacrifice, lengthened the time horizons of both society and government, and defined the direction of foreign economic policy. The anti-Soviet and pro-European content of Lithuanian national identity was widely agreed on. Lithuanian political parties enjoyed remarkable concord on matters of foreign economic policy.

HISTORY, INSTITUTIONS, AND LITHUANIAN NATIONAL IDENTITY

The content and contestation of post-Soviet Lithuanian national identity was both a historical outcome and a political process that in many ways began in the late 1980s. But it is also important to understand the historical sources of Lithuanians' collective identity because they contrast with the interpretation of history put forward by many Lithuanian nationalists themselves.

There are several misconceptions about the emergence of Lithuania's nationalist movement and its role in the fall of the Soviet Union and in framing societal debates about the fundamental purposes of the state. First, Lithuanians—or more precisely, the people who have lived on the territory of the state we now call Lithuania—have not always shared the particular content of their national identity that they do now. Lithuanians have not always defined their identity primarily in opposition to Russia, they have not always sought an independent state, and they were not always committed to their European-ness. These are characteristics primarily of late-twentieth-century Lithuanian nationalism.[4]

Second, although an independent Lithuanian state existed during the years between the two world wars, its existence by itself did not determine Lithuania's path to independence from the Soviet Union. Several kinds of arguments have been offered in relation to this interwar state, primarily

[4] See, for example, Leonidas Donskis, "Between Identity and Freedom: Mapping Nationalism in Twentieth-Century Lithuania," *East European Politics and Societies* 13, 3 (1999): 474–500.

because it distinguishes Lithuanian history from the histories of other republics, including Ukraine and Belarus. Some observers, including Lithuanians themselves, suggested that because many states never recognized the Soviet Union's annexation of Lithuania in 1940, the new Lithuanian state is not new at all but rather "restored," and that there was something inherent to the country's institutions or territory that required independence in 1991. But it is not the claim to a distinct legal status of the post-Soviet Lithuanian state that led Lithuanians to share their interpretation of their collective identity or to demand independence. Domestic social norms, not international legal norms, formed the basis of Lithuanians' nationalism.

It is also possible that Lithuania's interwar statehood was important because it meant that Lithuanians "remembered" their independence, unlike other post-Soviet societies that had never known independence in the twentieth century. There is some truth to this sentiment, but it should be incorporated into a general understanding of how national identities imply specific interpretations of history that become meaningful politically. Few Lithuanians alive during the late 1980s experienced the interwar statehood, and those who led the nationalist movement were, in general, not old enough to have remembered statehood. It was not the personal memories of Lithuanians that made the interwar state politically meaningful after 1988. Rather, it was a constructed, historical memory, shared among many Lithuanians, its symbols given meaning by an older to a younger generation.

Therefore, the interwar state mattered a great deal for Lithuania's nationalist politics of perestroika, but in two specific ways. First, the interwar state was important because it had provided the political space within which Lithuanian national identity, promoted by an independent government, first became widely shared among the population. Second, the symbol and mythology of a Lithuanian state lost to Soviet influence became important to politics during and after the collapse of Soviet political institutions.

The Rise and Fall of the Interwar Lithuanian State

The territory of contemporary Lithuania was once part of the Polish-Lithuanian Commonwealth, formally established in 1569 by the Treaty of Lublin and dating back to 1386, when the Lithuanian grand duke Jogaila married the Polish queen Jadwiga. Then, after the partitions of the commonwealth, 1772–95, most of what is now Lithuania became a western province of the Russian empire. This was well before nationhood had become widely institutionalized in the world and certainly before a modern Lithuanian national consciousness had emerged.

The first stirrings of nationalist activity in the Lithuanian territory came in the 1880s, when intellectuals created the publications *Auszra* (The

Dawn) and *Varpas* (The Bell). At the turn of the century, however, a coherently Lithuanian national consciousness was limited to the intelligentsia and, increasingly, a Lithuanian diaspora outside Russia. At this time, Lithuanians were not "more nationalist" than the populations of other western provinces of the empire, such as Ukrainians or Belarusians. As historian Ronald Grigor Suny argues, Lithuanians were similar to Belarusians in the empire, with their "peasant composition and low level of national consciousness." Indeed, the Lithuanian cultural elite was thoroughly Polonized, and people who considered themselves Lithuanians—with the ethno-national connotation the designation carries today—were noticeably absent from urban areas in the province.[5]

The goals of Lithuanian nationalists were modest: rather than statehood, in 1905 the Great Lithuanian Assembly in Vilnius demanded an autonomous and democratic Lithuanian province still within the tsarist empire. Lithuanians' pre–World War I nationalism could not therefore have caused their independent statehood. Suny concludes, "As in many other regions of the western borderlands, the creation of an independent Lithuania was not the result of a broad-based and coherent nationalist movement that realized long-held aspirations to nationhood."[6] Rather, the establishment of an independent Lithuanian state resulted from German eastern diplomacy, the weakness of the Russian state, and British policies in the Baltic region.[7]

The Emergence of the Lithuanian State.   Russia was in crisis and World War I was under way when the Lithuanian state emerged. In 1915, a year after the beginning of the war, the German army occupied Vilnius. Two years later political elites formed the Taryba, or Council, which then declared the formation of a Lithuanian state allied to Germany. In 1918 the Taryba declared the Lithuanian state to be independent of both Germany and Russia. By 1919, however, the Soviets had established the Lithuanian-Belorussian Soviet Republic, Litbel, in Vilnius, while the Taryba con-

---

[5] Ronald Grigor Suny, *The Revenge of the Past: Nationalism, Revolution, and the Collapse of the Soviet Union* (Stanford: Stanford University Press, 1993), 30, 35–38. See also Miroslav Hroch, *Social Preconditions of a National Revival in Europe*, trans. Ben Fowkes (Cambridge: Cambridge University Press, 1985), chap. 12; Alfred Erich Senn, *The Emergence of Modern Lithuania* (New York: Columbia University Press, 1959), chap. 1; A. S. Strazas, "Lithuania, 1863–1893: Czarist Russification and the Beginnings of the Modern Lithuanian National Movement," *Lituanus* 42, 3 (1996): 36–75; and Strazas, "From *Auszra* to the Great War: The Emergence of the Lithuanian Nation," *Lituanus* 42, 4 (1996): 34–73.

[6] Suny, *Revenge of the Past*, 37.

[7] See especially Stanley W. Page, *The Formation of the Baltic States: A Study of the Effects of Great Power Politics upon the Emergence of Lithuania, Latvia, and Estonia* (Cambridge: Harvard University Press, 1959); John Hiden, *The Baltic States and Weimar Ostpolitik* (Cambridge: Cambridge University Press, 1987); and Hiden, "From War to Peace: Britain, Germany, and the Baltic States, 1918–1921," *Journal of Baltic Studies* 19, 4 (1988): 371–82.

trolled most of western Lithuania.[8] Poland's victory over Soviet Russia in the Polish-Bolshevik War helped produce the power vacuum within which the Lithuanian state was institutionalized. Alfred Erich Senn, a scholar of Lithuania political history, concludes that "the decisive factor in the establishment of the Lithuanian national state was the existence of a titanic power struggle in Eastern Europe in 1918–20."[9]

In 1920 the Soviet Union recognized the Lithuanian state and signed a peace treaty with the new government. At the same time, Poland acceded to Lithuanian authority over Vilnius in the 1920 Suwalki Agreement. Within months, however, Polish forces had occupied Vilnius, which remained part of Poland throughout the interwar years. The question of Vilnius was the primary foreign policy preoccupation of the Lithuanian state during these years. In domestic politics the government concerned itself with nation making.

The Politics of Nationalism in Interwar Lithuania. During Lithuania's interwar statehood political elites succeeded in their project of consolidating a coherent Lithuanian national identity. Lithuanian nationalists took full advantage of the political opportunity created by the collapse of Germany and Russia, and Lithuanian nationalism became a broad-based cultural phenomenon.[10] Between 1920 and 1940 Lithuanians found themselves, for the first time in modern history, with the authority and space to "standardize their language, to establish an educational system and a literary culture based on that language, and to form institutions that strengthened Lithuanian national consciousness."[11] Before 1920 there were several contrasting cultural definitions of "Lithuania," as well as at least three competing literary dialects, with no predominant standard language. During the 1920s Jonas Jablonskis, a philologist whose face would appear on the five-litas note in 1993, continued his efforts of the previous decades to standardize a modern, literary Lithuanian, but with the firm support of the state.

Twenty years of the government's self-conscious efforts to turn the population of the Lithuanian territory into Lithuanians were consequential.

[8] In 1920 Litbel was renamed the Belorussian Soviet Socialist Republic, with its capital in Minsk.

[9] Senn, *Emergence of Modern Lithuania*, 231, and chap. 10 more generally.

[10] See Anatol Lieven, *The Baltic Revolution: Estonia, Latvia, Lithuania, and the Path to Independence* (New Haven: Yale University Press, 1993), chap. 3; Edvardas Tuskenis, ed., *Lithuania in European Politics: The Years of the First Republic, 1918–1940* (New York: St. Martin's, 1997); Georg von Rauch, *The Baltic States: Years of Dependence*, trans. Gerald Onn (Berkeley: University of California Press, 1974); V. Stanley Vardys and Romuald J. Misiunas, eds., *The Baltic States in Peace and War, 1917–1945* (University Park: Pennsylvania State University Press, 1978); and Nicholas Hope, "Interwar Statehood: Symbol and Reality," in *The Baltic States: The National Self-Determination of Estonia, Latvia, and Lithuania*, ed. Graham Smith (New York: St. Martin's, 1994).

[11] Alfred Erich Senn, introduction to *Lithuania in European Politics*, ed. Tuskenis, 1.

During these years the authority of a specific Lithuanian nationalist vision was relatively uncontested. Lithuania's nationalists were also involved in the state's turn toward authoritarian politics, when a military coup installed Antanas Smetona as president in 1926 and the Nationalist Union disbanded the parliament in 1927.[12]

Soviet Lithuania

The power vacuum in eastern Europe that created political space for Lithuania's interwar state was eventually filled, however, by the expansion of German and Soviet power. In August 1939 the first German-Soviet Non-Aggression Treaty, known as Molotov-Ribbentrop, assigned Lithuania to the German sphere of influence. A month later the second Molotov-Ribbentrop, the German-Soviet Treaty of Friendship, reassigned Lithuania to the Soviet sphere. In October the Soviets pressured Lithuanian leaders to sign the Treaty of Mutual Assistance, which provided for Soviet military bases and, significantly, the return of Vilnius from Polish to Lithuanian administration. Ostensibly dissatisfied with Lithuania's fulfillment of its treaty obligations, Soviet troops occupied Lithuania in June 1940, and the state was formally incorporated into the Soviet Union as a constituent republic two months later. Although the German army occupied Lithuania for most of the war, the Soviets returned in July 1944 and remained, despite the guerrilla war between anti-Soviet resistance and Soviet security forces that continued as late as 1952.[13]

The Soviets exerted firm control over Lithuania and transformed its domestic economic institutions and foreign economic relations. Within a few years the Lithuanian Soviet Socialist Republic shared the command economic institutions of the Union, and its commerce became Soviet. In 1938 79 percent of Lithuania's exports were sent to states of the present-day EU, which also accounted for 70 percent of Lithuania's imports. Exports to and imports from Russia were only 6 and 7 percent, respectively. Soon, however, almost all Lithuania's commerce was with other Soviet republics; in 1990 the figures for trade with Russia stood at 90 percent and had for decades.[14]

[12] See Alfonsas Eidintas, "The Presidential Republic," in *Lithuania in European Politics*, ed. Tuskenis.

[13] Leonas Sabaliunas, *Lithuania in Crisis: Nationalism to Communism, 1939–1940* (Princeton: Princeton University Press, 1981); and David M. Crowe, *The Baltic States and the Great Powers: Foreign Relations, 1938–1940* (Boulder, Colo.: Westview, 1993).

[14] On the integration of the Lithuanian economy into the Soviet, see Pranas Zune, "Lithuania's Economy: Introduction of the Soviet Pattern," in *Lithuania under the Soviets*, ed. V. Stanley Vardys (New York: Praeger, 1965).

THE RISE OF SAJUDIS AND THE FALL OF SOVIET LITHUANIA

An opportunity for change emerged with perestroika, the process of political restructuring initiated by Soviet leader Mikhail Gorbachev during the mid-1980s. A number of Lithuanian intellectuals in the Academy of Sciences created the Lietuvos Persitvarkymo Sajudis, or Lithuanian Movement for Restructuring (Perestroika), which at first merely sought to promote political change and independence from the Communist Party of Lithuania (CPL). The Movement, or Sajudis, as it came to be known, held its founding congress in October 1988, when it proclaimed its support of perestroika and proposed greater Lithuanian autonomy within the Soviet federation and more economic self-management. In November Sajudis elected Vytautas Landsbergis, a music professor, its president and adopted increasingly radical goals regarding Lithuania's place in the Soviet Union. Sajudis was transformed from a movement for perestroika into a nationalist front demanding independent statehood in the space of little more than a year.[15]

The CPL's reaction to Sajudis during its rise to prominence varied over time. Originally, the CPL sought to contain Sajudis's influence, but eventually it embraced Sajudis's support of a new model of Soviet federalism put forward by Estonian nationalists. The Party lacked Sajudis's resolve, at least early on. Under pressure from the Communist Party of the Soviet Union (CPSU), the CPL backed down from the Estonian federal model.

Algirdas Brazauskas, a young Party leader, pushed the Party to change more quickly with the times. Brazauskas's popularity and political savvy led to his appointment on 20 October 1988 as first secretary of the CPL, the Party's highest post. Brazauskas was clearly in touch with Lithuanian sentiment regarding the opportunity for change presented by perestroika. Two days after his appointment he addressed the founding congress of Sajudis, his first major public audience as first secretary. Attempting to connect with Lithuania's increasingly influential nationalists, he told Sajudis, "On matters of principle, we think alike."[16] A second speech he gave to the congress revealed his commitment to change, as he spoke of the "revival of Lithuanian national consciousness."[17] It is remarkable that the first secretary of the

---

[15] See Alfred Erich Senn, *Lithuania Awakening* (Berkeley: University of California Press, 1990); V. Stanley Vardys, "*Sajudis*: National Revolution in Lithuania," in *Toward Independence: The Baltic Popular Movements*, ed. Jan Arveds Trapans (Boulder, Colo.: Westview, 1995); and Nils R. Muiznieks, "The Influence of the Baltic Popular Movements on the Process of Soviet Disintegration," *Europe-Asia Studies* 47, 1 (1995): 3–25.

[16] Quoted in V. Stanley Vardys, "Lithuanian National Politics," *Problems of Communism* 38, 4 (1989): 53–76, at 65.

[17] Quoted in Senn, *Lithuania Awakening*, 222.

republic's Communist Party was intimately involved with the beginnings of the nationalist movement.

Although Brazauskas and the CPL became involved with Sajudis and the popular demands for perestroika, other political events showed that Lithuanians were unsatisfied with the pace of change under CPL leadership. In March 1989 Soviet republics held their elections to the All-Union Soviet Congress of People's Deputies. Sajudis won thirty-six of Lithuania's forty-two electoral districts, and the CPL faced the possibility of irrelevance to the future of Lithuanian politics.

When First Secretary Brazauskas called the twentieth congress of the CPL in December 1989, he proposed a dramatic break with the past: independence from the CPSU. Lithuania's Communists thus sent a clear message to the Lithuanian public and to Moscow, where Soviet authorities condemned the move. Afterward the CPL cooperated more intensively with Sajudis during the drive toward independence. Indeed, the memberships of Sajudis and the Communist Party of Lithuania increasingly overlapped: approximately half the Initiative Group that began Sajudis were Party members. And when the Party elected its new Central Committee in 1989, over half its members were of self-described "Sajudis orientation."[18] Later, in 1990, the CPL recast itself as a social democratic party, "in the west European tradition," and renamed itself the Lithuanian Democratic Labor Party (Lietuvos Demokratine Darbo Partija, or LDDP).[19]

Events moved quickly during 1990. Gorbachev visited Lithuania in January to campaign against secession from the Union. In the February 1990 elections to the Lithuanian Supreme Soviet, however, independence-minded Sajudis candidates won more than 70 percent of the seats. A month later the Supreme Soviet voted 124–0 to declare independence from the Soviet Union. Landsbergis of Sajudis was elected chairman of the Soviet, a parliamentary post that also made him the newly declared state's first president.

In response to the independence declaration, Gorbachev imposed a Soviet economic boycott of the republic that, beginning in April, cut off essential oil and gas supplies. In June Landsbergis announced a temporary suspension of the independence declaration, on the condition that negotiations regarding Lithuania's secession begin. Gorbachev ended the embargo, but the Soviet leadership still rejected any possibility of Lithuania's secession from the Union.

The republic's politics, however, were increasingly radicalized by Soviet authorities' intransigence as well as their use of violence to suppress

[18] Senn, *Lithuania Awakening*, 14, 70, and 254. Also see V. Stanley Vardys and Judith B. Sedaitis, *Lithuania: The Rebel Nation* (Boulder, Colo.: Westview, 1997), 149–52.

[19] A few Soviet loyalists retained the CPL name for their organization until the party was banned in August 1991.

demands for independence. In January 1991 Moscow dispatched Soviet special forces to take control of Lithuania's radio and television. The Soviet forces killed fourteen and wounded several hundred demonstrators in their taking of the television tower in Vilnius. In response, Landsbergis declared that the suspension of the independence declaration was over, and thus any possibility for compromise between Lithuanian politicians and Soviet authorities disappeared. In Moscow change took place rapidly also, particularly after Boris Yeltsin was elected president of Russia in June. After the hardliners' coup failed in Moscow in August 1991, Gorbachev resigned and the Soviet Union recognized Lithuania's independence.[20] A few months later, in December, the Soviet Union ceased to exist altogether.

THE POLITICS OF NATIONALISM IN POST-SOVIET LITHUANIA

Although other nationalist political parties emerged after independence, Sajudis was the most prominent and influential proponent of a vision for the future of the nation and set of purposes for the state. In 1993 Sajudis, which had been only a movement rather than an official party, reorganized itself as a political party called Homeland Union, which remained the dominant nationalist party throughout the decade.

Homeland Union, and most of Lithuania's other nationalists, organized their policy proposals around three main ideas. First, they argued that Lithuania's interwar state was lost to Soviet influence, which they associated with Russia, and that after the cold war Lithuania's newly regained statehood was threatened most by Russia. A strong state was therefore to be an important defense of the sovereignty of the Lithuanian nation.[21]

Second, Lithuania's nationalists argued that economic dependence on Russia was the state's primary security threat.[22] This was especially true after the last Russian troops left Lithuanian territory in 1993, after which it seemed unlikely that they would return any time soon. Economic dependence on Russia, in contrast to the military threat, was a serious, persistent, and immediate danger to the autonomy of Lithuanian decision makers and left the government open to Russian attempts at economic coercion, even undue influence on the country's politics.

[20] For a review of these events, see Alfred Erich Senn, *Gorbachev's Failure in Lithuania* (New York: St. Martin's, 1995); and Martha Brill Olcott, "The Lithuanian Crisis," *Foreign Affairs* 69, 3 (1990): 30–46.
[21] Arvydas Matulionis, "Nationalism and the Process of State-Building in Lithuania," *Sisyphus* 8, 2 (1994): 121–24. See also Terry Clark, "Nationalism in Independent Lithuania," unpublished manuscript, Creighton University, 2000.
[22] Author's interviews nos. 1 and 2, Homeland Union, Vilnius, July 1998.

Third, they argued that the state should therefore "reorient" its politics and economy from East to West.[23] That is, Lithuania should cultivate close economic relationships with "European" states and reduce its economic dependence on Russia. And while the Lithuanian government should become part of the EU, NATO, and other Western institutions, it should reject under all circumstances multilateral, institutionalized economic and political relationships with post-Soviet states as a group, especially the CIS. The reason for this reorientation, according to the nationalists, was that Lithuania is fundamentally "Western" and "European," both culturally and historically, whereas Russia is not. Thus, central to the idea of economic reorientation was the nationalists' interpretation of the country's "return to Europe," a righting of a historical wrong.

Sajudis, and later Homeland Union, essentially put forward specific proposals for the content of Lithuanian national identity. These ideas and policy proposals became popular between 1988 and 1991, when Lithuania was on its way to independent statehood. Almost all Lithuanians accepted the arguments of these nationalists, and there were no influential organized groups that contested them. Lithuanians largely agreed on what it meant to be Lithuanian, what the government should do in its relations with other governments, and what were the purposes of the state. As Soviet authority collapsed, the popularity of these ideas was reflected in the popularity of the Sajudis itself, which virtually swept the 1989 elections to the Congress of People's Deputies and 1990 elections to the parliament.

The coherence and consensus of Lithuanian national identity was even more clearly illustrated when Sajudis lost parliamentary and presidential elections to former Communists several years later. In October 1992, a little over a year after the Soviet authorities recognized Lithuanian independence, Lithuania was the first country in eastern Europe or the former Soviet Union to return its former Communists to power in an election. Lithuanians gave the LDDP a parliamentary majority in 1992 and elected former first secretary Brazauskas in the 1993 presidential election.[24] For five decisive years in the middle of the decade, Lithuania was ruled by essentially the same party that had controlled the republic during the Soviet era, and many of its leaders were the same people, the old nomenklatura.

[23] Author's interview no. 2, Homeland Union, July 1998. Also see Clark, "Nationalism in Independent Lithuania." On Baltic nationalists' pro-EU orientation in general, see Joan Lofgren, "A Different Kind of Union," *Transitions* 4, 6 (1997): 47–52. As in all three Baltic states, however, there were Euro-skeptics on the far right, and these radical nationalists generally opposed EU membership. Among Lithuanian nationalist parties, only one, Nationalist Union, opposed EU membership, although it favored NATO membership. See "Lithuania: Nationalist Union against Speedy Integration with EU," *Baltic News Service*, 22 February 1996; "Euro-skeptics Form Independence Movement, Back Moves to Join NATO," *ELTA*, 2 June 1997.

[24] The 1992 constitution created the presidency.

To many outside observers, particularly in the West, the return of the LDDP and Brazauskas was a shocking resumption of the Communist past, and the repetition of the "Lithuanian syndrome" in several other post-socialist states led to great concern about these societies' commitments to change.

Why did Lithuanians trust their former Communists to return to power? Lithuania's former Communists were unlike many former Communists throughout the region, Lithuanians seemed to believe. Of course, it helped that Brazauskas had cooperated with Sajudis and had broken with the CPSU even before formal independence had arrived. Most Lithuanians trusted the commitment of the LDDP and Brazauskas to an independent Lithuanian state.[25] After Brazauskas was elected president, he explained that Lithuanians knew they could trust the former Communists because "in the former Communist Party maybe three percent were communists and the rest were just members."[26] In other words, everyone knew that they never really meant it.[27]

Indeed, Lithuania's former Communists had become nationalists, in the sense that they used the symbol of the nation in the same ways Sajudis and Homeland Union did, and to legitimate the same foreign policy goals. Lithuanians elected a nationalist, pro-European LDDP in 1992 whose foreign policy goals were essentially identical to those of the original nationalists.[28] Thus, Lithuania's former Communists proclaimed the nationalists' main goals as their own as well. As an LDDP leader explained, in Lithuania "the Communists are more nationalist than the nationalists" because they are better at achieving the same goals.[29]

[25] See Alfred Erich Senn, "Post-Soviet Political Leadership in Lithuania," in *Patterns in Post-Soviet Leadership*, ed. Timothy J. Colton and Robert C. Tucker (Boulder, Colo.: Westview, 1995); Terry D. Clark, "The Lithuanian Political Party System: A Case Study of Democratic Consolidation," *East European Politics and Societies* 9, 1 (1995): 41–62; and Terry D. Clark, Stacy J. Holscher, and Lisa Hyland, "The LDLP Faction in the Lithuanian Seimas, 1992–1996," *Nationalities Papers* 27, 2 (1999): 227–46.

[26] Quoted in Tarmu Tammerk, "Brazauskas Storms into Office," *Baltic Independent*, 19–25 February 1993.

[27] See, for example, Alfred Erich Senn, "The Political Culture of Independent Lithuania: A Review Essay," *Journal of Baltic Studies* 23, 2 (1992): 307–16. On the ideology of Lithuania's Communist Party during the Soviet period and the tradition of "national communism," as well as the Party's transformation during perestroika, see Barbara Christophe, *Staat versus Identität: Zur Konstruktion von "Nation" und "nationalen Interesse" in den litauischen Transformationsdiskursen von 1987 bis 1995* (Cologne: Verlag Wissenschaft und Politik, 1997).

[28] See LDDP, "Platform of the Lithuanian Democratic Labor Party for the Parliamentary Elections," *Tiesa*, 7 October 1992, in FBIS-USR-92-149, 20 November 1992, 96–103, especially 102–3; and Alexandra Ashbourne, *Lithuania: The Rebirth of a Nation, 1991–1994* (Lanham, Md.: Lexington, 1999), 40–41. Also see Edward Tuskenis, "Brazauskas Returns," *Baltic Independent*, 30 October 1992; Tuskenis, "Sajudis Faces Clouded Future," *Baltic Independent*, 6 November 1992; Edward Lucas, "Sajudis Last Stand Ends in Defeat," *Baltic Independent*, 20 November 1992; Lucas, "LDDP Coasts to Easy Victory," *Baltic Independent*, 20 November 1992; and Lucas, "Brazauskas Takes Power," *Baltic Independent*, 27 November 1992.

[29] Author's interview, LDDP, Vilnius, August 1998.

In particular, although the LDDP and Homeland Union disagreed about a number of domestic issues, such as the pace of privatization and the relationships between state and economy and church and state, they did not disagree about the state's anti-CIS, pro-EU policy of political-economic reorientation. As Kornelija Jurgatiene and Ole Wæver point out, the LDDP offered a foreign policy program that "revealed no essential disparities in the attitudes of the contending political camps as to the strategy of the further development of the country."[30]

This consensus about the goals of the nation extended beyond Homeland Union and the LDDP. All five of Lithuania's major political parties (Table 4.1) advocated the same foreign policy objectives and used the same language of the nation to describe their purposes. Homeland Union, the LDDP, the Lithuanian Christian Democratic Party, the Center Union, and the Lithuanian Social Democratic Party all favored Lithuania's reorientation of its polity and economy toward the West and EU and NATO membership.[31] Homeland Union and LDDP were the two most dominant parties during the 1990s. And they, along with these other three influential parties, won over 90 percent of parliamentary seats in the 1992 and 1996 elections (Table 4.2).

In sum, Lithuanians, especially the Lithuanian political elites elected during the 1990s, agreed on the meaning of their national identity and on the fundamental purposes of their statehood, purposes derived from their shared historical memory of the interwar Lithuanian state and their shared interpretation of the Soviet Union as an empire that had denied them their sovereignty. In the late 1980s Sajudis emerged as a nationalist movement that proposed pro-European and anti-Soviet content for its society's identity, and it was successful. Most significantly, Lithuania's former Communists, the other major political force in the country, agreed and adopted the foreign policy goals and national symbolism of Sajudis. The prevailing construction of Lithuanian national identity was both clear and consensual.

THE POLITICS AND ECONOMICS OF EUROPE

Almost everyone agreed on the importance of returning to Europe, then, and Lithuanians were prepared to endure a great deal to accomplish

---

[30] Jurgatiene and Wæver, "Lithuania," 197–98. See also, for example, Mette Skak, *From Empire to Anarchy: Postcommunist Foreign Policy and International Relations* (New York: St. Martin's, 1996), chap. 5.

[31] See, for example, their party platforms for the 1996 parliamentary elections: Homeland Union, *Lithuania's Success* (Vilnius, 1996); Lithuanian Democratic Labor Party, *With Work, Concord, and Morality into the Twenty-First Century* (Vilnius, 1996); Lithuanian Christian Democratic Party, *To Serve for Lithuania* (Vilnius, 1996); Lithuanian Center Union, *The New Lithuania* (Vilnius, 1996); and Lithuanian Social Democratic Party, *Labor, Truth, and Justice* (Vilnius, 1996).

Table 4.1 Dominant Lithuanian Political Parties

Homeland Union–Lithuanian Conservatives (TS-LK)
Lithuanian Christian Democratic Party (LKDP)
Center Union (CS)
Lithuanian Social Democratic Party (LDSP)
Lithuanian Democratic Labor Party (LDDP)

Table 4.2 Distribution of Seats in the Lithuanian Parliament
in 1992 and 1996

	1992	1996
Homeland Union (Sajudis)	28	70
Lithuania Democratic Labor Party	73	12
Christian Democratic Party	18	16
Social Democratic Party	8	12
Center Union	2	13
Nationalist Union	3	3
Other	9	11

Note: There are 141 seats in the Lithuanian Parliament. In
1996 4 seats were vacant.

their reorientation. In many respects, Lithuania's economic relations with
Europe were the opposite of its economic relations with Russia and the
CIS. The government's central goal was EU membership, but multilateral
economic integration was itself a primary issue of state security. According
to the government, the two strategic goals of the country were "to ensure
national security through integration into the trans-Atlantic Community
and its institutions" and "to strengthen the national economy and improve
the nation's welfare by merging into the European market of goods and
capital."[32] Although the government clearly interpreted economic dependence on Russia as a security threat, it sought, as a fundamental strategic
goal, to become economically dependent on the EU.[33] The government

[32] Government of Lithuania, *Action Program of the Government of the Republic of Lithuania for
1997–2000* (Vilnius, 1997).

[33] Author's interviews nos. 1, 2, 4, and 5, Ministry of Foreign Affairs of Lithuania, Vilnius,
July and August 1998; author's interview, Administration of the President of Lithuania, Vil-
nius, July 1998. See also Ministry of National Defense, *White Paper '99* (Vilnius, 1999); and
Lithuanian Seimas, *Basics of National Security of Lithuania* (Vilnius, 1996). For more on the
issue of economic dependence in the security politics of Lithuania, see Evaldas Nekrasas,
"Lithuania and Her Neighbors," in *The Baltic States in International Politics*, ed. Nikolaj
Peterson (Copenhagen: Danish Institute of International Studies, 1993), 48–49; Ramunas
Vilpisaukas, "Trade between Lithuania and the European Union," in *Lithuania's Integration
into the European Union*, ed. Klaudijus Maniokas and Gediminas Vitkus (Vilnius: European In-
tegration Studies Center, 1997), 21–22; Jonas Cicinskas, Peter K. Cornelius, and Dalia
Treigiene, "Trade Policies and Lithuania's Reintegration into the Global Economy," in
Lithuanian Economic Reforms: Practice and Perspectives, ed. Antanas Buracas, Dean M. Larson,
and Joseph P. Kairys (Vilnius: Margi Rastai, 1997); and Christopher Marsh, "Realigning
Lithuanian Foreign Relations," *Journal of Baltic Studies* 29, 2 (1998): 149–64.

therefore was willing to engage only in "bilateral relations with Russia and other countries of the Commonwealth of Independent States."[34]

The foreign policy of President Landsbergis between independence in late 1991 and the election of Brazauskas in early 1993 was concerned almost exclusively with the removal of Russian troops from Lithuanian territory. Landsbergis adopted a hostile and uncompromising stance toward Moscow, essentially refusing to cooperate on any issues with Russia. As a result, tensions between the two states were high, and many Lithuanians believed that the economic costs of reorienting Westward were higher than necessary. The LDDP argued that some bilateral cooperation with Russia was necessary, if only because the country was so dependent on Russian energy.[35] According to Brazauskas, Lithuania should "not take any steps backward, but we have to define our relations with Russia more concretely."[36] Relations with Russia improved after Landsbergis left office. Still, under President Brazauskas the country solidified its Western orientation in security affairs when in 1994 Lithuania became the first post-Soviet state to apply for NATO membership.[37] When Homeland Union returned to power in its overwhelming victory in the 1996 parliamentary elections, Lithuania's domestic politics changed but its foreign policy again did not.[38]

Formal Ties

Thus, Lithuania's cultivation of European economic ties began immediately on the achievement of statehood. Responsibilities for Lithuania's relations with Europe were divided along their external and internal dimensions. Externally, the Ministry of Foreign Affairs was responsible for direct relations with the EU, and the Ministry's European Integration Department was responsible for integration strategy. The internal reforms necessary to qualify

---

[34] Ministry of Foreign Affairs, *Lithuania's Foreign Policy* (Vilnius, 1997). Also see "Republic Relations to Stay on Bilateral Treaties," *Baltfax*, 2 October 1991, in FBIS-SOV-91-192, 3 October 1991, 41; and "Lithuania: Foreign Minister Rules Out Joining CIS," *Baltic News Service*, 21 May 1996.

[35] Senn, "Post-Soviet Political Leadership," 134–35. See also Stephen Kinzer, "Lithuania Decides to Try Flexibility," *New York Times*, 3 January 1993.

[36] Quoted in Nikolai Lashkevich, "Kuda poidet Litva posle vyborov?" (Where will Lithuania go after the elections?), *Izvestiia*, 27 October 1992. See also Nikolai Lashkevich, "Litva na poroge smeny vlasti, no ne smeny kursa" (Lithuania on threshold of change of government, but not change of policy), *Izvestiia*, 17 November 1992; and Vladas Burbulis, "Algirdas Brazauskas: 'O vozvrate nazad rechi byt' ne mozhet'" (Algirdas Brazauskas: "There can be no question of returning to the past"), *Izvestiia*, 19 November 1992.

[37] "Lithuanian President and Prime Minister to Sign Official Application for Lithuanian Membership in European Union," *Baltic News Service*, 8 December 1995.

[38] See Saulius Girnius, "The Political Pendulum Swings Back in Lithuania," *Transitions* 3, 2 (1997): 20–21; and Terry D. Clark, "The 1996 Elections to the Lithuanian Seimas and Their Aftermath," *Journal of Baltic Studies* 29, 2 (1998): 135–48.

for EU membership were the responsibility of the European Committee, which briefly was part of the cabinet as the Ministry of European Affairs.[39] The government coordinated the efforts of these two organizations. In 1992 Lithuania and the European Union signed the Agreement on Trade and Commercial Cooperation, entered into force in 1993. Then, in June 1993 in Copenhagen, EU leaders confirmed their intention to enter into Europe (Association) Agreements with the three post-Soviet Baltic republics.

In July 1994 Lithuania and the EU concluded a free trade agreement, which came into effect in January 1995. In June 1995 the Lithuanian-EU free trade accord was incorporated into an agreement that Lithuania would become an associate member of the EU. This associate status was conferred by the Europe Agreement, which officially came into force in February 1998. Lithuania's pro-EU economic orientation was well institutionalized by the end of the decade, and the structure of Lithuania's trade had changed significantly (Tables 4.3 and 4.4).[40]

Clearly, Lithuania's nationalists sought to reorient the country's commerce. They also worried about possible influences of foreign owners of Lithuania's factors of production. Nationalists tend to attach significance to their territories, and to their land in particular, as discussed in chapter 2. Thus, article 47 of Lithuania's first constitution prohibited noncitizens from owning land in Lithuania. In 1996, however, after several years of internal debate and negotiations with the EU, the Seimas gave landownership a pro-European and anti-Russian direction, amending the constitution to allow citizens of other countries to own nonagricultural land for business purposes. Under the new amendment not all foreign citizens could own land in Lithuania, only members or associate members of the EU, NATO, and OECD, because they are, according to the Seimas, "foreign subjects meeting the criteria of European and trans-Atlantic integration."[41] In contrast, Russians, and citizens of other CIS countries, cannot own land in Lithuania.[42]

---

[39] Author's interview, European Committee, Vilnius, July 1998. See also Klaudijus Maniokas, "Political Aspects of Lithuania's Association with the European Union," in *Lithuania's Integration*, ed. Maniokas and Vitkus.

[40] See Ministry of Foreign Affairs of Lithuania, *Newsletter* 1, 2 (1998). Also see "Agreement on Free Trade with European Union Ratified," Vilnius Radio, 22 December 1994, in FBIS-SOV-94-247, 23 December 1994, 38–39; Vilpisaukas, "Trade between Lithuania and the European Union"; and William H. Meyers, Natlija Kazlauskiene, and Marcelo M. Giugale, eds., *Lithuania's Accession to the European Union* (Ames: Iowa State University Press, 1999).

[41] Seimas of the Republic of Lithuania, "Constitutional Law on the Subjects, Procedure, Terms, Conditions, and Restrictions of the Acquisition into Ownership of Land Plots Provided for in Article 47, Paragraph 2 of the Constitution of the Republic of Lithuania," No. I-1392, 20 June 1996.

[42] See Nikolai Lashkevich, "Inostrantsy smogut pokupat' zemliu v Litve, no tol'ko ne rossiiane" (Foreigners will be able to buy land in Lithuania, but just not Russians), *Izvestiia*, 25 June 1996. See also "Lithuanian Lawmakers Pass Constitutional Amendment on Land

Table 4.3 Lithuanian Exports to EU, CIS, and Russia as Percentages of Total Exports, 1991–99

	EU	CIS	Russia
1991	2	86	57
1992	16	66	32
1993	17	57	33
1994	26	47	28
1995	36	42	20
1996	33	45	24
1997	33	46	25
1998	38	36	17
1999	50	18	7

Source: Department of Statistics, Republic of Lithuania, *Foreign Trade 1999* (Vilnius, 2000).

Table 4.4 Lithuanian Imports from EU, CIS, and Russia as Percentages of Total Imports, 1991–99

	EU	CIS	Russia
1991	3	84	50
1992	10	80	58
1993	19	68	54
1994	26	50	39
1995	37	42	31
1996	42	33	26
1997	47	29	25
1998	50	26	21
1999	50	24	20

Source: Department of Statistics, Republic of Lithuania, *Foreign Trade 1999* (Vilnius, 2000).

Sacrifice for the Future

The Lithuanian government knew that its attempt to reorient the state's economy Westward would be costly in the short run. Although there was some debate about how costly the reorientation needed to be, and how much Lithuanian leaders needed to antagonize the Russian government in order to achieve the country's return to Europe, most Lithuanians acknowledged that this national purpose was worth some economic sacrifice. As Michael Wyzan argues: "Economic belt-tightening was associated with regaining political independence. People felt that they were sacrificing their living standards for a worthy cause."[43]

In the long run, a European state and economy for the Lithuania nation would pay off, Lithuanians argued. Reorientation was the most rational goal to pursue after the Soviet Union's collapse.[44] Economic policy making thus was a matter of time horizons, and Lithuanians, as well as Estonians and Latvians, economist Kalev Kukk argues, sought long-term over short-term economic goals, a fact that distinguished them from other post-Soviet societies.[45]

Purchase," *Baltic News Service*, 20 June 1996; "Lithuania Passes Foreigner-Friendly Land Law," *Reuters European Business Report*, 20 June 1996; and Vladas Burbulis, "Lithuania Permits Land Purchase by Foreigners Not from CIS," *ITAR-TASS*, 20 June 1996.

[43] Michael Wyzan, "Economies Show Solid Performance Despite Many Obstacles," *Transition* 3, 6 (1997): 11–14, at 14. See also Andrzej Jeziowski, "'Hardest Winter Ever' for Lithuania, Premier Predicts," *Baltic Independent*, 23 October 1992.

[44] Author's interviews nos. 1 and 2, Homeland Union, Vilnius, July 1998; author's interview, LDDP, Vilnius, August 1998. See Baltic Surveys, "Public Opinion on the European Union in Lithuania," in *Lithuania's Integration*, ed. Maniokas and Vitkus. See also, for example, Saulius Girnius, "Back in Europe, to Stay," *Transition* 3, 6 (1997): 7–10.

[45] Kalev Kukk, "The Baltic States," in *Going Global: Transition from Plan to Market in the World Economy*, ed. Padma Desai (Cambridge: MIT Press, 1997), especially 269.

CONCLUSION

Most remarkable about Lithuania's foreign economic policy orientation was its continuity, even as its presidents and parliaments changed. The first three heads of state, nationalist Vytautas Landsbergis (1990–93), the former Communist Party chief Algirdas Brazauskas (1993–98), and the émigré Valdas Adamkus (1998–), all pursued integration with the West. And when the nationalist Sajudis held the majority of parliamentary seats between 1989 and 1992, the LDDP between 1992 and 1996, and Homeland Union after 1996, the primary foreign policy goals never varied.

A European purpose, a "return to Europe" proposed by nationalists and accepted by former Communists and the rest of Lithuania's society, motivated the government's diplomacy during the 1990s. The range of debate about Europe was remarkably narrow, as political elites proposed conceptions of Lithuania's historical place in Europe and its "path" to Europe that differed only in emphasis. The central question was whether Lithuania was part of Central or Northern Europe.[46]

The North European path went through Scandinavia, though the Lithuanian territory historically had fewer ties with Scandinavian neighbors than did Latvia and Estonia. The Central European path, the most direct and, many argued, the most historically consistent, went through Poland. Lithuania's difficult shared history with Poland complicated the two states' post–cold war relations, however. For example, although the medieval Polish-Lithuanian Commonwealth predated specifically Polish and Lithuanian national identities, Poles tended to view the polity as having been a brotherly partnership between the two peoples whereas Lithuanians resented what they consider the commonwealth's excessively Polonizing, assimilating cultural influence. More recent, and violent, is the problem of Vilnius, which the interwar Polish state occupied and which was "returned" to Lithuania as part of the process of its annexation into the Soviet Union. For several years after the cold war ended, these national "myths" and unresolved historical disputes threatened cooperation between the two states.[47]

But the efforts of both Polish and Lithuanian governments to cultivate their Central European identities led to greater cooperation among them. Although interwar Lithuanian nationalism was as anti-Polish as it was anti-Russian, Lithuania's incorporation into the Soviet Union increased the im-

[46] Nekrasas, "Northern or Central European Country?" 22.

[47] See Tim Snyder, "National Myths and International Relations: Poland and Lithuania, 1989–1994," *East European Politics and Societies* 9, 2 (1995): 317–43; Stephen R. Burant, "Overcoming the Past: Polish-Lithuanian Relations, 1990–1995," *Journal of Baltic Studies* 27, 4 (1996): 309–29; and Burant, "International Relations in a Regional Context: Poland and Its Eastern Neighbors—Lithuania, Belarus, Ukraine," *Europe-Asia Studies* 45, 3 (1993): 395–418.

portance of Russia as Lithuania's most important "other." In addition, Poland's place in Central Europe fit the nationalists' sharp distinction between Europe and Russia. Thus, Lithuania's orientation toward Europe necessitated rapprochement with Poland.[48]

Meanwhile, by the end of the decade Lithuanian political elites agreed that bilateral economic ties with Russia should be normalized, as long as no multilateral institutions were involved and the Soviet-legacy production complexes were not to be reintegrated.[49] The Russian economic crisis of 1998 hurt the transitional Lithuanian economy, but it also helped solidify and justify the country's attempt to join an economic Europe. Those firms that by the late 1990s had entered European markets were largely insulated from the Russian crisis, but those, especially heavy industry, that remained focused on Russian and CIS markets faced disaster.

Thus, after ten years of independent statehood Lithuanians had managed to institutionalize their political-economic relationships with Europe and with Russia on different terms. EU leaders knew that Lithuania ardently sought membership, and Russian leaders became convinced that they had lost Lithuania from the Eurasian political-economic space. It took some time for this realization to reach Russian political elites, however. One interesting and surreal event of post-Soviet international relations occurred when Russia offered security guarantees, a "security umbrella," to the Baltic republics, insisting that it could protect them as well as NATO, as though it were not Russia that Baltic leaders perceived to be the state from which they needed protection. Of course, Lithuania and the Baltic states turned down Russia's offer.[50] Russia still opposed Lithuania's membership in NATO but had accepted that the Baltic states' membership in the EU might soon come and that its own political-economic relations with Lithuania would not be organized by multilateral institutions of Russian creation. Sixty years after Molotov-Ribbentrop assigned their fate to the Soviet Union, Lithuanians had extricated themselves from the Russian sphere of influence, primarily because they agreed among themselves, and with their most vocal nationalists, what their nation meant.

---

[48] See Tim Snyder, *Peace in the Northeast* (New Haven: Yale University Press, forthcoming), chaps. 2 and 3.

[49] Author's interviews nos. 4 and 5, Ministry of Foreign Affairs of Lithuania, Vilnius, July and August 1998. See "Lithuania Hopes to Settle Economic Problems with Russia," *ELTA*, 23 October 1997; "Brazauskas on Successes, Problems in Foreign Policy," *ELTA*, 17 November 1997; "Lithuania: Landsbergis Promises Better Ties with Russia If Elected," *Interfax*, 1 December 1997; and "Lithuanian-Russian Bilateral Trade Commission Meets," *ELTA*, 24 February 1998.

[50] See Boris Vinogradov, "Baltii ne nuzhen rossiiski 'zontik'" (Baltics do not need Russian "umbrella"), *Izvestiia*, 11 November 1997.

CHAPTER FIVE

Ukraine: Between East and West

No one won the contest over Ukraine's foreign economic policy. Ukraine's indecisive middle path between East and West, between Russia and Europe, was an outcome very few Ukrainians preferred. The Ukrainian state's ambivalence resulted from Ukrainians' collectively ambivalent interpretation of their nation. The nationalists wanted Ukraine to turn Westward both economically and politically. They were influential, so powerful and committed in several parts of the country that political elites could not ignore or marginalize them. But Ukrainian nationalists were merely influential; they neither won, like Lithuania's nationalists, nor lost, like Belarus's, the debate about their country's proper place in the post–cold war world. As a result, Ukraine failed to institutionalize its place in "Europe," as Lithuania did, or in "Eurasia," as Belarus did. Ukraine, whose name—*Ukraina*—means "borderland" in several Slavic languages, remained on the border of both regions, as they were defined by the choices made by Ukraine's post-Communist neighbors. Location on the border between East and West was a cliché for many east-central Europeans, but for Ukraine it was also a political and economic reality.

The economic results of Ukraine's political struggle were dire. Its indecisiveness cost society dearly since the economy received neither the potential longer-term benefits of institutional reform and reorientation toward Europe nor the shorter-term benefits of stability and Russian subsidies. For most Ukrainians, then, their state's ambivalence was an unhappy outcome, politically and economically. Economic welfare and autonomy from Russia were competing principles of Ukraine's foreign economic policy during the 1990s.[1] And Ukrainians could not agree among themselves which principle should guide policy. Recall List's argument, discussed in chapter 2, that a shared national identity lengthens a society's time horizons, thereby creating the political will necessary for economic sacrifice in the pursuit of long-term national goals. Collectively, as a society, Ukrainians were not prepared to make enormous sacrifices for their state, as they indicated in a 1993 opinion poll (Table 5.1).

It was not that Ukraine completely lacked citizens willing to sacrifice for independence. As the poll indicates, almost 20 percent of respondents were prepared to endure any necessary economic hardship. The problem was the lack of agreement on the goal itself, since more than 40 percent felt that Ukrainian autonomy was not worth any economic sacrifice. Many Ukrainians simply did not see the point of allowing the post-Soviet regional economy to continue to disintegrate. To them, the costs of autonomy seemed foolish and irrational, and even avoidable, as neighboring Belarus demonstrated.

Ukrainians' debate about the guiding principle of their foreign economic policy—either welfare or autonomy—was connected to their interpretation of the Ukrainian nation. For Ukrainian nationalists, most influential in western Ukraine, Russia was the Ukrainian nation's constituting "other," against which identity was defined. Many east and south Ukrainians, however, contested this anti-Russian content of Ukrainian national identity. For them, a distinctively Ukrainian national identity overlapped with several other identities, including regional, pan-Slavic, and even Soviet identities. These overlapping identities were neither necessarily nor coherently discrete from a Russian identity. In other words, many Ukrainians did not agree that being Ukrainian also meant being separate from Russia, and certainly not that it necessitated economic sacrifice for the sake of greater autonomy from their Slavic neighbor to the east. The content and contestation of Ukrainian national identity was a historical outcome.

HISTORY, INSTITUTIONS, AND UKRAINIAN NATIONAL IDENTITY

The most common misconception about Ukraine is that its territory was always part of the Russian empire and then the Soviet state and that it is therefore fated to remain in the Russian sphere of influence. Russia itself has perpetuated this idea of a Ukraine intimately integrated with Russia since 1654, when the Treaty of Pereiaslav institutionalized the tsar's

---

[1] See Volodymyr Sidenko, "Economic Independence or Economic Efficiency," *Politychna Dumka* 2 (1994): 160–66; and Paul D'Anieri, *Economic Interdependence in Ukrainian-Russian Relations* (Albany: SUNY Press, 1999), chap. 2.

Table 5.1 Ukrainians' Commitment to Independence (in Percent)

Are You Willing to Endure Economic Hardships for the Sake of Maintaining the Independence of Ukraine?	
I am willing to endure as much as is necessary	18.5
I am willing to endure for 1–2 years	30.9
I am not willing to endure any hardships	43.8
Difficult to answer	6.8

Source: Democratic Initiatives Foundation, *The Current Political Situation and the Future Political and Economic Development of Ukraine* (Kyiv, November 1993).

authority over Ukrainian territory. Pereiaslav incorporated only parts of what is now eastern Ukraine into the tsarist empire, however. Central Ukraine was incorporated almost one hundred fifty years later, in 1793–95, after the last partition of Poland. Then, in the middle of the twentieth century, the Soviet Union annexed western Ukraine, which includes Galicia and Volhynia (1939), Bukovina (1940), and Ruthenia (1945). Galicia, Bukovina, and Ruthenia had never been part of a Russian or Soviet state before their incorporation into the Ukrainian SSR. Thus, Ukraine, as it exists after 1991, does not have a singular history, much less a single type of historical relationship to Russian authority and identity.[2]

The most distinctive feature of Ukrainian history is its regional diversity, which ultimately influenced the content and contestation of Ukrainian national identity in powerful ways. This diversity of historical experience produced diverse interpretations of Ukrainian national identity after 1991. Just as it is difficult to tell a single history of Ukraine, it is problematic for Ukrainians themselves to tell a single story about how their past, their historical memory of their relations with other nations and states, should influence the choices they must make after Soviet rule. The regional contestation of Ukrainian national identity is a result of the shifting boundaries and changing institutional contexts within which Ukrainian nationalists, as well as Russian and Soviet bureaucrats, have sought their cultural, economic, and political goals.

Ukrainian Nationalists under the Romanovs and the Habsburgs

Although the western regions of post-Soviet Ukraine eventually became the country's stronghold of nationalist sentiment, nationalists first attempted to construct a Ukrainian identity distinct from Russia's in central and eastern Ukraine, under Romanov rule, in the 1820s and 1830s.

---

[2] For a recent review of Ukrainian history and historiography, see Mark von Hagen, "Does Ukraine Have a History?" *Slavic Review* 54, 3 (1995): 658–73.

In 1846 the first Ukrainian nationally minded organization, the Society of Saints Cyril and Methodius, was founded in Kyiv, then a part of the Russian empire.[3]

These first Ukrainian nationalists elicited a severe reaction from the tsarist authorities. The Polish Insurrection of 1863 had brought nationality issues in the western borderlands of the empire to the attention of the tsarist regime. As one measure to deal with the problem, the empire banned the Ukranian language in 1876. The development of a distinctively Ukrainian identity, independent, as the nationalists proposed, of a broader Russian identity, was a serious threat to the identity project that motivated Moscow. The regime of the Russian empire considered both Ukrainians and Belarusians to be part of a Russian identity that included them all—Great Russians, Little Russians (Ukrainians), and White Russians (Belarusians). Thus, Russian authorities effectively hindered the development of Ukrainian national consciousness by Russifying the language, eliminating distinctively Ukrainian institutions, and as Laitin observes, giving Ukrainian elites favored positions in the empire's administration to win their loyalty.[4]

Meanwhile, the Ukrainian-speakers living under Habsburg rule in the west also began to propose specific content for a Ukrainian national identity that included east and central Ukrainians and was defined by its differences from both Poles and Russians, and thus against the Polonophile and Russophile identities embraced by many elites in their society. This attempt, and the rising national consciousness associated with it, began later than it had in the east. Only in the late nineteenth and early twentieth centuries did the Ukrainian-speaking population in these eastern territories of the Habsburg empire begin to refer to themselves as "Ukrainians." This identity project, the fashioning of Ukrainian national identity within Austrian territory but for a population that lived outside Austrian territory as well, required considerable intellectual flexibility on the part of nationally conscious Ukrainians, who had never shared a province, much less a state, with Ukrainians who lived in the Russian empire.

During this Ukrainian nationalist revival the most influential region of what would become western Ukraine was Galicia, then part of the Habsburg empire. According to historian Orest Subtelny, in Galicia "nationally

---

[3] See Roman Szporluk, "Ukraine: From an Imperial Periphery to a Sovereign State," *Daedalus* 126, 3 (1997): 85–119. Also see Orest Subtelny, *Ukraine: A History*, 2d ed. (Toronto: University of Toronto Press; Canadian Institute of Ukrainian Studies, 1994), chaps. 12, 13, and 17; and Paul Robert Magocsi, *A History of Ukraine* (Seattle: University of Washington Press, 1996), chaps. 28 and 29.

[4] David D. Laitin, *Identity in Formation: The Russian-Speaking Populations in the Near Abroad* (Ithaca: Cornell University Press, 1998), chap. 3.

conscious Ukrainian intellectuals took advantage of the relative freedom allowed by the Habsburgs" to engage in the cultural politics of nation making.[5] Not only was the Habsburg regime more liberal than that of the Romanovs to the east; it also tolerated, and occasionally encouraged, the rise of Ukrainian nationalism in Galicia as a counterweight to Polish influence in the region. As Suny concludes, Austrian Galicia thus became the "center for literary expression and popular nationalism" whereas Ukrainians in Russia developed "neither a coherent mass-based national movement nor even a widely shared sense of a Ukrainian nation."[6] Some of east Ukraine's persecuted nationalists fled to Austrian Galicia, strengthening both the nationalist movement and their sense of solidarity across the boundary between the two empires.[7]

The Russian Revolution in 1917 and the end of World War I initiated chaotic years on the territories of the collapsed Habsburg and Romanov empires and the several nascent Ukrainian states that emerged. The Ukrainian Central Rada declared an independent state based in Kyiv in January 1918, but this Ukrainian People's Republic lasted less than a year. After several more years of ebbing and flowing independence and war, Soviet authorities subjugated the territories that had been part of the Romanov empire and incorporated them into the Ukrainian Soviet republic, also based in Kyiv. West Ukrainian nationalists based in L'viv, in Galicia, declared independence for the short-lived West Ukrainian National Republic in November 1918, only to become part of Poland in 1919. A few small provinces populated predominantly by Ukrainian-speakers were annexed to neighboring states—Bukovina to Romania, Ruthenia to Czechoslovakia.

Essentially, however, Ukrainian territories were divided between interwar Poland, which included most of western Ukraine, and the Soviet Union, which controlled central and eastern Ukraine, still ruled from Russia after several centuries. Historically separate before the war, western and eastern Ukraine also remained apart between the world wars, and their cultural and political experiences under the Poles and Soviets continued to diverge.

[5] See Subtelny, *Ukraine*, 241–42. Also see Ivan L. Rudnytsky, "The Ukrainians in Galicia under Austrian Rule," in *Nation Building and the Politics of Nationalism: Essays on Austrian Galicia*, ed. Andrei S. Markovits and Frank E. Sysyn (Cambridge: Harvard University Press, for Harvard Ukrainian Research Institute, 1982); and Paul Robert Magocsi, "The Ukrainians of Galicia under Habsburg and Soviet Rule," in *Nationalism and Empire: The Habsburg Empire and the Soviet Union*, ed. Richard L. Rudolph and David F. Good (New York: St. Martin's, 1992).

[6] Ronald Grigor Suny, *Revenge of the Past: Nationalism, Revolution, and the Collapse of the Soviet Union* (Stanford: Stanford University Press, 1993), 43.

[7] See Hugh Seton-Watson, *Nations and States: An Enquiry into the Origins of Nations and the Politics of Nationalism* (Boulder, Colo.: Westview, 1977), 187–88.

Uniting Ukraine under the Soviets

Many Ukrainian nationalists, in both the eastern and western regions, had sought to unify all Ukrainians into a single state for a century or more. Soviet leader Joseph Stalin achieved the goal for them in 1939, when Soviet authorities incorporated western Ukraine into the Ukrainian SSR. As historian Roman Szporluk notes, the Soviet annexation of western Ukraine "may have been one of Stalin's most fateful decisions during the years from 1939 to 1945."[8]

Western Ukraine had not by World War II become any less nationalist. Indeed, in reaction to the interwar Polish state's attempts to Polonize its eastern borderlands, west Ukrainians had in general become even more committed to their Ukrainian identity and to projects such as autonomy and independent statehood, with which they increasingly connected their nation.

Thus, after its incorporation into the Soviet Union, western Ukraine profoundly influenced how the content of national identity was constructed and debated in the Ukrainian SSR.[9] Moreover, Soviet authorities, wary of powerful nationalist sentiment in western Ukraine, treated the new region carefully after 1945, allowing the local press to continue to publish in Ukrainian and in general seeking to influence the meaning of Ukrainian national identity rather than Russifying the language and population, as they did in western Belarus after the war.[10] Western Ukraine, once the Piedmont of Ukrainian nationalism in the late nineteenth and early twentieth centuries, again influenced the trajectory of Ukrainian nationalism in the late 1980s, when perestroika and glasnost opened up the Soviet political and economic system to nationalist contention.

PERESTROIKA AND RUKH

After Gorbachev initiated the Soviet Union's perestroika and glasnost, several existing and new Ukrainian organizations began to mobilize

[8] Roman Szporluk, "The Soviet West—or Far Eastern Europe?" *East European Politics and Societies* 5, 3 (1991): 466–82, at 474.

[9] See Yaroslav Bilinsky, "The Incorporation of Western Ukraine and Its Impact on the Politics and Society of Soviet Ukraine," in *The Influence of East Europe and the Soviet West on the USSR*, ed. Roman Szporluk (New York: Praeger, 1975); Ivan L. Rudnytsky, "Soviet Ukraine in Historical Perspective," in *Essays in Modern Ukrainian History*, ed. Peter L. Rudnytsky (Cambridge: Harvard University Press, 1987); and Subtelny, *Ukraine*, 486–92.

[10] Roman Szporluk, "West Ukraine and West Belorussia: Historical Tradition, Social Communication, and Linguistic Assimilation," *Soviet Studies* 31, 1 (1979): 76–98. See also Taras Kuzio and Marc Nordberg, "Nation and State Building, Historical Legacies, and National Identities in Belarus and Ukraine: A Comparative Analysis," *Canadian Review of Studies in Nationalism* 26, 1–2 (1999): 69–90.

support for goals linked to the survival of the Ukrainian nation, that is, to connect the symbol of the Ukrainian nation to specific projects. The Ukrainian Writers' Union changed its public stance on cultural issues in 1986, when its leadership proposed the "rebirth" of Ukrainian culture and language. In 1987 the Ukrainian environmental movement, Green World (Zelenyi Svit), linked the renewal of the Ukrainian nation to ecological issues and sought to use the Chernobyl nuclear disaster to rally Ukrainians' support for their goals.[11] In 1988 the Ukrainian Helsinki Union, formed by recently released political prisoners, began to call for more rapid change. In addition, a number of so-called informal organizations, not legally sanctioned, began to promote political autonomy, especially in western Ukraine. Ukraine's Communist Party opposed the rising tide of nationalist sentiment, however, and its First Secretary, Volodymyr Shcherbytsky, remained among the most conservative in the union republics.

The year 1989 was a turning point. The most important event was the creation of the Popular Movement of Ukraine for Restructuring, or Rukh, in early 1989. In September 1989 Shcherbytsky was removed from his post as First Secretary. Rukh held its founding congress in Kyiv in the same month, by which time it had almost three hundred thousand members. Initially, Rukh was careful to operate within the framework of Gorbachev's perestroika, supporting democratization, cultural and linguistic renewal, and economic autonomy but not political independence.

As Subtelny reports, popular support for Rukh was "unevenly distributed. To an overwhelming extent it was based in western Ukraine and among the Kyiv intelligentsia. In eastern and southern Ukraine, where the Party maintained an iron grip, support for Rukh was minimal."[12] Thus, western Ukraine became a vanguard for the Ukrainian nationalist movement during the late 1980s, as it had been earlier in the century.[13]

As throughout most of the Soviet Union, the attempted coup in Moscow in August 1991 brought the Ukrainian republic's politics to a moment of choice. By then it was clear that the Soviet Union was unraveling, and Ukraine's Supreme Soviet declared the state's independence on 24 August 1991. The independence declaration was made subject to ratification by a referendum on 1 December 1991, when more than 90 percent of Ukrainian voters supported an independent state. Although it seemed then that the nationalist agenda had emerged triumphant, it soon became clear that Ukrainians understood their new independence in starkly contrasting ways.

[11] See Jane I. Dawson, *Eco-Nationalism: Anti-Nuclear Activism and National Identity in Russia, Lithuania, and Ukraine* (Durham: Duke University Press, 1996).

[12] Subtelny, *Ukraine,* 576.

[13] Alexander Motyl and Bohdan Krawchenko, "Ukraine: From Empire to Statehood," in *New States, New Politics: Building the Post-Soviet Nations,* ed. Ian Bremmer and Ray Taras (Cambridge: Cambridge University Press, 1997), 251–52.

THE POLITICS OF NATIONALISM IN POST-SOVIET UKRAINE

Ukraine's nationalists sought to define the content of Ukrainian national identity. After 1991 two traditions of nationalist ideology reemerged. Most prominent was Ukrainian society's so-called national democratic tradition (represented by Rukh, the Democratic Party of Ukraine, the Ukrainian Republican Party, and the Congress of National Democratic Forces), which was much more influential than Ukraine's national radical tradition (represented by the Ukrainian National Assembly, Congress of Ukrainian Nationalists, and Nationalist Union for Ukrainian State Independence).[14] The national democrats and national radicals competed to some extent in their proposals for Ukrainian national identity. For example, national radicals tended to emphasize ethnic definitions of the Ukrainian nation instead of the combined ethnic and civic definition favored by national democrats.[15] National radicals also tended to be less oriented toward Europe than national democrats. Nevertheless, the traditions shared several key ideas, especially their emphasis on Russia as the nation's constituting "other."[16]

The national radicals, despite their political marginality, were important for two reasons. First, their interpretations of Ukrainian national identity prompted concern in the West about the apparent aggressiveness of Ukrainian nationalism. Second, their arguments, which undercut the mainstream conservatism of the national democrats, alienated many east and south Ukrainians from the more moderate claims embedded in Ukrainian nationalist ideology.

Nationalists' Proposals for the Content of Ukrainian National Identity

"Most Ukrainian leaders now accept the need for a national idea," Taras Kuzio explains, but "the question is how to define its content."[17] The single most important proposal for the content of Ukrainian national identity was that of Rukh.[18] Rukh was influential because it was widely recognized as

[14] See Taras Kuzio, "Radical Nationalist Parties and Movements in Contemporary Ukraine before and after Independence: The Right and Its Politics, 1989–1994," *Nationalities Papers* 25, 2 (1997): 211–42.

[15] See Motyl and Krawchenko, "Ukraine," 250–51; and Andrew Wilson, *Ukrainian Nationalism in the 1990s* (Cambridge: Cambridge University Press, 1997), 153.

[16] For a historical reflection on the changing content of Ukrainian nationalist ideology, see John A. Armstrong, "Whither Ukrainian Nationalism?" *Canadian Review of Studies in Nationalism* 23, 1–2 (1996): 111–24. On nationalist ideology in post-Soviet Ukraine, see Taras Kuzio, *Ukraine: State and Nation Building* (London: Routledge, 1998), chap. 6.

[17] Kuzio, *Ukraine*, 53.

[18] See *The Popular Movement of Ukraine for Restructuring "Rukh": Program and Charter* (Baltimore: Smoloskyp Publishers, for the Ukrainian National Association, [1989] 1990),

Ukraine's most important nationalist party. Rukh also enjoyed the most electoral success of any nationalist party, winning twenty seats in the 1994 parliamentary elections and forty-six in the 1998 elections.[19]

Statehood and Its Meaning.   Statehood was necessary but not sufficient
for nationalists to be satisfied. After all, almost all Ukraine's political parties agreed that the Ukrainian state should continue to exist. With the exception of some separatists in Crimea, few political actors in Ukraine promoted outright separatism or political reintegration with Russia. Although
many political parties situated in eastern Ukraine sought close economic
relations with Russia and within the CIS, the boundaries and existence of
the Ukrainian state itself were not up for debate. "Where they differ,"
Mykola Ryabchuk argues, "is in their conception of how this state is to be
built, with which priorities."[20]

Ukrainian nationalists argued that Ukraine had a long history of statehood,[21] although it eluded them until 1991. Ukrainian nationalists traced
the political lineage of contemporary Ukraine to the medieval state of
Kievan Rus, which in Russian historiography has long been considered the
origin of the modern Russian state. This put Ukrainian nationalists in direct competition with Russia for ownership of these historical memories, a
fact that led, as D'Anieri shows, to political conflict between the two
states.[22] In Ukrainian nationalist ideology Russia was directly implicated in

---

especially 11; and Ivan Lozowy, *The Popular Movement of Ukraine "Rukh" 1994: Statehood, Democracy, Reforms* (Kyiv: International Relations Secretariat, Popular Movement of Ukraine
"Rukh," 1994), especially 21–22.

[19] Ukraine's parliament comprises 450 seats, which are filled with proportional representation of political parties and single-member districts. Only 338 seats were filled in 1994, of
which 5.9 percent represented Rukh. In 1998 Rukh's 46 seats accounted for 10.2 percent of
the total 450.

[20] Mykola Ryabchuk, "Between Civil Society and the New Etatism: Democracy and State
Building in Ukraine," in *Envisioning Eastern Europe*, ed. Michael Kennedy (Ann Arbor: University of Michigan Press, 1994), 142.

[21] John A. Armstrong, *Ukrainian Nationalism, 1939–1945* (New York: Columbia University
Press, 1955), chap. 1. This central argument of nationalist historiography was explicated by
Ukraine's most important historian, Mikhailo Hrushevsky, in his *History of Ukraine* (New
Haven: Yale University Press, 1941). See also Stephen Velychenko, *National History as Cultural
Process* (Edmonton: Canadian Institute of Ukrainian Studies, 1992).

[22] Paul D'Anieri, "Nationalism and International Politics," *Nationalism and Ethnic Politics* 3,
2 (1997): 1–28. See also Zenon Kohut, "History as Battleground: Russian-Ukrainian Relations
and Historical Consciousness in Contemporary Ukraine," in *The Legacy of History in Russia and
the New States of Eurasia*, ed. S. Frederick Starr (Armonk, N.Y.: M. E. Sharpe, 1994); Andrew
Wilson, "Myths of National History in Belarus and Ukraine," in *Myths and Nationhood*, ed. Geoffrey Hosking and George Schöpflin (London: Hurst, 1997), 187; and Peter J. Potichnyj, ed.,
Ukraine and Russia in Their Historical Encounter (Edmonton: Canadian Institute of Ukrainian
Studies, 1992).

Ukrainian nationalists' debates about the causes of brief and failed states between 1917 and 1921. These tenuous moments of statehood also became part of some Ukrainians' historical memory.

Therefore, post-Soviet Ukrainian statehood was not new, in the nationalists' conception; it was restored, regained. Most important, Russia was *from whom* statehood has been regained. Ukraine's nationalists, like Lithuania's, considered both tsarist Russia and the Soviet Union to have been occupying regimes and empires, and Soviet and post-Soviet Ukrainian nationalism was about the liberation of Ukraine from Russian imperial rule. As Kuzio argues, Ukraine's nationalists were "intrinsically hostile towards Russians and Russia, whom they perceive as imperialistic, chauvinistic, and the major threat to Ukrainian independence."[23]

The nationalists' interpretation of Russia as Ukraine's "other" also shaped their preferences about state building. Radical nationalists, haunted by Ukraine's failed states of 1917–21, were prepared to sacrifice democracy for a strong state. For example, the campaign slogan of the Ukrainian National Assembly for the 1994 parliamentary elections was, "Vote for us and you'll never have to vote again."[24] Even the national democrats, whose democratic ideology distinguished them from the national radicals, envisioned a strong, centralized Ukrainian state.[25] Such a state, indivisible, would be able to protect the national community from threats to its identity and security.

Economic Dependence and Autonomy. Ukrainian nationalists argued that economic dependence on Russia was a threat to state security.[26] Nationalists were most interested in creating autonomy from Russia, and economic means were Russia's most effective for influencing politics in many post-Soviet states. Few nationalists seriously feared Russian military invasion in the short run: Russia's economic influence was considered to be a much

---

[23] Taras Kuzio, "Radical Right Parties and Civic Groups in Belarus and Ukraine," in *The Revival of Right-Wing Extremism in the Nineties,* ed. Peter H. Merkl and Leonard Weinberg (London: Frank Cass, 1997), 203. See also Mykola Ryabchuk, "Civil Society and Nation Building in Ukraine," in *Contemporary Ukraine: Dynamics of Post-Soviet Transformation,* ed. Taras Kuzio (Armonk, N.Y.: M. E. Sharpe, 1998), 82–83.

[24] Quoted in Anna Reid, *Borderland: A Journey through the History of Ukraine* (Boulder, Colo.: Westview, 1999), 108.

[25] See especially Armstrong, "Whither Ukrainian Nationalism?" 114–15; and Ryabchuk, "Between Civil Society," 135–37.

[26] Author's interview, Rukh, Kyiv, July 1998. See the election platforms of several nationalist parties and coalitions: Rukh, *New Way for Ukraine* (Kyiv, 1998); Ukrainian National Assembly, *Economic Program of UNA* (Kyiv, 1998); and the National Front (a coalition of the Congress of Ukrainian Nationalists, Ukrainian Conservative Republican Party, and Ukrainian Republican Party), *Ukraine Needs Ukrainian Power!* (Kyiv, 1998). Also see, for example, "Nationalists Denounce CIS Economic Committee," *Uniar,* 26 September 1994, in FBIS-SOV-94-187, 27 September 1994, 57–58.

more pernicious influence on Ukrainian politics. Therefore, the nationalists warned against any economic integration with Russia or the CIS.[27] For example, Rukh, when it became an official political party in 1992, demanded that Ukraine withdraw from the CIS and its economic structures, a move that would be the "only way of getting rid of colonial status."[28] Similarly, the Ukrainian Republican Party emphasized the necessity of "securing the self-sufficiency of the national economy and its independence from the influence of external economic competitors or political maneuverings."[29] In December 1998, when parliamentary speaker Tkachenko traveled to Russia and publicly urged that Ukraine and Russia integrate their economies by creating a "common economic space" and monetary union, Ukraine's nationalist parties demanded that he be removed from office.[30]

The nationalists were not unaware of the costs of economic autonomy. Ukrainian nationalists, Dominique Arel observes, were prepared to endure economic deprivation to preserve autonomy from Russia.[31] Such deprivation, according to the nationalists, would have to be borne only in the short run: in the longer term, Ukraine's integration into Europe would make the nation wealthy.[32] The time horizons of nationalists were thus lengthened by their sharing of a national identity and vision for their society: future generations of Ukrainians would benefit from the costs of Westward reorientation borne by the first post-Soviet generation.

Europe and "Europe."   Nationalists contended that Europe was fundamental to the content of Ukrainian national identity. The nationalists' external agenda, Andrew Wilson shows, was "clear and can be neatly summarized as

[27] See "Nationalists Warn of Threats against Independence," *Intelnews*, 26 August 1995, in FBIS-SOV-95-168, 30 August 1995, 52; "Nationalists Appeal for Withdrawal from CIS," *Radio Ukraine*, 11 June 1992, in FBIS-SOV-92-115, 15 June 1992, 41; "Nationalists Reject Cooperation Accord," *Narodna hazeta*, March 1992, in FBIS-USR-92-045, 22 April 1992, 47; and "Statement by the Ukrainian National Assembly in Connection with the Intentions to Sign the CIS Statute and the Russian-Ukrainian Agreement on Good-Neighborly Relations, Cooperation, and Partnership," reprinted in *Molod Ukrainiy*, 6 January 1993, in FBIS-SOV-93-008, 13 January 1993, 43–44. Also see Andrew Wilson, "Foreign Policy Orientation of Ukrainian Political Parties," *Politychna Dumka* 1 (1993): 204–6, especially 204–5.

[28] Quoted in Vladimir Skachko, "Rukh Becomes a Political Party while Remaining a Public Organization," *Nezavisimaia gazeta*, 8 December 1992, in *Current Digest of the Post-Soviet Press* 44, 49 (1992): 24–25.

[29] Quoted in Wilson, *Ukrainian Nationalism*, 170–71.

[30] "Ukrainian Nationalists Demand Tkachenko's Ouster," *RFE / RL Newsline* 2, 245, part 2, 22 December 1998.

[31] Dominique Arel, "Ukraine: The Temptation of the Nationalizing State," in *Political Culture and Civil Society in Russia and the New States of Eurasia*, ed. Vladimir Tismaneanu (Armonk, N.Y.: M. E. Sharpe, 1995), 179. See also Sergei Tikhy, "Ukraine: The Political Economy of Nationalism," *Moscow News*, 3 September 1993; and Tor Bukkvol, *Ukraine and European Security* (London: Royal Institute of International Affairs, 1997), especially 5–6.

[32] Author's interview, Rukh, Kyiv, July 1998.

Table 5.2 Foreign Policy Preferences of Ukrainian Political Parties and Factions, 1993–98

Pro-CIS	Neutral	Anti-CIS
Communist Party	Constitutional	Rukh Party
Socialist Party	Democratic Party	Ukrainian Republican
Civic Congress	Green Party	Party
Party of Slavic Unity	Social Democratic Party	Democratic Party
Peasant Party	People's Democratic Party	Peasant Democratic
	Inter-Regional Bloc Reforms	Party
	Liberal Party	Christian Democratic
	New Ukraine	Party
	Hromada	Congress of Ukrainian
		Nationalists
		Reform Parliamentary
		Faction
		Ukrainian National
		Assembly
		Nationalist Union for
		Ukrainian State
		Independence

anti-Russian and pro-European."[33] The idea of "Europe" meant several things to Ukraine's nationalists. Most important, it was a means to ensure Ukraine's security by integrating into Western, democratic structures that would prevent the state's incorporation into a new Russian empire.[34]

In addition, Europe was the central orienting concept of nationalists' sense of history and destiny. Europe was both future and past. The nationalists claimed that Ukraine, like other states in the region, was not going to Europe as much as it was "returning" to Europe. Europe symbolized a cultural space that Ukraine supposedly shared before Soviet Communism.[35] Ukrainian nationalists thus sought to build a European state, by which they meant democratic, civilized, and rich, the characteristics that would cause other European states to recognize Ukraine's European identity.[36]

The Contestation of Ukrainian National Identity

The nationalists' proposals for the content of Ukrainian national identity were accepted by some Ukrainians and rejected by others along

[33] Wilson, *Ukrainian Nationalism,* 173. Some radical nationalists, including the Ukrainian National Assembly, argued that Kyiv should be the center of a new East Slavic empire rather than integrate into Europe. See the discussion in Kuzio, "Radical Nationalist Parties."

[34] See Ryabchuk, "Between Civil Society," 147–48; and Taras Kuzio, "The East Slavic Conundrum," in *Contemporary Ukraine,* ed. Kuzio, 240.

[35] See the discussion of Ukraine's "Return to Europe" in Rukh, *New Way for Ukraine.* Also see Ilya Prizel, *National Identity and Foreign Policy: Nationalism and Leadership in Poland, Russia, and Ukraine* (Cambridge: Cambridge University Press, 1998), 367; and Wilson, *Ukrainian Nationalism,* 179–80.

[36] See Ryabchuk, "Between Civil Society," 136.

Table 5.3 Self-Identification in Four Ukrainian Cities (in Percent)

	To Which Population Do You Attribute Yourself?			
	L'viv	Kyiv	Donetsk	Simferopol
Ukraine	75.4	64.9	29.6	12.2
CIS	3.8	8.2	9.2	9.0
USSR	8.5	11.9	32.8	32.5
Russia	0.5	0.2	2.0	3.5
Region	8.0	8.0	20.4	38.3
Europe	3.0	4.7	2.7	3.2
Don't know	0.8	2.1	3.2	2.3

Source: Democratic Initiatives Foundation, *Socio-Political Portrait of Four Ukrainian Cities* (Kyiv, May 1995).

Note: L'viv is in western Ukraine; Kyiv is in central Ukraine; Donetsk is in eastern Ukraine; Simferopol is in Crimea.

regional lines, primarily the historical differences that separated western from eastern Ukraine.[37] Nationalist political parties and their identity and policy proposals enjoyed wide support in western regions, especially Galicia, and urban and central regions, including Kyiv. Nationalist parties generally received 20 to 30 percent of Ukrainians' votes in parliamentary elections, with those votes concentrated in the west.[38] Few other Ukrainian political parties agreed with the nationalists' goals, however.

East and south Ukrainians largely rejected the nationalist parties in favor of the Communist and Socialist Parties, which disagreed with the nationalists' emphasis on a Ukrainian identity defined in opposition to Russia and in concord with Europe.[39] These parties also rejected the nationalists' argument that economic autonomy from Russia was necessary for state security. In general, the Communist, Socialist, and Peasant Parties were anti-reform, anti-Western, and pro-CIS (Table 5.2).

East and south Ukrainians tended to embrace multiple identities that overlapped with three others: a pan-Slavic identity, a residual Soviet identity, and their regional identity within Ukraine (Table 5.3).[40] None of these three was

[37] See especially Kuzio, *Ukraine*, 152–60. See also Paul Kubicek, "Dynamics of Contemporary Ukrainian Nationalism: Empire Breaking to State-Building," *Canadian Review of Studies in Nationalism* 23, 1–2 (1996): 39–50.

[38] Valeri Khmelko and Andrew Wilson, "Regionalism and Ethnic and Linguistic Cleavages in Ukraine," in *Contemporary Ukraine*, ed. Kuzio. See also Andrew Wilson and Artur Bilous, "Political Parties in Ukraine," *Europe-Asia Studies* 45, 4 (1993): 693–703.

[39] See the discussion of the platforms of the Communist, Socialist, and Peasant Parties in Taras Kuzio, *Ukraine under Kuchma* (New York: St. Martin's, 1997), 19–20; Wilson, "Foreign Policy Orientation," 205–6; and Prizel, *National Identity*, 367–68.

[40] See Paul S. Pirie, "National Identity and Politics in Southern and Eastern Ukraine," *Europe-Asia Studies* 48, 7 (1996): 1079–1104; Paul Robert Magocsi, "The Ukrainian National Revival," *Canadian Review of Studies in Nationalism* 16, 1–2 (1989): 45–62; and Kuzio, *Ukraine*, chap. 7.

defined in opposition to Russia. In fact, each allowed for the possibility that Ukrainians and Russians are more similar than different, that they are not each other's "others."[41] Any characterization of east Ukrainians as "pro-Russian" is therefore misleading. More accurately, most east and south Ukrainians were *not anti-Russian*. East and south Ukrainians did not long to rejoin Russia in a new state or empire;[42] they simply had a different idea of what it means to be Ukrainian. As Arel points out, east and south Ukrainians were "less likely to worry about what a close integration with Russia would do to their identity, since they already identify at least as much with Russian culture as with Ukrainian culture."[43] The pro-CIS stance popular in the eastern and southern regions was primarily based on an economic argument for living better and avoiding economic pain by cooperating more with the East.[44]

For much of the decade, the Communist and Socialist Parties dominated in the eastern regions whereas Rukh and other nationalist parties did well in the west. Thus, the Ukrainian political spectrum was polarized with regard to the most fundamental foreign economic policy choice the government had to make. Indeed, approximately 35 percent of members of parliament favored an exclusively Eastern foreign policy orientation, and around 20 percent urged a Western foreign policy orientation.[45] A centrist position was not well institutionalized in party competition, and the societal and political debates were dominated by two opposing and irreconcilable arguments about the purpose of the Ukrainian state and economy after 1991. Thus, as Ilya Prizel observes, Ukrainian national identity was contested regionally, "leading to different 'national' agendas advocated by different regions." Ukrainians agreed that their state was permanent, but there was "little agreement as to the purpose of that statehood."[46]

---

[41] For a closely related discussion, see Stephen Shulman, "Competing versus Complementary Identities: Ukrainian-Russian Relations and the Loyalties of Russians in Ukraine," *Nationalities Papers* 26, 4 (1998): 615–32.

[42] See Taras Kuzio, "National Identity in Independent Ukraine: An Identity in Transition," *Nationalism and Ethnic Politics* 2, 4 (1996): 582–609, at 599. Also see Roman Solchanyk, "The Post-Soviet Transition in Ukraine: Prospects for Stability," in *Contemporary Ukraine*, ed. Kuzio, 30–31. This is true except for Crimea, which remains a significant exception to most generalizations about Ukraine and where explicit pro-Russianism and separatism exist. Crimea was settled primarily by Russians and was part of the Russian SSR from 1922 to 1953; it was transferred to the Ukrainian SSR in 1954.

[43] Arel, "Ukraine," 179.

[44] Orest Subtelny, "Russocentrism, Regionalism, and the Political Culture of Ukraine," in *Political Culture and Civil Society*, ed. Tismaneanu, 194. See also Stephen R. Burant, "Foreign Policy and National Identity: A Comparison of Ukraine and Belarus," *Europe-Asia Studies* 47, 7 (1995): 1125–44; and Steven Erlanger, "Economic Protest Seen in Ukrainian Election," *New York Times*, 29 March 1994.

[45] Pro-CIS and anti-Western parties accounted for 118 of 338 seats (35 percent) in 1994 and 158 of 450 seats (35 percent) in 1998. Anti-CIS and pro-West parties accounted for 40 of 338 seats (12 percent) in 1994 and 95 of 450 seats (21 percent) in 1998.

[46] Prizel, *National Identity*, 371.

THE POLITICS OF ECONOMIC AUTONOMY

These divisions within Ukrainian society played an important role in the government's approach to the issue of economic autonomy after the Soviet Union collapsed. Before 1991, however, when the nationalists began to argue that economic autonomy was worth the short-term costs, Ukrainian nationalists had insisted that Ukraine's economy would benefit from independence. According to this argument, economic reorientation toward the West would be rapid and relatively costless. After Ukrainians escaped the Soviet economic system that had exploited them, and that they had subsidized, the country would become part of economic Europe. The "breadbasket of Europe," rich in Donbas coal, and the soul if not the heart of Soviet industry, Ukraine would achieve its economic autonomy from Russia lucratively.[47] It was a plausible argument partly because everyone believed the Soviets had grossly mismanaged the economy.

The nationalists' argument was at least partly strategic. West Ukrainian nationalists wanted east Ukrainians to join the independence movement. Wisely, they convinced the eastern half of the country that they would all be richer as an independent state. The December 1991 referendum on independence, in which over 90 percent of Ukrainians voted for a new Ukrainian state, thus meant very different things in different parts of Ukraine.[48] East and south Ukrainians wanted the wealth of statehood. The nationalists wanted the autonomy of statehood. The poverty and economic chaos that east and south Ukrainians received instead seriously undermined what had previously been widespread support for a statehood autonomous from Russia.[49]

After political independence in late 1991 the Ukrainian government, influenced by the nationalist agenda, interpreted economic dependence on Russia as a security threat.[50] The government defined state security broadly, including economic autonomy as a central foundation of policy. For example, Vladimir Selianinov, President Leonid Kravchuk's national security adviser in 1993, argued that Ukraine's "economic security is becoming the basis of national security as a whole."[51] Therefore, in 1992

[47] See the discussion in Subtelny, *Ukraine*, 589–93; and Wilson, *Ukrainian Nationalism*, 150–51.

[48] Zenovia Sochor, "Political Culture and Foreign Policy," in *Political Culture and Civil Society*, ed. Tismaneanu, 210; and Victor Stepanenko, "Ukrainian Independence: First Results and Lessons," *Ukrainian Review* 40, 2 (1993): 3–7.

[49] See Peter Ford, "West Tugs, Russia Yanks at Ukraine's Identity," *Christian Science Monitor*, 6 June 1995.

[50] Author's interview, Ministry of Foreign Affairs of Ukraine, Kyiv, June 1998; author's interview, Administration of the President of Ukraine, Kyiv, June 1998.

[51] Quoted in Vladimir Mayevskiy, "Economy Must Be Secure," *Pravda Ukrainy*, 29 January 1993, in FBIS-USR-93-023, 3 March 1993, 79. Ukraine's first post-Soviet military doctrine

Ukraine's government chose, apparently decisively, to pursue the Lithuanian model of trade reorientation away from Russia and toward the West. As discussed briefly in chapter 3, in March 1992 President Kravchuk articulated a coherent plan for Ukrainian economic security, understood primarily as security from Russia and Russian economic influence.

Ukraine's search for economic autonomy from Russia coincided with the post-Soviet economic crisis and collapse in industrial production that was common to all post-Soviet states. As the economic crisis unfolded, Ukrainian politics began to divide on the issue of economic autonomy and the importance of a European reorientation. Ukrainian nationalists remained committed to the autonomy policies. For them, economic autonomy was almost synonymous with state security.

Many Ukrainians rejected this nationalist interpretation of the necessity of sacrifice. The post-Soviet economic crisis heightened Ukraine's regional divisions. Heavy industry's concentration in the eastern regions meant that the people who suffered the highest costs of autonomy were the same people who were least willing to bear them merely for reasons of identity. Industrialists lobbied vigorously for the government to reconsider its attempt to achieve economic autonomy from Russia. In the end, the demands of citizens in the eastern and southern regions of the country, as well as the lobbying of Ukraine's most influential economic actors, led the government to abandon the economic autonomy plan.[52] The director of a Donbas mine expressed eastern Ukraine's reaction to western Ukraine's perspective on economic relations with Russia: "Nationalism blinds intelligence."[53] As Kuzio summarizes, "In western Ukraine the drop in living standards has

---

identified "the problem of the national economy's dependence on other countries for resources and technology" as an issue of state security. See Vladimir Buida, "Military Doctrine Adopted," *Nezavisimaia gazeta,* 21 October 1993, in *Current Digest of the Post-Soviet Press* 45, 42 (1993): 25–26. The 1997 national security doctrine adopted by parliament also emphasized the problem of economic dependence on Russia, particularly Russian oil and gas. See Oles M. Smolansky, "Fuel, Credit, and Trade: Ukraine's Economic Dependence on Russia," *Problems of Post-Communism* 46, 2 (1999): 49–58. See also Charles J. Dick, "The Military Doctrine of Ukraine," *Journal of Slavic Military Studies* 7, 3 (1994): 507–20. The text of the doctrine is reprinted in *Ukrainian Review* 40, 4 (1993): 77–83. According to one recent survey, approximately 70 percent of Ukraine's foreign policy elites consider economic factors to be most important for Ukraine's security whereas only 10 percent emphasize military factors. See Ukrainian Center for Peace, Conversion, and Conflict Resolution Studies, *Monitoring Foreign and Security Policy of Ukraine, 1997–1998* (Kyiv, 1998), supplement 1, table 3.

[52] See Rawi Abdelal and Jonathan Kirshner, "Strategy, Economic Relations, and the Definition of National Interests," *Security Studies* 9, 1–2 (1999–2000): 119–56; and Paul D'Anieri, "Dilemmas of Interdependence: Autonomy, Prosperity, and Sovereignty in Ukraine's Russia Policy," *Problems of Post-Communism* 44, 1 (1997): 16–26.

[53] Quoted in Henry Kamm, "Struggling Ukrainian Miners Are Put Off by Diet of Nationalism," *New York Times,* 16 February 1992. Also see Jane Perlez, "Ukraine's Miners Bemoan the Cost of Independence," *New York Times,* 17 July 1993.

been offset by the strength of the national idea," but in eastern Ukraine the "drop in living standards is blamed largely on the disintegration of the former USSR or the breakdown in economic ties with Russia caused by the former 'nationalist' President Kravchuk."[54]

KRAVCHUK, KUCHMA, AND THE "PARTY OF POWER"

Although institutionalized centrist political parties did not mediate Ukraine's polarized foreign economic policy debate during the 1990s, the state's post-Communist elite came to achieve something of a balance between the western and eastern regions. Ukraine was ruled largely by formerly Communist elites, both elected officials and members of Ukraine's bureaucracies. These elites, whose ranks included Presidents Kravchuk and Kuchma, adopted substantial elements of the nationalist program in 1990–91 in order to insulate themselves from revolutionary change in Moscow and to find a way to maintain power in the context of a political-economic system that clearly was no longer working. As a result, these "national communists," or "communist-sovereigntists," ostensibly adopted the state-building goals of the nationalists as their own. Kravchuk, for example, appropriated much of the nationalist agenda for his 1991 presidential campaign.[55] Until then Rukh had held a monopoly on the nationalist agenda. During the election campaign, journalists asked Rukh's presidential candidate, Viacheslav Chornovil, about the differences between his and Kravchuk's political programs. Chornovil answered: "No difference, except one. My program is thirty years old, while his—thirty days."[56]

The "Party of Power" (a more cynical appellation) was an informal group of elites whose continuity of influence across the 1991 divide was a defining feature of Ukrainian politics. These former Communists were the swing vote

---

[54] Kuzio, *Ukraine*, 85.

[55] Kuzio, *Ukraine*, chap. 2. See also, for example, Fred Hiatt, "Ukrainian Changes His Course: New President Was Party Ideologue," *Washington Post*, 3 December 1991; and Chrystia Freeland, "Unholy Alliance of the Heart Robs Ukraine of Its Head: Nationalists Back the Old Communists Where Independence Is the Deal and Policy the Price," *Financial Times*, 16 June 1992. For a more general assessment, see Alexander Motyl, "The Conceptual President: Leonid Kravchuk and the Politics of Surrealism," in *Patterns of Post-Soviet Leadership*, ed. Timothy J. Colton and Robert C. Tucker (Boulder, Colo.: Westview, 1995), which argues that the Communists, left on the Soviet periphery without a legitimating center, turned to their ethnic constituencies. Georgiy Mirsky suggests that there are two kinds of nationalism in Ukraine: the genuine nationalism of the nationally conscious intelligentsia and west Ukrainians and the "career nationalism" of former Communists "anxious to hold their positions and privileges." See Mirsky, *On Ruins of Empire: Ethnicity and Nationalism in the Former Soviet Union* (Westport, Conn.: Greenwood, 1997), 119–20.

[56] Quoted in Ryabchuk, "Between Civil Society."

in the political struggle between western and eastern Ukraine. Ukraine's former Communists thus consciously mediated Ukraine's regional and political divisions, which, in addition to the stalemate at the societal level, kept Ukraine between East and West during the 1990s.[57]

Perhaps the most remarkable feature of the Ukrainian-Russian economic relationship since 1993 was its continuity across two very different Ukrainian presidents.[58] Ukraine's rejection of CIS economic integration was consistent even after 1994, when Leonid Kuchma defeated the incumbent Kravchuk in a presidential election that politicized both the economy and foreign policy. Because Kuchma campaigned on a platform of closer relations with Russia, Kravchuk's supporters portrayed Kuchma as pro-Russian. Ukrainian nationalists called him a traitor, dangerous for Ukrainian independence. Against the contrary expectations of Western observers and many Ukrainians themselves, however, Kuchma continued Ukraine's policies of bilateral cooperation with Russia but consistent rejection of multilateral economic integration with any CIS states.[59]

The culmination of Kuchma's policy of bilateral ties with Russia, a policy begun by Kravchuk when his administration retreated from its economic autonomy plan in 1993, was a treaty on bilateral economic cooperation signed in 1998. The treaty was designed to create a closer and more stable bilateral economic relationship between the two Eurasian powers, but it was accompanied by Kuchma's assurances that Ukraine's foreign policy goals had not changed. Although Kuchma recognized the economic

[57] On the Party of Power and foreign policy, see Sherman Garnett, *Keystone in the Arch: Ukraine in the Emerging Security Environment of Central and Eastern Europe* (Washington, D.C.: Carnegie Endowment for International Peace, 1997), 53–54; Oleh Bilyi and Yevhen Bystrytsky, "State-Building in Ukraine: Ways of Legitimation," *Politychna Dumka* 7 (1996): 122–33; and Burant, "Foreign Policy and National Identity," 1127–28. Furtado makes this argument slightly differently: Ukraine's foreign policy elites borrowed the statism and civic nationalism of Ukrainian nationalists' ideology because other, stronger versions of Ukrainian national identity were not widely shared. See Charles F. Furtado, Jr., "Nationalism and Foreign Policy in Ukraine," *Political Science Quarterly* 109, 1 (1994): 81–104. See also Andrei Kapustin and Viktor Timoshenko, "Communists Win in Ukraine," *Nezavisimaia gazeta*, 31 March 1998; and Olga Ansimova, "Party of Power Looks West—Rivals Are Looking in Other Direction," *Nezavisimaia gazeta*, 18 June 1994, both in *Current Digest of the Post-Soviet Press* 50, 13 (1998): 19; and 46, 24 (1994): 23.

[58] On the foreign policy continuity between Presidents Kravchuk and Kuchma, see Kuzio, *Ukraine under Kuchma*, especially 187–88.

[59] See Vladimir Skachko, "Ukraine's Goal Is Full Membership in European Union—Leonid Kuchma Gives New Interpretation to His Country's Nonaligned Status," *Segodnia*, 8 June 1996; "Kiev Is Not Averse to Becoming a Special Partner of NATO," *Kommersant'*, 26 June 1996; Arkady Moshes, "Ukraine's Shifting Neutrality," *Moskovskie novosti*, no. 26, 30 June–7 July 1996; and Andrei Kapustin, "Leonid Kuchma on Foreign Policy," *Nezavisimaia gazeta*, 17 July 1996; all in *Current Digest of the Post-Soviet Press* 48, 24 (1996): 23; 48, 26 (1996): 15; 48, 26 (1996): 15–16; and 48, 29 (1996): 25. Also see Chrystyna Lapychak and Ustina Markus, "Ukraine's Continuing Evolution," *Transition* 3, 2 (1997): 29–32; and "Ukraine: Between East and West," *The Economist*, 28 September 1996.

necessity of cooperation with Russia, he insisted that the new treaty would not divert Ukraine from its "strategic course—integration into European structures."[60] With his toughness on Russia, Kuchma solidified his state-building reputation and won the grudging support of west Ukrainians, who had given him only 4 percent of the region's votes in the 1994 election.[61] "We have to cooperate with Russia," Kuchma observed, "but that doesn't mean that we have to trust them."[62]

A consistent theme in Ukraine's evolving economic relationship with Russia was the potential alternative of "the West." Officially, Ukraine sought to integrate into Europe and all its political and economic institutions; that is, "integration" was a concept used only in reference to Ukraine's economic relations with Europe, not with Russia or Eurasia. At the first Ukraine-EU Cooperation Council meeting in Luxembourg in June 1998, Ukraine applied for associate membership in the EU, thus giving definite institutional meaning to the Western vector of its foreign policy. Of all the post-Soviet states, Ukraine certainly was the only one in the 1990s to attempt to have partial membership in *both* the CIS and the EU. Boris Hudyma, the representative of Ukraine to the EU, expressed the fundamental components of Ukrainian foreign economic policy and their interrelationship. Although some Western observers interpreted President Kuchma's election as a sign of Ukraine's having turned Eastward after its initial gambit under Kravchuk to pursue the Baltic model of reorientation, Hudyma dissented: "But in fact, while maintaining good economic ties with Russia, Ukraine's policy is aimed at developing a wider and deeper relationship with the European Union."[63] By the end of the decade, however, Ukraine was not nearly as far along as the Baltic states in reorienting its state and economy toward the EU and away from Russia (Tables 5.4 and 5.5).

[60] Kuchma, at a press conference in Kyiv, quoted in "Kuchma ubezhden v neobkhodimosti rasshiriat' kontakty s Rossiei, sokhraniaia strategicheskii kurs na integratsiiu v evrostruktury" (Kuchma convinced of necessity to broaden contacts with Russia, maintaining strategic course toward integration into European structures), *Interfax*, 3 March 1998. Also see Evgeny Lakoza, "Rossiia i Ukraina dogovorilis' soglasovat' strukturnuiu perestroiku ekonomik" (Russia and Ukraine agree to coordinate structural reorganization of their economies), *Finansovye izvestiia*, 3 March 1998. On the events leading up to the treaty, see Boris Vinogradov, "Yeltsin i Kuchma provedut dva sammita—Prezidenty nadeiutsia reshit' vse ostavshiesia problemy" (Yeltsin and Kuchma conduct two summits—The presidents are hoping to resolve all remaining problems), *Izvestiia*, 21 January 1998. On Kuchma's insistence that the bilateral treaty would not affect Ukraine's fundamental foreign policy goals, see also Aleksandr Bovin, "Problemy v otnosheniiakh s Ukrainoi ostalis'" (Problems in relations with Ukraine remain), *Izvestiia*, 5 March 1998.

[61] James Rupert, "Ukraine's Kuchma Gains in Nationalistic Region despite Hard Winter, People Back Reforms," *Washington Post*, 16 March 1995.

[62] Quoted in Chrystia Freeland and Matthew Kaminski, "In the Shadow of the Russian Bear," *Financial Times*, 25 November 1995.

[63] Boris Hudyma, "Ukraine Seeking Membership in EU," *Financial Times*, 13 June 1998.

Table 5.4 Ukrainian Exports to EU, CIS, and Russia as Percentages of Total Exports, 1991–98

	EU	CIS	Russia
1991	—	—	—
1992	8	56	—
1993	10	59	—
1994	10	55	40
1995	10	53	43
1996	10	51	39
1997	12	39	26
1998	15	33	23

Source: Interstate Statistical Commission of the Commonwealth of Independent States, *Official Statistics of the Countries of the Commonwealth of Independent States* (Moscow, various years).

Table 5.5 Ukrainian Imports from EU, CIS, and Russia as Percentages of Total Imports, 1991–98

	EU	CIS	Russia
1991	—	—	—
1992	10	70	—
1993	7	72	—
1994	10	73	59
1995	13	65	53
1996	15	63	50
1997	18	58	46
1998	17	54	48

Source: Interstate Statistical Commission of the Commonwealth of Independent States, *Official Statistics of the Countries of the Commonwealth of Independent States* (Moscow, various years).

CONCLUSION

It was common during the 1990s to hear that Ukraine had a "weak" sense of itself as a nation and state. Identity was the correct variable, but the description seems imprecise. Ukrainian nationalists were quite strongly attached to their proposals for Ukrainian national identity. Indeed, they were adamant, frequently uncompromising. The more useful way to understand the influence of Ukrainian national identity is with the conceptual tools offered here: its content and contestation. Ukrainian national identity was important because of the ways in which its content was contested, especially regionally. This meant that Ukrainians disagreed among themselves about the meaning of the Ukrainian nation and purpose of the Ukrainian state. Different views were predominant in different regions. Thus, division and disagreement, rather than collective vagueness or weakness, characterized Ukraine's internal debates.

As Kuzio argues, Ukraine could not adopt the Baltic or the Belarusian foreign policy models.[64] Ukraine's national identity was too contested and fragmented regionally for the government to make a decisive break from the CIS and toward Europe, as did the Baltics. At the same time, Ukraine's nationalism was too well developed to be marginalized while the government sought to trade political autonomy for economic gain, as did Belarus. Neither a purely pro-Western nor a purely pro-Eastern foreign policy was possible because it would have divided the country. The former entailed economic costs east Ukrainians were unwilling to bear. The latter was unacceptable to west Ukrainians for reasons of identity.

The outcomes of the societal debates in Lithuania, Belarus, and Ukraine—Lithuania's turning Westward, Belarus's turning Eastward, and Ukraine's inability to choose either—suggest the possibility that Lithuania *actually is* more Western and European than Ukraine, which in turn actually is more Western and European than Belarus. Samuel Huntington's influential and controversial *Clash of Civilizations* argues precisely that.[65] For Huntington, the "Eastern Boundary of Western Civilization" leaves Lithuania on the side of the West whereas the dividing line runs through both Belarus and Ukraine. In contrast, I argue that the cultural boundary Huntington identifies is real but is not defined by the essential civilizational attributes of Lithuanians, Ukrainians, and Belarusians. Rather, the cultural boundary is a result of institutional history and its influence on national identity.

For Huntington, these states' foreign policy choices reflected civilizational and cultural affinity, not nationalism. Balancing and bandwagoning were questions primarily of cultural similarity.[66] The Baltic states are different, he argues: "The usefulness of differentiating among countries in terms of civilization is manifest with respect to the Baltic republics. They are the only former Soviet republics which are clearly Western in terms of their history, culture, and religion, and their fate has consistently been a major concern of the West."[67] The Baltics, located West of Huntington's civilizational fault line that divides Western Christendom from Eastern Orthodoxy, are predominantly Catholic and Protestant.

Ukraine, in contrast, is unlucky enough to be a "cleft country." According to Huntington, the "civilizational fault line between the West and

---

[64] Kuzio, "National Identity," 600. Moreover, policy makers I interviewed self-consciously rejected what they referred to as the "Belarusian option" and the "Baltic option" for the very reason of Ukraine's internal divisions. Taras Kuzio elaborates this argument in "The Domestic Sources of Ukrainian Security Policy," *Journal of Strategic Studies* 21, 4 (1998): 18–49.

[65] Samuel P. Huntington, *The Clash of Civilizations and the Remaking of World Order* (New York: Simon and Schuster, 1996), especially 157–68.

[66] "Countries tend to bandwagon with countries of similar culture and to balance against countries with which they lack cultural commonality." Huntington, *Clash of Civilizations*, 155.

[67] Huntington, *Clash of Civilizations*, 162.

Orthodoxy runs through its heart and has done so for centuries."[68] Western Ukraine is the home of the Uniate Church, which is something of a compromise between the Catholic and Orthodox Churches: it acknowledges the pope's authority but practices Orthodox rites. The fact that Ukraine is so divided leads Huntington to address the possibility that the country will split along its "fault line."

Thus, there are two distinct parts of Huntington's argument: the civilizational approach offers an alternate interpretation of why Lithuania, Ukraine, and Belarus chose such different post-Soviet foreign policies and, at the same time, a coherent explanation for how they were interpreted by the EU and the West. Both parts together are plausible. And the divide that separates Lithuania, western Ukraine, and western Belarus from eastern Ukraine and the rest of Belarus, a boundary Huntington identifies, seems important. Ultimately, however, the civilizational argument, as an alternative to a more narrow account based on national identity, is unsatisfactory for three reasons.

First, it cannot make sense of these states' actual political struggles during the 1990s—the causal mechanisms are ill defined. It is true that religion was an important part of national identity in all three states. But that is precisely how religion was important: as a part of national identity. Lithuanian and west Ukrainian nationalists traditionally, under tsarist and Soviet rule, used their religious institutions (Catholic and Uniate, respectively) as a means to organize an identity distinct from Russian identity. But religion alone as an identity variable cannot explain why Belarus's Catholics, who live primarily in western Belarus and on the Western side of Huntington's civilizational divide, are not substantially more nationally conscious than the rest of the population. By Huntington's own map and logic, western Belarus should be a hotbed of Belarusian nationalism, just as western Ukraine is its state's Piedmont. But Belarus is not a "cleft country," as Ukraine is, and western Belarus is not particularly nationalist. Belarus's pro-EU nationalists instead are predominantly Russian-speaking, Orthodox, cultural elites from Minsk. One possible reason that western Belarus is not a hotbed of nationalism, moreover, is the fact that Soviet authorities vigorously pursued their identity project in the region after incorporating it into the Belorussian SSR. As I show in chapter 6, Soviet authorities linguistically Russified western Belarus after 1945, though they did not do the same to western Ukraine, which they incorporated at the same time.

This raises the second problem with the civilizational argument: a number of very plausible historical counterfactuals would redraw Huntington's civilizational divide, a fact that implies that civilizational attitudes do not inhere

[68] Huntington, *Clash of Civilizations*, 166 and generally 165–67.

to these societies. The Soviet Russification of western Belarus but not western Ukraine is one example. What if the Soviets had Russified western Ukraine and smothered the distinctiveness of its identity, as they did in Belarus? Other examples are even more telling. One of the reasons western Ukraine became the Piedmont of Ukrainian nationalism was that it remained, first as part of the Habsburg empire and then as part of interwar Poland, outside Moscow's cultural influence until 1939–45. Ukraine's first nationalists, however, arose not in western Ukraine but in eastern Ukraine, which was then under tsarist rule. When the tsarist regime banned the Ukrainian language and subdued the nascent movement, at the same time pursuing policies of cultural and linguistic Russification, it succeeded in molding east Ukrainians into a population with an identity complementary to Russian identity. What if western Ukraine had been incorporated into the tsarist empire in the late eighteenth century, after the partitions of Poland, instead of the middle of the twentieth century? Western Ukraine would now look much more like eastern Ukraine, and the Uniate Church would not exist.

Also troublesome for Huntington's argument is Lithuania's interwar statehood. As I argued in chapter 4, Lithuania's interwar statehood was not the result of a mass-based nationalist movement that demanded independence from tsarist Russia; Lithuania's nationalist movement was no more popular than Belarus's in the early twentieth century. Again, religion was not politically meaningful until nationalism made it so: despite their Catholicism, Lithuanians under tsarist rule did not organize a mass movement for independence. Only during the interwar years did Lithuanian nationalists succeed in linking their religion to an identity defined in opposition to Russia. Also, Lithuania's interwar statehood certainly was not supported by the "West." In fact, Lithuania was to have been part of a German empire. Its statehood instead was an accident of the geopolitics of the time, and no great power supported statehood for the Baltic peoples. The immediate reincorporation of the Baltic territories into the Bolshevik state was a very real possibility, and this is of course what happened to the independent Ukrainian and Belarusian states proclaimed in 1917–18. But it is precisely the twenty years of interwar statehood that allowed a distinctively Lithuanian national identity to become widely shared among Lithuanians. Furthermore, when European states protested the incorporation of the Baltic states into the Soviet Union in 1940, it was certainly the first time there had been coherent Western support for independent states on the Baltic littoral. Another accident of history became part of the mythology of "Europe," defined against Russia. What if Lithuanians had never had an interwar state?

These reflections about historical counterfactuals suggest the third and most general reason that the civilizational argument is unsatisfactory. As these states' histories, and especially Ukraine's, make clear, the cultural differences are a result of the complex institutional, and therefore political, history of the region. Lithuanian nationalists finally succeeded in turning Catholicism into a politically salient identity marker only during the interwar years; before that, Lithuanians were Catholics, but it did not matter for their politics. The national ambiguity of western Belarus's own Catholics demonstrates that a different institutional history can ensure that religion, for Huntington the fundamental source of the East-West divide in Europe, is unimportant instead of all-important. These societies are not discrete units with homogenous civilizational identities. They could have turned out differently had their institutional histories been different. Ukraine's contested national identity and the institutional history that underlies it make that clear.

CHAPTER SIX

Belarus: Toward Russia and the East

Belarusian nationalists believe Belarus's national interest is influenced by history, culture, and destiny. During the first post-Soviet decade the Belarusian Popular Front (BPF), the most influential organization of Belarusian nationalists, argued that Belarusian society is inherently European and Western, in contrast to its Eurasian and Eastern neighbors, the Russians. The BPF desperately sought to convince Belarus's society and political elite that their state should "return to Europe." The BPF wanted what Lithuania's Sajudis and Ukraine's Rukh wanted, but they were less successful and less popular than their neighboring nationalists. Undeterred throughout the 1990s, the BPF proposed anti-Soviet, anti-Russian, and pro-European content for their society's national identity.

Most Belarusians rejected the BPF's proposals. Although the content of Belarusian national identity was contested vigorously by the BPF, other Belarusians passively observed the dispute between political elites and nationalists over their competing concepts of the nation and state. Collectively, Belarusians' interpretation of their national identity was both ambiguous and ambivalent. In the repertoire of Belarusians' identities, pan-Slavic and even residual Soviet identities were more widely and coherently shared than a distinctively Belarusian identity defined in opposition to Russia. Put simply, most Belarusians rejected the anti-Russian content that the BPF proposed for Belarusian national identity. But there was no coherent alternative proposed. Although Belarusian nationalist groups such as the BPF were ardent, collectively Belarusians did not share a coherent sense of their nation in relation to either Russia or "Europe." No

Belarusian political party, except the BPF, used the symbol of the Belarusian nation to legitimate economic sacrifice, to describe the destiny of the people, or to define the fundamental purposes of the new Belarusian state.

As a result, there was no national purpose that underlay the government's foreign economic policy. The government did not interpret economic dependence on Russia as a problem to be solved. Rather, economic relations with Russia were interpreted as mutually beneficial exchange, and the government sought only to improve the society's standard of living and solve the post-Soviet economic crisis. The government's solution was to reintegrate the post-Soviet economic space. Russia was willing to reintegrate and to pay handsomely for Belarusian loyalty. Russia forgave Belarus's mounting energy debts, offered subsidies, and generally eased the costs of the dissolution of the Soviet economy. As production collapsed in many post-Soviet states, some observers wondered how Belarus managed to maintain high levels of employment and exports to Russia. The answer seemed to lie in the absence of significant change.[1]

To the nationalists, the government's policies seemed decadent and near-sighted. The BPF accused the government of "selling out," of putting short-term material goals above the fundamental purposes of the Belarusian state, at least as they interpreted them. Belarus's first president (1994–), Aleksandr Lukashenko, found these criticisms irrelevant. Indeed, from his and the government's justifications of Belarusian-Russian economic reintegration, it was clear that the nationalists and the administration were speaking different languages. Lukashenko explained that reintegration just made good economic sense: "The main thing is interest. We have an interest in Russia. There is no altruism in the Belarusian president's policy here: it is absolutely in our interest. Yes, as always the opposition criticizes me for this—and not just for this, either—saying that I am selling our interest. You know, I'm an economist, not a photographer. I understand perfectly what interest is. Interest is subject to accounting."[2] Lukashenko's idea that the national interest is something calculable from the material consequences of policy was exactly the opposite of the Belarusian nationalists' understanding of the national interest.

Lithuania's Sajudis, Ukraine's Rukh, and the BPF sought essentially the same things for their states: primarily, more autonomy from Russia. Sajudis got what it wanted because Lithuania's Communists adopted the movement's

---

[1] See Matthew Kaminski, "Is Belorussian Dictator's Growth for Real? 'Lukanomics' and Easy Credit Help Nation to Outpace Russia," *Wall Street Journal*, 23 February 1998. For a review, see David R. Marples, *Belarus: A Denationalized Nation* (Amsterdam: Harwood, 1999), chap. 2.

[2] Quoted in "Lukashenko on the CIS and the Belovezh Forest Agreements," Moscow television, 15 February 1995, in *Russia and the Commonwealth of Independent States: Documents, Data, and Analysis*, ed. Zbigniew Brzezinski and Paige Sullivan (Armonk, N.Y.: M. E. Sharpe, 1997), 246–47.

foreign policy goals. Rukh got some of what it wanted because it was power-ful enough in the western half of the country to influence politics and en-courage some of Ukraine's Communists to turn into nationalists. In contrast, virtually none of Belarus's Communists became nationalists, and the former Communists, many of them members of Belarus's *two* post-Soviet Commu-nist parties, remained in control of the Belarusian government throughout the decade. The failure of the BPF to galvanize Belarusian society for pur-poseful sacrifice shows what was missing in Belarusian politics, what allowed the distinctively Belarusian approach to post-Soviet political economy. Pres-ident Lukashenko's description of the crass material interests of his state would have been inconceivable in Lithuania because most Lithuanians as-cribed national meaning and purpose to their state and economy. Belaru-sians, and their government, simply interpreted post-Soviet material reali-ties differently. As a result, Belarusian political elites followed the material incentives to cooperate closely with Russia, and their policies were popular among most Belarusians, who were more interested in returning to an in-creasingly mythologized Soviet past, stable and wealthy, than in endorsing the nationalists' own mythologized past of a European Belarus that was au-tonomous from Russia.[3]

Belarus's cultural and institutional history influenced Belarusians' in-terpretation of their nation, though differently than has commonly been assumed. The historical context helps make sense of the unpopularity of the Popular Front and its ideas and policy proposals, and the ambiguity and contestedness of Belarusians' view of themselves in relation to Russia.

HISTORY, INSTITUTIONS, AND BELARUSIAN NATIONAL IDENTITY

The ambiguity and contestation of Belarusian national identity in the 1990s resulted from the policies of Russian and Soviet governments over the past several centuries. Post-Soviet Belarus is composed of territories that were integral parts of the Russian empire and the Soviet Union. Both tsarist and Soviet leaders sought to mold the identity of Belarusian popu-lations to serve their political needs, first by emphasizing the unity among Eastern Slavs, especially Great Russians, White Russians (Belarusians), and Little Russians (Ukrainians). Then Soviet leaders sought to create a non-national, Soviet identity for its citizens. Both these identity projects suc-ceeded more fully in Belarus than in any other region of the tsarist and Soviet states.

---

[3] See Astrid Sahm, "Political Culture and National Symbols: Their Impact of the Belaru-sian Nation-Building Process," *Nationalities Papers* 27, 4 (1999): 649–60.

Nevertheless, Belarus shares a potentially important feature with Ukraine: contemporary Belarus contains territories that were incorporated into the USSR only after World War II. The territories known collectively as western Belarus were, like western Ukraine and the three Baltic republics, brought into the Soviet polity relatively late.[4] Like western Ukraine, western Belarus was part of interwar Poland. Unlike western Ukraine, however, western Belarus did not become a regional stronghold of national sentiment; it did not become Belarus's "Piedmont," its place of national revival. The institutional histories of the Russian empire and the Soviet Union help explain why that was so.

One common interpretation of Belarusian acquiescence in Russian regional hegemony is quite problematic. Namely, it is common to hear that Belarusians had no modern tradition of statehood on which to draw and that therefore they sought reintegration. But Ukraine also had no modern tradition of statehood, and its government resisted Russian hegemony and sought economic autonomy. This contrast suggests that it was not the histories of Belarusian and Ukrainian *territories* that were influential in their post-Soviet policy making. Rather, it was the histories of the identities of the populations of those territories, and the political and institutional contexts within which those identities developed, that eventually influenced Belarusians' interpretation of the economic choices they faced after 1991.

The Incorporation into Tsarist Russia

The territories of contemporary Belarus were part of the Grand Duchy of Lithuania and later the Polish-Lithuanian Commonwealth, formally established in 1569, until the three partitions of 1772–95. During the seventeenth and eighteenth centuries Russia and the commonwealth competed for supremacy in central Europe. After the last partition of the commonwealth in 1795, the Belarusian territories and population were incorporated into the Russian empire. During the nineteenth century tsarist authorities imposed policies of cultural and linguistic Russification.[5]

Small groups of Belarusian nationalists emerged during the late nineteenth century, but their influence was as minimal as their goal, which was not to establish a Belarusian state but merely to reintegrate Poland and Lithuania in a new commonwealth. The Belarusian national movement

[4] Belarus is made up of six regions: Brest, Vitebsk, Homel', Hrodno, Minsk, and Mahileu. Western Belarus refers to Brest and Hrodno, which were formally incorporated into the Belorussian SSR in 1939. See Jan Gross, *Revolution from Abroad: The Soviet Conquest of Poland's Western Ukraine and Western Belorussia* (Princeton: Princeton University Press, 1988).

[5] See Piotr S. Wandycz, *The Lands of Partitioned Poland, 1795–1918* (Seattle: University of Washington Press, 1974).

remained weak until the end of tsarist rule.[6] The Russian empire's linguistic and cultural policies were successful in Belarus, as they had been in eastern Ukraine. The populations of Belarus and eastern Ukraine considered themselves not necessarily "Russian" but rather part of a broader Slavic identity that included Belarusians, Russians, and Ukrainians. At the time of the Russian Revolution in 1917, there were no other territories currently part of the Belarusian state that lay outside the Romanovs' empire.

After the Russian Revolution a number of states appeared on the map during the ebb of Moscow's authority, including the Belarusian Democratic Republic (BDR) in 1918. The BDR's independent existence ended in 1919. According to the historian Nicholas Vakar, who was sympathetic to Belarusian nationalist historiography, "It has been said that nationhood came to the Belorussians as an almost unsolicited gift of the Russian Revolution. It was, in fact, received from the hands of the Austro-German occupation army authorities and depended on their good will."[7] Then, when war between Poland and the Soviet Union ended in 1920–21, Belarusian territories were divided between the two states by the Treaty of Riga. Western Belarus became part of interwar Poland and was subject to the Polish government's own attempts to Polonize its eastern territories during the 1920s and 1930s.

Uniting Belarus under the Soviets

Stalin formally incorporated western Belarus into the Belorussian SSR in 1939 but did not solidify Soviet rule over the territories until after the German occupation of Belarus ended in 1944.[8] The inclusion of western Belarus into the SSR did not significantly affect the development of Belarusian national identity, however. Western Belarus did not, like western Ukraine, transform the republic into which it was incorporated after World War II. In particular, western Belarus did not become the location of a Belarusian cultural or national revival during the 1980s. Belarus's Brest and Hrodno provinces were no Galicia, the stronghold of Ukrainian nationalism in the western regions of the republic.

[6] See Steven L. Guthier, "The Belorussians: National Identification and Assimilation, 1897–1970," Parts 1 and 2, *Soviet Studies* 29, 1 and 2 (1977): 37–61 and 270–83; Richard Pipes, *The Formation of the Soviet Union: Communism and Nationalism, 1917–1923*, rev. ed. (Cambridge: Harvard University Press, 1964), 11–12, 74–75, and 150–54; and Ronald Grigor Suny, *Revenge of the Past: Nationalism, Revolution, and the Collapse of the Soviet Union* (Stanford: Stanford University Press, 1993), 36.

[7] Nicholas P. Vakar, *Belorussia: The Making of a Nation* (Cambridge: Harvard University Press, 1956), 105.

[8] See Vakar, *Belorussia*, chaps. 9–11.

Historian Roman Szporluk shows that Soviet authorities treated the incorporation of the western regions of the Ukrainian and Belorussian SSRs differently, particularly in terms of policies regarding language and nationality. Because Soviet leaders were concerned about the difficulties of incorporating nationalist Galicia into Ukraine, they allowed the local press to continue to publish in Ukrainian. In contrast, Soviet authorities banned the use of Belarusian in the local press of western Belarus and engaged in extensive cultural and linguistic Russification of the region. Although it was undoubtedly true that the Belarusian national movement was weak before 1944, it is also true that west Belarusians and, at that time, most Belarusians in the BSSR spoke primarily Belarusian, not Russian. Soviet authorities changed all that, and their different treatment of western Ukraine and western Belarus reflected their divergent assessments of the national resistance in the two regions.[9]

Whether Soviet authorities were right or not about which of the two were more nationalist, the choice they made based on those assessments was consequential. By the 1980s most Belarusians spoke Russian as their primary language. Although nationalist ideas were marginally more popular in western Belarus than in other regions of the country during the 1990s, western Belarus never became a regional stronghold for the nationalist movement.

Despite the fact that both regions had been part of interwar Poland, then, western Belarus and western Ukraine had very different historical and cultural experiences. Western Ukraine had been part of the Habsburg empire before incorporation into Poland, and it was under the Habsburgs that Ukrainian national activists enjoyed a relatively liberal political space in which to pursue their nation-making project. Western Belarus, in contrast, was part of Russia before and after the interwar years, and therefore it had not been separate from Russian political authority and cultural influence during the nineteenth century, when nationhood was becoming the dominant idiom of world politics. Significantly, western Belarus, unlike western Ukraine, had never produced a nationalist movement. Thus, the difference in historical sequence between the Habsburg-Polish-Soviet authority experienced by western Ukraine and the Romanov-Polish-Soviet context of western Belarus influenced their divergent cultural and political roles in the Soviet and post-Soviet republics of which they were a part. The existence of a modern tradition of statehood was obviously not what distinguished Ukraine from Belarus. Rather, it was the identities of the societies that inhabited Belarusian and Ukrainian territories, and the

---

[9] See Roman Szporluk, "West Ukraine and West Belorussia: Historical Tradition, Social Communication, and Linguistic Assimilation," *Soviet Studies* 31, 1 (1979): 76–98.

internal and external influences on the development of those identities. In sum, as the Ukrainian author Viktor Zalizniak comments, "They do not say it for nothing that Belarus is Ukraine minus Galicia."[10]

PERESTROIKA AND THE BELARUSIAN POPULAR FRONT

Just as in the Lithuanian and Ukrainian SSRs, during Gorbachev's perestroika and glasnost of the mid and late 1990s a nationalist movement began to take shape in Belarus. Indeed, an articulate nationalist movement emerged in Belarus even before similar movements mobilized in Ukraine and other parts of the Soviet Union. Belarusian nationalists began to demonstrate over issues of language and culture in 1987. Then, in 1988, Belarusian archaeologists discovered mass graves linked to Stalinist purges of Belarusian citizens in the Kurapaty Forest near Minsk. The discovery galvanized the small opposition movement, and one of the archaeologists, Zenon Pazniak, helped mold the movement into a national front. The Belarusian Popular Front (Belarusky Narodny Front), also known as Rebirth (Adradzhenie), was founded in 1988 in the politically charged context of the Kurapaty excavation.

Under serious pressure from the Communist Party of Belarus, the BPF was forced to hold its founding congress outside Belarus and with the help of nationalists from neighboring states. The BPF thus held its first congress in June 1989 in Vilnius, Lithuania.[11] The contrast between the BPF's experience and that of Lithuania's Sajudis is remarkable. The First Secretary of Lithuania's Communist Party, Algirdas Brazauskas, had addressed the founding congress of Sajudis to express his sympathy with the nationalists' goals. Meanwhile, Belarus's Communist Party opposed the emergent nationalist movement at every stage of its development.

[10] Quoted in Taras Kuzio, "The Sultan and the Hetman: Democracy-Building in Belarus and Ukraine in a Gray Security Zone," paper presented at the conference Democratic Consolidation in Eastern Europe, European University Institute, Florence, December 1997, 14. See also David R. Marples, *Belarus* (New York: St. Martin's, 1996), 16–18; and Taras Kuzio and Marc Nordberg, "Nation and State Building, Historical Legacies, and National Identities in Belarus and Ukraine: A Comparative Analysis," *Canadian Review of Studies in Nationalism* 26, 1–2 (1999): 69–90.

[11] See Jan Zaprudnik, "Belorussian Reawakening," *Problems of Communism* 38, 4 (1989): 36–52; and Ralph Clem, "Belarus and the Belarusians," in *The Nationalities Question in the Post-Soviet States*, 2d ed., ed. Graham Smith (London: Longman, 1996), especially 216–17. On the first program of the BPF, see *Grazhdanskie dvizheniia v Belorussii: Dokumenty i materialy, 1986–1991* (Civic movements in Belorussia: Documents and materials, 1986–1991) (Moscow: TsIMO, 1991), especially 119–56.

THE POLITICS OF NATIONALISM IN POST-SOVIET BELARUS

Nowhere in the former Soviet Union was there a larger gap than in Belarus between the beliefs of a society's nationalist movement and the beliefs of society as a whole about the political meaning of a collective identity. Belarusian nationalists offered a set of proposals for the content of national identity, but Belarusian political elites, as well as most Belarusians in general, rejected them.[12]

Russian scholars Dmitri Furman and Oleg Bukhovets offer a compelling summary of the differences in popular support for nationalists in Lithuania, Ukraine, and Belarus: "Whereas the people's fronts in the Baltic region really were movements of the peoples as a whole, and while Rukh in Ukraine has, together with its intellectual social base in Kiev, a powerful regional base in western Ukraine as well, the BPF in fact has a base only among the mass of Minsk intelligentsia and that of other large cities."[13] Thus, the local nationalist movement's ideas were ascendant in Lithuania, contested regionally in Ukraine, and marginalized in Belarus.

The Belarusian Popular Front

The BPF was essentially the only nationalist political party in Belarus, the only group that consistently linked the symbol of the nation to the political and economic projects it proposed. Therefore, the BPF was the central cultural location for the production of nationalist ideology. The BPF, like nationalists throughout the post-Soviet region, concentrated on the history and purposes of the Belarusian state, the threat of economic dependence on Russia, and the necessity of reorienting the polity and economy away from Russia and toward Europe and the West. For the BPF, Russia was the nation and the state against which Belarusian identity should be defined. "Europe," especially Central Europe, was a broad cultural identity with which Belarusians had a historical affinity.

Statehood. Although Belarus lacks a modern tradition of independent statehood, Belarusian nationalists sought to attach political importance to the Belarusian state (the Belarusian Democratic Republic) that appeared briefly between 1918 and 1919. Despite the precariousness and brevity of

---

[12] For recent reviews of the issue, see Marples, *Belarus*; and Sherman W. Garnett and Roberg Legvold, "Introduction: Assessing the Challenge of Belarus," in *Belarus at the Crossroads*, ed. Garnett and Legvold (Washington, D.C.: Carnegie Endowment for International Peace, 1999), 3–4.

[13] Dmitri Furman and Oleg Bukhovets, "Belorusskoe samosoznanie i belorusskaia politika" (Belarusian self-awareness and Belarusian politics), *Svobodnaia mysl'* 1 (1996): 57–75, in *Russian Politics and Law* 34, 6 (1996): 5–29, at 14.

the republic, for nationalists it was a moment of statehood, true independence from Russia, which Russia snatched from Belarusians' grasp. According to Vakar, "It cannot be denied that the ten-month period of symbolic independence has left an indelible impression on the Belorussian mind. A fact, historically accidental and trivial, has grown into a historic legend."[14]

Moreover, Belarusian nationalists claimed an even longer tradition of statehood: the Grand Duchy of Lithuania.[15] According to the nationalists, the elites of the Grand Duchy were primarily Belarusian-speakers, and the Grand Duchy's statutes, written in Belarusian, reflect the influence of Slavs on the politics and culture of the government. As a result of this historical claim, in 1918 the Belarusian Democratic Republic adopted as its state emblem the state symbol of the Grand Duchy—a coat of arms depicting a knight on horseback—which also became an official symbol of post-Soviet Lithuania. Lithuanians call the coat of arms "Vytis" (the White Knight), and Belarusians call it "Pahonia" (the Chase), but it is the same. During the 1990s the BPF adopted Pahonia as its emblem and kept it after Belarusian voters rejected it in a 1995 referendum. Regardless of the plausibility of either the Lithuanians' or Belarusians' claim to medieval historical stateness, the Grand Duchy supposedly represents a time when the people and territories of contemporary Belarus were outside the sphere of influence of tsarist Russia. Even after the Grand Duchy officially united with Poland to create the Polish-Lithuanian Commonwealth in 1569, Belarus was, the argument runs, in the cultural and political space of Europe. When, after the partitions of Poland, Russia absorbed Belarusian territories and began to Russify their populations, that was the first time Russia was responsible for the loss of statehood; 1919 was the second.

Therefore, like Lithuanian nationalists, Belarusian nationalists claimed that their state was "restored," not new. And Russia, linked to Soviet authority in Moscow, was the "empire" from which Belarusian statehood was regained. Belarusian nationalists thus adopted the "anti-imperial master frame" of Soviet and post-Soviet nationalist movements throughout the region.[16] Tsarist and Soviet leaders were empire builders who subjugated and imprisoned the Belarusian nation, depriving it of its rightful state and stealing its historical memory and culture. Clearly Russia, according to Belarusian nationalists, was the Belarusian nation's most important "other." It was

---

[14] Vakar, *Belorussia*, 105, and chaps. 7 and 8 generally. For a contemporary discussion, see Petr Petrikov, "Byla li BNR gosudarstvom?" (Was the BNR a state?), *Sovetskaia Belorussiia*, 25 March 1993.

[15] See Andrew Wilson, "Myths of National History in Belarus and Ukraine," in *Myths and Nationhood*, ed. Geoffrey Hosking and George Schöpflin (London: Hurst, 1997).

[16] See Mark Beissinger, "How Nationalisms Spread: Eastern Europe Adrift the Tides and Cycles of Nationalist Contention," *Social Research* 63, 1 (1996): 97–146.

the only state in the region that threatened Belarus's independence and statehood.[17]

Economic Dependence.   The BPF's first platform called for the "complete economic independence" of Belarus as well as the "integration of the republic's economy into the European and world economic system."[18] The BPF called economic dependence on Russia "the main problem of the security of the Belarusian state."[19] Belarusian nationalists did not believe Russian troops would cross their shared border to take over the country, but they feared that economic dependence on Russia would lead to two unhappy scenarios. The first was that Belarus would lose its ability to act autonomously in international affairs. The second and more serious concern was that the government would continue to offer political deals to Russia in exchange for favorable economic treatment; in other words, the nationalists feared the government itself would trade away sovereignty for economic gain. Therefore, Belarusian nationalists wanted the country to diversify its external supplies of oil, gas, and raw materials and maintain the state's monetary sovereignty.[20]

The policies that the Belarusian government pursued instead, policies of economic integration with Russia and with other CIS states, vexed the nationalists. At every step of Belarus's primrose path to integration, Belarus's nationalists objected. The security and autonomy of the state was always the primary reason for objecting. In 1992 BPF leader Pazniak announced that Belarus should be wary of its economic relations with Russia and that Belarusians should seek a prize more suitable to their history and culture, namely, economic integration into Europe, a turn away from Russia.[21] In 1993 the BPF issued a statement demanding that Belarus immediately withdraw from the CIS. "Any further orientation toward Russia," the statement continued, "will bring destruction to Belarus."[22] When Prime

---

[17] Zenon Pazniak, "O russkom imperializme i ego opasnosti" (Of Russian imperialism and its dangers), *Narodnaia gazeta*, 15–17 January 1994. See also Adrian Karatnycky, "The 'Nearest Abroad': Russia's Relations with Ukraine and Belarus," in *Russia: A Return to Imperialism?* ed. Uri Ra'anan and Kate Martin (New York: St. Martin's, 1996); and Roman Szporluk, "Belarus, Ukraine, and the Russian Question: A Comment," *Post-Soviet Affairs* 9, 4 (1993): 366–74.

[18] See the discussion of the BPF's platform in Art Turevich, "Elections in Byelorussia," *Byelorussian Review* 2, 1 (1990): 5–8, especially 5. See also the BPF's first official economic program, "The Concept of Economic Reform in Belarus," published in April 1992 and reprinted in Joe Price, "Belarus's Program for Transition," *Belarusian Review* 4, 1 (1992): 5–11.

[19] Author's interview no. 1, Belarusian Popular Front, Minsk, July 1998.

[20] See Jan Zaprudnik and Michael Urban, "Belarus: From Statehood to Empire?" in *New States, New Politics: Building the Post-Soviet Nations*, ed. Ian Bremmer and Ray Taras (Cambridge: Cambridge University Press, 1997), 286–88 and 297–98.

[21] Zenon Pazniak, "Belarus' i dorozhe" (Belarus and a higher prize), *Narodnaia gazeta*, 29 October 1992.

[22] "Popular Front Warns against Pro-Russia Orientation," *Vecherny Minsk*, 24 December 1993, in FBIS-SOV-93-249, 30 December 1993, 61.

Minister Viacheslav Kebich emphasized the necessity of post-Soviet economic reintegration in 1993, Pazniak demanded his resignation, claiming that his policies "pose a threat to our sovereignty."[23]

The BPF also staunchly opposed the Belarusian government's first steps toward monetary integration with Russia.[24] In 1994 Pazniak argued, "Unification of the monetary systems of Belarus and Russia is impossible without Belarus's losing its independence and statehood."[25] Parliamentary debate about monetary unification with Russia in 1994 was characteristic, in both its intensity and its lopsidedness. Pazniak was unable to rally members of parliament to oppose monetary unification despite his rhetoric and calls for mass protest. The affront to the nationalists' ideas did not stop there: Pazniak's rhetoric was rejected figuratively and literally. While Pazniak was in mid-speech, the speaker of the Belarusian parliament, Mechislav Gryb, ordered that Pazniak's microphone be turned off. In the end, the BPF and Pazniak demanded that criminal charges be brought against Prime Minister Kebich for violating four articles of the Belarusian constitution by giving up the sovereignty of the country in the monetary union deal with Russia.[26] The central accusation made by the nationalists was that the Belarusian government, under both Kebich and Lukashenko, has sold out the Belarusian national interest.[27]

"Europe." Finally, Belarusian nationalists believed that the state's rightful and historical place is in Europe, not the "East," represented by Russia. According to this interpretation of history, Belarus was historically a part of cultural Europe until Russia wrested it from the influence of the West.[28] The nationalists' foreign policy goals reflected that interpretation: the BPF wanted Belarus to join the EU and NATO and to integrate fully into the institutions

[23] "Popular Front Wants Resignation of Kebich," *Interfax,* 15 October 1993.

[24] Vitaly Tsygankov, "Russia and Belarus Unite Monetary Systems—Opposition Sees This as a Threat to Independence," *Nezavisimaia gazeta,* 20 November 1993, in *Current Digest of the Post-Soviet Press* 45, 47 (1993): 23. See also Valentin Zhdanko, "The Unification of the 'Bunny' and the Ruble Draws a Stormy Reaction," *Segodnia,* 15 April 1994, in *Current Digest of the Post-Soviet Press* 46, 15 (1994): 3–4.

[25] See Valentin Zhdanko, "Belarus: Just You Wait, 'Rabbit'!—Prime Minister Intends to Sign Agreement with Moscow on Any Terms," *Segodnia,* 5 February 1994, in *Current Digest of the Post-Soviet Press* 46, 5 (1994): 24–25.

[26] Aleksandr Starikevich, "Opposition in Belorussia Demands that Criminal Charges Be Brought against Prime Minister," *Izvestiia,* 20 April 1994, in *Current Digest of the Post-Soviet Press* 46, 16 (1994): 22.

[27] See, for example, Mikhail Shimansky, "Oppozitsiia obviniaet pravitel'stvo v rasprodazhe Belarus'" (Opposition accuses government of selling off Belarus), *Izvestiia,* 14 April 1994.

[28] See Wilson, "Myths of National History." See also Zenon Pazniak, "Al'ternativa vsegda sushchestvuet . . ." (Alternatives always exist . . .), *Narodnaia gazeta,* 23–30 October 1990; Art Turevich, "Byelorussia: Its Government and the Opposition," *Byelorussian Review* 3, 1 (1991): 10–13; and "Pazniak: The Opposition's Point," *Belarusian Review* 3, 4 (1992–93): 5–6.

of the West.[29] The nationalists thus sought to create a European identity for their state, by which they meant democratic, civilized, and ultimately, rich.

The Contestation of Belarusian National Identity

Although Belarusian nationalists emerged during the late 1980s to articulate a coherent vision of a new state free from external domination, according to political scientist Mark Beissinger, they "ultimately failed in their attempts to mobilize the [Belarusian] population around the anti-imperial master frame" of the region's ascendant nationalist ideologies during the 1980s and 1990s.[30] In Beissinger's metaphor, Belarusian nationalism barked but did not bite.

The ideas of Belarusian nationalists were unpopular among most Belarusians, particularly Belarusian political elites.[31] In the parliamentary elections of 1990 the BPF won less than 8 percent of the total number of seats, and of those, half were in urban Minsk. Thus, the BPF essentially was alone in its foreign policy preferences for breaking with Russia and turning the country Westward; the 8 percent of the seats the BPF held was the full extent of members of parliament who opposed integration with Russia.

The political divide of Belarus in the 1990s separated those who saw the Belarusian population as a community of shared and distinct identity, on the one hand, from those who saw the population as part of a larger community of Slavs, on the other. Thus, the central axis of contention in

[29] Author's interviews nos. 1 and 2, Belarusian Popular Front, Minsk, July 1998. "In contrast to Belarusian officials," Burant shows, "the nationalist opposition would like to secure a European identity for Belarus" ("Foreign Policy and National Identity," 1134). See also "Belarus—To Europe! A Strategy of Defense of Independence," in *Documents of the Fifth Congress of the Belarusian Popular Front*, Minsk, 20–21 June 1997; Piatro Pankratovich, "Popular Front Activist on Union with Russia," *Svoboda*, 1 February 1995, in FBIS-SOV-95-031, 15 February 1995, 62–63; Vasily Romanovsky, "Should Belarus Leave the CIS?" *Vecherny Minsk*, 24 December 1993, in FBIS-SOV-93-249, 30 December 1993, 61; Andrei Makhovski, "Zenon Pazniak: 'We Are Ready to Cooperate with Everyone Who Supports Independence,'" *Belorusskaia delovaia gazeta*, 21 September 1995, in FBIS-SOV-95-186, 26 September 1995, 89–90; and Eve-Ann Prentice, "Opposition Leader Promises to Break Belarus's Links with Moscow," *The Times*, 4 February 1995.

[30] Beissinger, "How Nationalisms Spread," 124. Also see 122–23, where he finds: "But even when nationalisms do bark, it is far from certain that they will bite, and even if they do snap a bit, that the bite will find its intended target. Intellectuals who propagate nationalist ideas may indeed be in place; they may even attempt to mobilize populations in pursuit of nationalist aims. But whether their messages resonate within populations is another matter." See also Beissinger's excellent survey of the issue, "Nationalisms that Bark and Nationalisms that Bite: Ernest Gellner and the Substantiation of Nations," in *The State of the Nation*, ed. John A. Hall (Cambridge: Cambridge University Press, 1998).

[31] See Furman and Bukhovets, "Belorusskoe samosoznanie," 12–13; and Kathleen Mihalisko, "Political-Economic Assessments: Belarus," in *The Former Soviet Union in Transition*, ed. Richard F. Kaufman and John P. Hardt (Armonk, N.Y.: M. E. Sharpe, 1993), 1005.

Belarusian politics during the 1990s was the interpretation of the state's political-economic relationship to Russia. Belarus's nationalists favored autonomy, the former Communists ever closer ties.[32]

Moreover, Belarusian nationalists acknowledged their unpopularity. The Belarusian Popular Front complained that "few political parties" shared the foreign policy goals of the organization and that their support was "certainly less" than 25 percent of the population.[33] The nationalists' recognition of the low levels of national awareness among Belarusians was, according to Ed Jocelyn, "one of the defining characteristics of Belarusian nationalism." Unlike nationalist movements in the Baltics that appealed to images of their "reawakening" dormant national consciousness among their populations, Belarusian nationalists sought to "restore the lapsed marker of Belarusian collective identity," which everyday Belarusians have forgotten over years of Russification and the rewriting of history. Thus, in Belarus, nationalist imagery is of "rebirth" and "renewal," of giving nationality back to the Belarusians rather than discovering it already within them.[34]

Belarusian nationalist intellectuals complained of Belarusians' "national nihilism."[35] BPF leader Pazniak remonstrated that the majority of Belarusians were indifferent to their national culture and their newly regained statehood, "a consequence of colonial thinking and the absence of a national consciousness."[36] In Belarusian social and political discourse, *nationalist* and *nationalism* were pejorative words from which even the Popular Front sought to distance itself as well. In sum, Belarusian society did not embrace the BPF.

Belarusian political elites also reacted negatively, even angrily, to the BPF. As Prime Minister Kebich insisted, "There are not, and never will be, roots of nationalism in Belarus."[37] In 1992 members of the Belarusian parliament

---

[32] See Viacheslau Pazniak, "Belarus's Foreign Policy Priorities and the Decision-Making Process," in *The Making of Foreign Policy in Russia and the New States of Eurasia*, ed. Adeed Dawisha and Karen Dawisha (Armonk, N.Y.: M. E. Sharpe, 1995), 150–52; Clem, "Belarus and the Belarusians," 219–20; and Anatolii Rozanov, "Belarusian Perspectives on National Security and Belarusian Military Policy," in *State Building and Military Power in Russia and the New States of Eurasia*, ed. Bruce Parrott (Armonk, N.Y.: M. E. Sharpe, 1995), 196, 197, and 203.

[33] Author's interview no. 2, Belarusian Popular Front, Minsk, July 1998.

[34] See Ed Jocelyn, "Nationalism, Identity, and the Belarusian State," in *National Identities and Ethnic Minorities in Eastern Europe*, ed. Ray Taras (New York: St. Martin's, 1998), 74–77, quotations from 76, 77. See also Algimantas Prazauskas, "The Influence of Ethnicity on the Foreign Policies of the Western Littoral States," in *National Identity and Ethnicity in Russia and the New States of Eurasia*, ed. Roman Szporluk (Armonk, N.Y.: M. E. Sharpe, 1994).

[35] Alexander Bely, "Belarus: A Real or Fictitious Nation?" *Cross Current* 47, 4 (1997): 3–6, at 4.

[36] Zenon Pazniak, "Belarus, Russia, and the CIS," *Narodnaia gazeta*, 14 January 1993, in FBIS-USR-93-020, 25 February 1993, 139–43.

[37] "Kebich Outlines Government Policy toward Minorities," *Respublika*, 7 June 1994, in FBIS-SOV-94-112, 10 June 1994, 46–47.

Table 6.1 Foreign Policy Preferences of Main Belarusian Political Parties

Pro-CIS and Anti-West	Non-bloc	Anti-CIS and Pro-West
Agrarian Party of Belarus	United Civil Party	Belarusian Popular Front
Belarusian Patriotic	Belarusian Party	
Movement	of Women, "Nadezhda"	
Belarusian Peasants' Party	Belarusian Social	
Belarusian People's Party	Democratic Party,	
Communist Party of Belarus	"New Hromada"	
Party of Communists of Belarus	Belarusian Green Party	
Belarusian Party		
"For Social Justice"		
Liberal Democratic Party		

began labeling the BPF "extremist" for its arguments in favor of autonomy from Russia and the continued disintegration of post-Soviet economic interdependence.[38] In contrast to the BPF's pro-European and anti-Russian foreign policy stance, all major Belarusian political parties emphasized in their platforms that they did not oppose close economic integration and political cooperation with Russia (Table 6.1).[39]

The politics and results of the May 1995 referendum and parliamentary elections are illustrative. The debate over both was clearly cast as a contest between those politicians opposed to integration with Russia and those in favor. According to some observers, President Lukashenko had organized the referendum to demonstrate the Belarusian public's support of his pro-Eurasian and integrationist policies and its disdain for the program of the nationalists.[40] Although the nationalists exhorted Belarusians to support national revival and autonomy from Russia, Belarusian voters rejected both. In the referendum over 80 percent of Belarusian voters approved of the government's proposal to give the Russian language legal status equivalent to Belarusian *and* the president's policies of economic integration with Russia. Lukashenko's interpretation of the referendum was that Belarusians

[38] V. Letankov, "Popular Front Criticized as Extremist," *Sel'skaia zhizn'*, 27 November 1992, in FBIS-USR-92-158, 11 December 1992, 119–21. See also Yevgeny Rostikov, "Zenon Pazniak's Anti-Russian Accent," *Rossiiskaia gazeta*, 16 June 1994, in FBIS-SOV-94-118, 20 June 1994, 57–59.

[39] V. A. Bobkov, N. V. Kuznetsov, and V. P. Osmolovsky, *Politicheskie Partii Belarusi* (Political parties of Belarus) (Minsk: BGEU, 1997), 3–98. See also Jan Zaprudnik, "Political Parties in Belarus: An Overview," *Belarusian Review* 10, 4 (1998): 2–6.

[40] See Matthew Kaminski, "Russian Links Tempt Belarus Voters," *Financial Times*, 15 May 1995. See also "In the Slav Shadowlands," *The Economist*, 20 May 1995; Margaret Shapiro, "Belarus Voters Support Resumed Ties to Russia," *Washington Post*, 16 May 1995; Matt Warshaw, "Reintegration with Russia, Soviet Style," *Transition* 1, 20 (1995): 58–62; Ustina Markus, "Lukashenko's Victory," *Transition* 1, 14 (1995): 75–78; and "Belarus Leader Gains More Power, Strengthens Links to Russia," *Reuters*, 15 May 1995.

Table 6.2 Results of the May 1995 Referendum(Percent answering yes)

1. Do you support giving the Russian language equal status with Belarusian?	83
2. Do you support the establishment of a new state flag and symbol of the Republic of Belarus?	75
3. Do you support the actions of the president toward economic integration with the Russian Federation?	83
4. Do you agree with the necessity of changing the constitution of the Republic of Belarus to provide for the possibility of the president's disbanding the Supreme Soviet before the end of its term in case of systematic or serious breaches of the constitution?	78

Source: Narodnaia gazeta, 19 April 1995, 16 May 1995.

"cannot conceive of themselves without close, intimate ties with Russia. To ignore this fact, as the national radicals do, would be a big mistake."[41] Indeed, the BPF had apparently made the tactical error of emphasizing the threat of Russia's "imperial" ambitions in reintegrating with Belarus in their campaign to influence the outcome of the referendum. Obviously, their concerns did not resonate with the Belarusian public (Table 6.2).

The parliamentary elections of 1995 were also a choice about economic integration with Russia, and Belarusians again voted for integration.[42] The elections were disastrous for the BPF, which did not win a single seat, including that of Pazniak himself. The result was that the Belarusian parliament by 1995 had not a single member, nationalist or otherwise, who favored a pro-EU and anti-CIS economic orientation for the country.[43]

In sum, the nationalists proposed a specific vision for the Belarusian nation, and Belarusian political elites contested it, offering instead a more ambiguous interpretation of the Belarusian nation that did not contradict the closest of economic and political ties with Russia. It was not that Belarus as an entire country or society lacked a national identity or that Belarusians believed themselves to be Russian. More accurately, most Belarusians, like

[41] Quoted in Vladimir Yefanov, Pavel Gurin, and Anatoly Yurkov, "We Separated. The Time Has Come to Reunite," *Rossiiskaia gazeta,* 24 August 1996, in FBIS-SOV-96-169, 29 August 1996, 38–41.
[42] See Irina Bugrova and Svetlana Naumova, "Parliamentary Elections and Foreign Policy Orientations of Belarus," *Vector* 1, 1 (1996): 4–9, especially 7.
[43] The elections themselves were controversial, and opposition parties claimed the government tampered with the electoral process. This became a moot point in 1996 when President Lukashenko dismissed the popularly elected parliament and replaced it with a new parliament that would be more responsive to his policy initiatives. Lukashenko's move was greeted with widespread condemnation by European governments, which have yet to recognize the new parliament as legitimate.

east Ukrainians, had mixed identities, combinations of multiethnic and multilingual identities that did not preclude a significant overlap between Belarusian and Russian identities.[44]

THE POLITICS OF BELARUSIAN-RUSSIAN INTEGRATION

As the post-Soviet economic crisis worsened, the usefulness of independent statehood became less and less clear to Belarusians. The Belarusian government looked to Russia for economic assistance and to the Soviet past for policy guidance.[45] According to the annual poll conducted by the Belarusian Public Opinion Center, 48 percent of Belarusians approved of the breakup of the Soviet Union in 1992. Three years later only 6 percent approved.[46] Thus, for most Belarusians neither independent statehood nor autonomy from Russia was a sufficient motivation for economic sacrifice, which they increasingly associated with the dissolution of the Soviet Union. In Belarusian popular parlance the trade-off between autonomy and higher living standards was summarized by the phrase "sausage psychology," which implied a society more concerned with relative prosperity and the days when sausage was plentiful and inexpensive. The Belarusian government chose a policy that was "sausage first."[47]

The Belarusian government interpreted economic dependence on Russia not as a security threat but as mutually beneficial exchange.[48] There were no nonmaterial goals that the government considered more important than its material goals. Whereas the Lithuanians claimed that history and destiny demanded their return to Europe, Belarus's President

[44] Author's interview no. 2, Belarusian Popular Front, Minsk, July 1998. See George Sanford, "Belarus on the Road to Nationhood," *Survival* 38, 1 (1996):131–53, at 137–38.

[45] See Ustina Markus, "Imperial Understretch: Belarus's Union with Russia," *Current History* 95, 603 (1996): 335–39.

[46] See *Nezavisimaia gazeta*, 10 February 1996.

[47] See the discussion in Jan Zaprudnik, "Development of Belarusian Identity and Its Influence on Belarus's Foreign Policy," in *National Identity and Ethnicity*, ed. Szporluk, 142–43. For a general assessment of the trade-off between autonomy and living standards, see Vladimir Novakov, "Obyknovennyi . . . natsionalizm?" (Ordinary . . . nationalism?), *Sovetskaia Belorussiia*, 27 March 1993.

[48] See, for example, the article by Belarus's then minister of foreign affairs, Vladimir Senko, "Foreign Policy of the Republic of Belarus: Directions and Prospects," *Belarus' v mire* 1, 1 (1996): 45–46; Viacheslau Pazniak, "Belarus: In Search of a Security Identity," in *Security Dilemmas in Russia and Eurasia*, ed. Roy Allison and Christopher Bluth (London: Royal Institute of International Affairs, 1998), 153–56; Anatoli Tozik, "V konseptsii natsional'noi bezopasnosti razrabotchiki postavili tochku" (National security concept is finalized), *Narodnaia gazeta*, 6 June 1995; and Aleksandr Sharapo, Aleksandr Cheliadinsky, and Anatoli Rozanov, "The Concept of the Foreign Policy of Belarus: What Kind Is It to be?" *Sovetskaia Belorussiia*, 11 February 1993, in FBIS-USR-93-031, 13 March 1993, 62–63.

Lukashenko argued that the goal of foreign economic policy was "the well-being of the man, the citizen of Belarus."[49] As Vladimir Senko, the former foreign minister of Belarus, has argued, the policy of Eurasian integration is pragmatic and rational: "It is a matter of fact that in the early 1990s we lost the market for Belarusian goods and failed to find new markets in the West. It was the logic of circumstances, plain common sense, and the need to keep our industry and agriculture operational that prompted further improvement in our relations with Russia."[50] What seemed pragmatic and rational in Belarus was anathema in the Baltics, however, where the rationality of their own European orientation seemed just as obvious. Interestingly, in Belarus, as throughout the former Soviet Union, "pragmatism" became code for regional reintegration policies, as opposed to the "idealism" of nationalist goals.

Belarus's Communists neither showed the political inclination to recast themselves as nationalist elites nor faced the electoral incentives to do so. As Kathleen Mihalisko observes, "Belarus's Party elite did not find it expedient or necessary to co-opt the national-democratic agenda of their opponents."[51] Moreover, there was no middle ground in Belarusian politics, only the unpopular nationalists and the popular former Communists. The Belarusian political elite produced no leaders like Kravchuk and Brazauskas, the Ukrainian and Lithuanian Communists-turned-nationalists who became their countries' first presidents and who adopted many of the nationalists' goals as their own, mediating the political division between the nationalists and the old nomenklatura.

Thus, the foreign policy of the nascent Belarusian state in 1992 immediately turned Eastward, though the first few years were a moment of choice. Prime Minister Kebich vied for control over the direction of the country's politics with Stanislav Shushkevich, the speaker of the parliament. Kebich was consistently pro-Eurasian whereas Shushkevich, a centrist who was neither pro-Western nor pro-Eurasian, was not committed to any foreign policy direction.[52] When Shushkevich demurred at Kebich's plans for

---

[49] Quoted in Pazniak, "Belarus: In Search of a Security Identity," 155.

[50] Senko, "Foreign Policy," 45.

[51] See Kathleen J. Mihalisko, "Belarus: Retreat to Authoritarianism," in *Democratic Changes and Authoritarian Reactions in Russia, Ukraine, Belarus, and Moldova*, ed. Karen Dawisha and Bruce Parrott (Cambridge: Cambridge University Press, 1997), 240. The stronger Ukrainian national movement could not have been pushed aside as easily, partly because of its electoral and popular support in several key regions of the country. Also see Jan Zaprudnik, *Belarus: At a Crossroads in History* (Boulder, Colo.: Westview, 1993), 133, and see 137 for the similarity of goals of Baltic Communists and nationalists in the late 1980s.

[52] See Igor Siniakevich, "Shushkevich, Kebich Differ on Confederation," *Nezavisimaia gazeta*, 19 September 1992, in *Russia and the Commonwealth of Independent States*, ed. Brzezinski and Sullivan, 297–98. Shushkevich outlined three possible options for Belarusian statehood: the

economic reintegration with Russia in 1993–94, Kebich and his political supporters orchestrated a parliamentary vote that ousted Shushkevich from his speaker's seat. Thus, the most influential voice for a neutral Belarusian foreign policy was removed, and Kebich continued to solidify the Eastern orientation for Belarusian policy.[53]

Even under Prime Minister Kebich, the Belarusian government's reaction to the post-Soviet economic crisis was economic integration with Russia. Economic union, according to Kebich, was Belarus's only possible "salvation" because of Belarusians' "deep-rooted blood relationship and age-old unity with the Russian people" and the fact that Belarusians and Russians were "united economically."[54] Improved living standards were, for Kebich, the central goal of foreign policy. "We will live even worse without the economic union," Kebich explained, because Russia "is the only source to satisfy our energy needs."[55] Thus, Kebich's administration pursued plans for trade cooperation and monetary integration during 1994 to prove that the government was doing something to respond to the crisis and safeguard the living standards of the citizenry. By February 1994 Kebich announced that his central political goal was to reunify Belarus's economy with Russia's.[56]

By the time of the 1994 presidential elections in Belarus, the first of the post-Soviet era, Kebich had already institutionalized the country's orientation toward reintegration with Russia. And though the 1994 election was an important turning point in the political system of the country, since the winner, Aleksandr Lukashenko, turned the government sharply authoritarian, the election itself was not a turning point economically.

---

creation of a "national state," the "Slavic option" of integrating with Russia, and neutrality. See "Shushkevich Addresses Supreme Soviet," Minsk radio, 9 April 1993, in *Russia and the Commonwealth of Independent States,* ed. Brzezinski and Sullivan, 245–46. As president of the Belorussian SSR, Shushkevich joined with his Ukrainian and Russian counterparts Kuchma and Yeltsin in December 1991 to dissolve the USSR by withdrawing their republics from the union and creating the CIS. Also see "Stanislav Shushkevich: 'Nuzhen krepkii ekonomicheskii soiuz'" (Stanislav Shushkevich: "A strong economic union is necessary"), *Sovetskaia Belorussiia,* 19 March 1993.

[53] See Oleg Stepanenko, "The First 'Belovezhskaia Wisent' Is Down," *Pravda,* 29 January 1994; Larisa Saienko, "Belarus: Does It Want to Be the Belorussian SSR?" *Moskovskie novosti,* no. 5, 30 January–6 February 1994, both in *Current Digest of the Post-Soviet Press* 46, 4 (1994): 11–13.

[54] Kebich quoted in Oleg Stepanenko, "Viacheslav Kebich: Vykhod iz krizisa—v soiuze s Rossiei" (Viacheslav Kebich: The way out of crisis—Union with Russia), *Pravda,* 29 April 1994.

[55] "Kebich Stresses Need for Economic Treaty with Russia," *ITAR-TASS,* 14 September 1993, in FBIS-SOV-93-178, 16 September 1993, 45. Also see "Kebich Promotes Economic Integration with Russia," *Respublika,* 1 February 1994, in FBIS-SOV-94-023, 3 February 1994, 52.

[56] Viacheslav Kebich, "Moia glavnaia politicheskaia tsel'—vosstanovlenie ekonomicheskogo soiuza s Rossiei" (My main political goal—Restoration of economic union with Russia), *Sel'skaia zhizn',* 5 February 1994.

In fact, it is a measure of how entrenched Belarus's foreign economic orientation had already become that presidential candidates competed to show how pro-Eurasian and pro-Russian they were. In the first round of voting there were six candidates, five of whom advocated economic integration with Russia. The nationalist candidate, BPF leader Pazniak, received only 13 percent of the vote and, along with four other candidates, was eliminated after the first round of the elections, on 23 June 1994. Prime Minister Kebich and Lukashenko were left to compete in the second round, on 10 July 1994. During the few weeks between the first and second rounds of voting Kebich and Lukashenko competed against each other, but their foreign economic plans were identical: reintegration with Russia.[57] Critical of Kebich's role in the creation of the CIS in the USSR's stead in 1991, Lukashenko demanded, "Why did you break up the country?" Kebich, explaining that he was doing his best to reunify the fractured economic area of the union, responded that he was "not to blame if nationalists in all these countries started pulling every which way."[58] "We ourselves don't know what we want when we talk about independence," Lukashenko announced during the 1994 presidential election campaign. "Independence has given nothing to Belarus."[59] It was with such rhetoric that Lukashenko defeated Kebich with over 80 percent of the popular vote on 10 July 1994.[60] Such an electoral competition, to decide the most pro-Eurasian president, would have been unimaginable in many other post-Soviet states, certainly including Ukraine and Lithuania.

Clearly, then, the administration of President Lukashenko (1994–) by itself is not sufficient explanation for Belarus's reintegrationist foreign economic orientation. Nor can it be argued that Lukashenko's authoritarianism pushed the country further Eastward than it otherwise would have gone; Lukashenko's foreign economic policies were a continuation of Kebich's.[61] Lukashenko himself was a product of the Belarusian political elite, and his pro-integration policies, if not his authoritarianism, enjoyed the wide support of the Belarusian population. Lukashenko was not

---

[57] Yaroslav Shimov, "Favorit belorusskikh izbiratelei ne imeet yasnoi ekonomicheskoi programmy" (The Belarusian voters' favorite has no clear economic program), *Izvestiia*, 7 July 1994.

[58] Quoted in "Belarus Contenders Vie to Show Pro-Russian Stand," *Reuters*, 8 July 1994. See also Vitaly Tsygankov, "Prime Minister Has Determined His Life's Goal—To Merge Minsk and Moscow Monetary Systems," *Nezavisimaia gazeta*, 25 March 1994, in *Current Digest of the Post-Soviet Press* 46, 12 (1994): 22.

[59] Quoted in Wendy Sloane, "Populist Wins Big in Belarus Poll, Vows to Restore USSR," *Christian Science Monitor*, 27 June 1994.

[60] Lee Hockstader, "Belarus Votes to Go Back to the Future; Winner Reflects Nostalgia for Good Old Soviet Days," *Washington Post*, 16 July 1994.

[61] See Ustina Markus, "Belarus: Missed Opportunities in Foreign Policy," *Transition* 1, 15 (1995): 62–66, especially 63; and Bugrova and Naumova, "Parliamentary Elections," 5.

an accident or an anachronism but "a symptom of Belarusian history," a product of Belarusians' ambiguous national identity.[62] Put differently, "it is the absence of nationalism," Mihalisko argues, "that makes Lukashenko possible."[63]

As discussed in chapter 3, Belarus and Russia, along with several other post-Soviet states, attempted to institutionalize the economic links among them during the 1990s. Remarkably, as the trade flows among post-Soviet states collapsed during the early and middle 1990s, Belarus managed to strengthen its economic relationship with Russia, becoming more dependent on it over time (Tables 6.3 and 6.4).

In addition, Belarusian-Russian "reintegration" was so popular among the mass publics of both Belarus and Russia that Belarusian president Lukashenko and Russian president Yeltsin reached almost yearly agreements to unify their states economically and politically. In April 1996 the two presidents signed a treaty on formation of the Russian-Belarusian Community. A year later, after some last-minute changes made by Russian negotiators to dilute many of the provisions of the new agreement, Lukashenko and Yeltsin agreed to a treaty of "Closer Union."[64] In December 1998 the two leaders announced their plans for a common policy on economic and military issues, a common currency, and a single budget.[65] Finally, in December 1999 Belarus and Russia completed their most ambitious, though still ambiguous, agreement to form a "confederation," still less than a state.[66]

---

[62] See David R. Marples, "Belarus: An Analysis of the Lukashenka Regime," *Harriman Review* 10, 1 (1997): 24–28, at 28. See also Dmitri Vodotynsky, "Analysis: Belarusian Residents' Attitudes towards Russia Are Quite Ambivalent—In Large Part, This Determined the Outcome of the Presidential Election," *Nezavisimaia gazeta*, 21 July 1994, in *Current Digest of the Post-Soviet Press* 46, 28 (1994): 16.

[63] Mihalisko, "Belarus," 224. On the continuing popularity of Lukashenko and his policies throughout the decade, see Larissa Titarenko, *Public Opinion in Belarus* (Washington, D.C.: International Foundation for Election Systems, 1999), especially 3, 36, and 61.

[64] See Vladimir Konobeyev, "The Union of Russia and Belarus: New Phase of Cooperation in Foreign Policy," *Belarus' v mire* 2, 2 (1997): 51–53; "Slavic Symbolism," *The Economist*, 5 April 1997; Alessandra Stanley, "Russia Dilutes a Treaty with Belarus, then Signs," *New York Times*, 3 April 1997; and Lee Hockstader, "Belarus, Russia Move toward a New Union," *Washington Post*, 3 April 1997.

[65] Michael Wines, "Russia and Belarus Move toward Economic Integration," *New York Times*, 26 December 1998; and Wines, "Belarus's Chief Pursues Dream to Revive the Soviet Union," *New York Times*, 27 December 1998.

[66] Michael Wines, "Russia and Belarus Agree to Join in a Confederation," *New York Times*, 9 December 1999; and Charles Clover, "Russia and Belarus in New Treaty on Reunification," *Financial Times*, 9 December 1999.

Table 6.3 Belarusian Exports to EU, CIS, and
Russia as Percentages of Total Exports, 1991–98

	EU	CIS	Russia
1991	—	—	—
1992	10	69	42
1993	13	72	47
1994	13	61	48
1995	13	62	44
1996	10	67	54
1997	7	73	65
1998	7	73	65

Source: Interstate Statistical Commission of the
Commonwealth of Independent States, *Official
Statistics of the Countries of the Commonwealth of
Independent States* (Moscow, various years).

Table 6.4 Belarusian Imports from EU, CIS, and
Russia as Percentages of Total Imports, 1991–98

	EU	CIS	Russia
1991	—	—	—
1992	8	78	54
1993	24	71	56
1994	17	71	64
1995	16	63	51
1996	18	66	51
1997	16	67	54
1998	17	65	55

Source: Interstate Statistical Commission of the
Commonwealth of Independent States, *Official
Statistics of the Countries of the Commonwealth of
Independent States* (Moscow, various years).

CONCLUSION

At the end of the 1990s the economic results of Belarus's reintegration with Russia were unclear. Because Belarus had chosen to reintegrate with Russia, it was hardest hit by Russia's disastrous financial and economic crisis, which erupted in August 1998 and continued through the end of the decade. The short-run strategy seemed to have failed the Belarusian economy. The government's commitment to the East, however, did not waver, even if more Belarusians began to question the desirability of seeking an economic bailout from their giant but poor neighbor.[67]

[67] See especially Roman Yakovlevskii, "Integratsionnyi realizm na novoi volne" (Integration realism on a new wave), *Belorusskaia gazeta*, 21 September 1998; and Mikhail Miasnikovich, "'Strategicheskikh partnerov ne vybiraiut na odin den'" ("Strategic partners are not chosen for one day"), *Narodnaia gazeta*, 17 September 1998.

Belarusian politics were also unstable. The BPF joined with other opposition groups that responded to President Lukashenko's increasing control over the apparatus of the state during the mid and late 1990s. And as the BPF grew more assertive during the 1990s, Lukashenko's administration cracked down on the organization's activities. But not all of Lukashenko's opposition was nationalist or shared the BPF's political goals. Gennady Karpenko, a former member of the Belarusian parliament and head of the National Executive Committee, an umbrella organization designed to coordinate the efforts of all forces opposing Lukashenko, explained that the opposition was not against close integration with Russia, as Lukashenko had argued. "There is not one sensible politician in our country," Karpenko explained, "who today would object to the tightest integration with Russia. In the first place because it is what the Belarusian people themselves want."[68] The democratic opposition to Lukashenko was not equivalent to the nationalist opposition.

Outside Belarus, Belarusian-Russian integration increasingly posed a difficult problem for the United States and the European Union, not least because for Lukashenko, allying with Russia also meant standing up to the West. Lukashenko opposed NATO expansion, called on rising powers to "balance" against the hegemonic United States, and according to the EU, flouted European norms of democracy and human rights. Of all the post-Soviet states, Belarus has the most strained relations with the United States and EU. Belarus's location made this disharmony even more significant. Poland will be a member of both the EU and NATO, but in 2000 Belarus's membership in either organization seemed quite unlikely. Unlike its neighbor to the north, Lithuania, and to the south, Ukraine, Belarus expressed antagonism toward both the EU and NATO. If the boundary of "Europe" and the "West" comes to be defined by the EU and NATO, it will be at the Polish-Belarusian border.

The final irony is that Belarus represents just what many U.S. policy makers had hoped for in the collapse of the Soviet Union: the weakness of nationalism, especially of the so-called suicidal variety. Belarus is the very model of ethnic harmony. The government championed a civic identity for the country, embraced bilingualism, and rejected the nationalists' proposals for "Belarusification" of state institutions. Indeed, most Belarusians considered the lack of ethnic content and external directionality in their national identity to be a sign of their modernity, of a rationality that stands

---

[68] Karpenko also argues that Lukashenko's promotion of Belarusian-Russian integration is cynical because Lukashenko covets the presidency of a unified Slavic republic. Karpenko is quoted in El'mar Guseinov, "Gennady Karpenko: Lukashenko pridet k vlasti v Rossii, esli ego ne ostanovit'" (Gennady Karpenko: Lukashenko will come to power in Russia if he is not stopped), *Izvestiia*, 22 October 1997.

above the emotional, ethnic contents of the national identities of their neighbors. From the perspective of the West, and in comparison with Lithuania, for example, it seems that Belarus's politics would have been better off with a little more nationalism—at least, more agreement about what the specifically national purposes of the state should be. A more coherent, collective *national* identity, along the lines proposed by the BPF, would have unified the electorate around a purpose and pushed the government to attempt to break out of the Russian orbit, to reform the economy, and to improve relations with Europe.

Instead, however, the contestedness and ambiguity of Belarusian national identity meant that Belarusians did not agree about the content of their identity or about the fundamental purposes of their national statehood. Without a shared sense of purpose, history, or destiny, Belarusians did not choose long-term goals for their state's economy. The government focused primarily on stability and growth, not reform or reorientation. The Belarusian government thus responded to the short-term material incentives to reintegrate with Russia.

CHAPTER SEVEN

Political Economy after Empire

Within post-Soviet states societal actors struggled over the meaning of their nations, a struggle that implicated the purposes of their economies and the necessity of change. Similar political struggles over change and continuity influenced the foreign economic policies of postimperial states throughout the twentieth century. In newly independent states there were always those who advocated the breaking of economic ties with the rest of the empire, and especially with the former metropole, for the sake of an economic autonomy complementary to their new political independence. And there were others who disagreed, demanding that the imperial economic ties be maintained so that the new state could avoid economic collapse. The issue of economic sacrifice made these political struggles compelling because it was difficult to reorient the production and commerce of a state without imposing costs on its society in the short run.

What motivates people to pay such a cost willingly? The people who demanded change and autonomy legitimated the economic distress with the symbol of the nation, linking it politically to the social purposes of statehood. These nationalists never thought that the costs of autonomy would be permanent. They argued that present sacrifice would produce future rewards, if only society would bear it. Rupert Emerson, a Harvard political scientist writing about imperial collapse after World War II, captured the essence of this economic choice for the societies of newly independent states:

The prime rival to nationalism as a driving force is presumed to be the desire for an improved standard of living. From time to time it is asserted that the ordinary poverty-stricken Asian and African is interested only in seeing an end put to his poverty. This is a highly dubious proposition. The evidence indicates that he regards at least temporary economic privation as an appropriate price to pay for national salvation. . . . Furthermore, the issue between nationalism and material advancement here posed is seen as a quite unreal one, since the nationalist creed normally embraces the belief that material improvement will surely follow in the wake of national self-realization.[1]

Here again is a central theme of this book: national identities influence how societies interpret the material facts of their foreign economic relations. Nationalism engenders sacrifice for a purpose, and it privileges the prospective over the present, lengthening the time horizons of a society and government. Thus, the nationalists of newly independent states almost invariably proposed the former metropole of the empire as the most threatening "other" against which identity was defined and the state from which economic autonomy must be pursued. Postimperial nationalists also argued that their economies must be made more "national," organized more for the benefit of the nation, whose membership they themselves defined.

Just as in the former Soviet states, however, the nationalists' arguments did not consistently convince everyone in society. The content of national identity was not simply what the nationalists said it was; it was always, to some extent and in some way, contested. Sometimes the nationalists disagreed among themselves. There were many other reasons that the national identities of these societies were contested. In particular, two kinds of arguments were made against the nationalists in newly independent states, and therefore two reasons why some societal groups were content with their economic dependence on the former metropole. Some people shared a larger, non-national, or supranational identity that included the metropolitan state and population; such people, like the pan-Slavs of Belarus and eastern Ukraine, derided their nationalist compatriots as parochial and irrational. This is the opposite of a national identity that engenders sacrifice; it is a shared identity that leads people to see their economic dependence as irrelevant to politics.

The second force in favor of continuity was commerce and industry, for there were powerful business interests that benefited from the profits of political acquiescence.[2] Commercial and industrial interests, on balance and in the short run, almost always urged the maintenance of previous economic ties, if not their cultivation and intensification. The benefits of

---

[1] Rupert Emerson, "Nationalism and Political Development," *Journal of Politics* 22, 1 (1960): 3–28, at 3, 4.

[2] As the post-Soviet cases indicated, these need not be capitalist profits. For a related assessment that explores cases not dealt with here, see Robert L. Tignor, *Capitalism and Nationalism at the End of Empire: State and Business in Decolonizing Egypt, Nigeria, and Kenya, 1945–1963* (Princeton: Princeton University Press, 1998).

radically reorienting the commerce of a state were distant and uncertain. So the commercial interests in newly independent states have not usually been very nationalist, even if they were sometimes narrowly protectionist of their own industries. This was especially true for *organized* commercial, industrial, and financial interests because those who lose by a policy of radical economic reorientation have been quite identifiable, by themselves most of all. The most organized economic actors consistently lobbied for economic continuity. The preferences of these organized economic lobbies did not vary a great deal from state to state, nor did the intensity of their preferences. But the influence of those lobbies varied, and it depended on other kinds of politics.

The nationalists sometimes simply won the political struggle outright and chose to reorient the economy and redistribute its wealth to those whom they recognized as members of the nation. At other times the nationalists were able to influence policy choice but were not powerful or influential enough to sustain it. Infrequently, the nationalists were marginalized and could not influence policy at all. Finally, in some cases it was not the nationalists' power that won the day but their argument itself—when the consensus of elites and society on the fundamental content of their national identity defined and framed postimperial politics. It is clear that the immediate, short-term costs and benefits of possible economic strategies were never decisive because societies' national identities led them to different interpretations of the trade-offs. National identity—its content and contestation—was the most important explanatory variable for understanding the outcomes of these political struggles. Thus, the Nationalist perspective provides the best theoretical interpretation of the political economy of postimperial international relations in the twentieth century.

NATIONS, STATES, AND EMPIRES

"Empires," according to Michael Doyle, "are relationships of political control imposed by some political societies over the effective sovereignty of other political societies."[3] This definition raises a crucial question: How can we tell one political society from another? States often have identity projects—they seek to give their populations an identity that will produce both consent and legitimacy.[4] Since the late eighteenth century, nation

---

[3] Michael W. Doyle, *Empires* (Ithaca: Cornell University Press, 1986), 19.
[4] Here I use the standard Weberian definition of state: a political form with a relatively fixed territory, a claim to a single sovereignty and monopoly over the use of legitimate violence, and a set of authority relationships between rulers and ruled.

making has been the central and most common identity project of states. But nations do not exist before they are constructed by cultural elites and by states. Therefore, the process of nation making necessarily involves the transformation of the identities of several distinct societies into a single cultural and national identity. Successful nation making can turn what was an empire, by Doyle's definition, into a nation-state. The distinction between an empire and other political forms depends on the identity of its subjects. Thus, as Beissinger shows, empires are intersubjective constructs, not objectively defined political units.[5]

The distinction between an empire and a nation-state depends in part, therefore, on the goals of political authorities. In a nation-state the government claims to govern on behalf of the nation. An empire is a state in which the government does not claim to govern for a nation. Instead, empires claim their ideological legitimacy from a source other than national identity, and they tend not to seek to mold a single nation within their boundaries. So empires are states, but they are not nation-states, or states that legitimate their authority on the basis of the nationhood of their societies.[6] Empires may be states that failed in their nation-making projects, or much more commonly, empires are states that did not even try to construct a nation within their boundaries. Empires therefore do not seek to homogenize their populations; they seek to manage heterogeneity.[7]

The Soviet Union was an empire in that sense: it did not seek to make a Soviet nation. Soviet authorities instead sought to manage the state's heterogeneous population. This is not to say that the Soviet Union lacked an identity project or that it was not a single ideological space. Rather, it attempted to create a supranational Soviet identity that would transcend the merely national identities of its citizens. These citizens were to become a Soviet people made up of its constituent nations.

The Soviet Union's collapse, like that of other empires, was coincident with the rise of nationalism in peripheral areas.[8] The most important

[5] Mark Beissinger, "The Persisting Ambiguity of Empire," *Post-Soviet Affairs* 11, 2 (1995): 149–84.

[6] See the excellent discussion in Ronald Grigor Suny, "Ambiguous Categories: States, Empires, and Nations," *Post-Soviet Affairs* 11, 2 (1995): 185–96.

[7] See Alain de Benoist, "The Idea of Empire," *Telos* 98–99 (1993–94): 81–98.

[8] See especially Rogers Brubaker, "Nationalizing States in the Old 'New Europe'—and the New," *Ethnic and Racial Studies* 19, 2 (1996): 411–37; Karen Barkey, "Thinking about Consequences of Empire," in *After Empire: Multiethnic Societies and Nation-Building*, ed. Karen Barkey and Mark von Hagen (Boulder, Colo.: Westview, 1997); and Bruce Parrott, "Analyzing the Transformation of the Soviet Union in Comparative Perspective," in *The End of Empire? The Transformation of the USSR in Comparative Perspective*, ed. Karen Dawisha and Bruce Parrott (Armonk, N.Y.: M. E. Sharpe, 1997). See also Alexander Motyl, "From Imperial Decay to Imperial Collapse: The Fall of the Soviet Empire in Comparative Perspective," in *Nationalism and Empire: The*

reason that nationalisms rise as empires fall is quite straightforward: if empires claim a non-national legitimacy that fails to unite a society, those who seek independence will claim a national legitimacy for the new states they hope to acquire or govern. As John Hall suggests, "Nationalism flourishes as the result of the collapse of empires." And the collapse of the Soviet Union has brought us the "fourth great moment in the history of nationalism."[9] The first three great ages of nationalism were the foundation of new states in Latin America early in the nineteenth century, interwar Europe, and postwar decolonization.

Soviet authorities themselves were responsible for some of the patterns of the union's disintegration. The Soviet Union institutionalized the national identities of its constituent societies in the form of national-federalism, whereby the union consisted of fifteen republics given administrative functions, demarcated territory, and a titular nationality. This institutionalization of national identities, at the same time that the Soviet regime repressed alternate organizational possibilities, ensured that the end of Soviet rule would create disintegrative pressures organized at the republic level.[10] Thus, in addition to the fact that empires tend to fall apart amid nationalist demands for sovereignty, the Soviet Union's demise was even more likely than that of other empires to be patterned along ostensibly national lines. The way Soviet authorities organized the union contributed to the importance of post-Soviet nationalisms as an alternate source of legitimacy for post-Soviet states.

In sum, post-Soviet politics during the 1990s were postimperial in the following sense: many of the governments in the region considered the Union to have been an empire, and so, therefore, it was—at least for them. In fact, nationalists in every Soviet republic tried to rally their societies around the

Habsburg Empire and the Soviet Union, ed. Richard L. Rudolph and David F. Good (New York: St. Martin's, 1992); Motyl, "Imperial Collapse and Revolutionary Change: Austria-Hungary, Tsarist Russia, and the Soviet Empire in Theoretical Perspective," in *Die Wiener Jahrhundertwende*, ed. Jürgen Nautz and Richard Vahrenkamp (Vienna: Böhlau Verlag, 1993); and Motyl, *Revolutions, Nations, and Empires* (New York: Columbia University Press, 1999). In addition to the volumes edited by Barkey and von Hagen and Dawisha and Parrott, an overview that puts the fall of the Soviet Union in comparative historical perspective is Geir Lundestad, ed., *The Fall of Great Powers: Peace, Stability, and Legitimacy* (Oslo: Scandinavian University Press; Oxford: Oxford University Press, 1994).

[9] John A. Hall, "Nationalisms: Classified and Explained," *Daedalus* 122, 3 (1993): 1–28, at 2–3.

[10] See especially Valerie Bunce, *Subversive Institutions: The Design and Destruction of Socialism and the State* (Cambridge: Cambridge University Press, 1999). Also see Rogers Brubaker, "Nationhood and the National Question in the Soviet Union and Post-Soviet Eurasia: An Institutionalist Account," *Theory and Society* 23, 1 (1994): 47–78; Yuri Slezkine, "The USSR as a Communal Apartment, or How a Socialist State Promoted Ethnic Particularism," *Slavic Review* 53, 2 (1994): 414–52; and Philip G. Roeder, *Red Sunset: The Failure of Soviet Politics* (Princeton: Princeton University Press, 1993).

idea that they had just been liberated from Moscow's imperial grasp. The nationalists' assessment of the past as empire and the future as national liberation was very popular in some republics, less popular in others, but was in every republic the dividing line between those who did and those who did not want radical change in the foreign economic relations of the new state. This same dividing line, this national axis of debate, has characterized nearly all newly independent states throughout the twentieth century.

Among the fallen empires of the twentieth century, one might choose a number of possible cases for comparison, including those that fell at the end of World War I, at the end of World War II, and during the 1960s decolonizations. In the interests of thoroughness, I have chosen one case from each period: 1920s central and eastern Europe, 1950s Indonesia, and 1960s French West Africa. With these comparisons, I hope to demonstrate the usefulness of this book's Nationalist analytical framework for post-imperial politics throughout the century and across several regions.

Post-Habsburg Eastern Europe, 1919–1939

Post-Habsburg eastern Europe is the most similar historical comparison for understanding the dynamics of nationalism and regional economic disintegration in the former Soviet Union. This is not because the Habsburg case is necessarily a close analogy or because what ultimately happened in interwar central Europe will happen in post–cold war eastern Europe, Caucasus, and Central Asia.[11] But both were continuous, overland empires, and both went through similar phases of collapse, nationalism, and proposals

[11] Economists have frequently offered a Habsburg analogy for what has happened in the post-Soviet economy, emphasizing how nationalism leads to monetary separation and trade conflict. For elaborations of the Habsburg analogy, see Oleh Havrylyshyn and John Williamson, *From Soviet disUnion to Eastern Economic Community?* (Washington, D.C.: Institute for International Economics, 1991), 11–12, also 2 and 5–7; Peter M. Garber and Michael G. Spencer, *The Dissolution of the Austro-Hungarian Empire: Lessons for Currency Reform*, Princeton Essays in International Finance, no. 191 (Princeton, 1994); and Rudiger Dornbusch, "Monetary Problems of Post-Communism: Lessons from the End of the Austro-Hungarian Empire," *Weltwirtschaftliches Archiv* 128, 3 (1992): 391–424. Sociologists and political scientists have offered other analogies, depending on their substantive interests. For example, the weakness of post-Soviet state institutions is most frequently compared with the case of postcolonial Africa. The dynamics of imperial collapse are compared, again, with the Habsburgs but also with tsarist Russia. See, for example, Motyl, *Revolutions.* Comparison with the Ottoman empire is less frequent, perhaps because its decline was so protracted. See, however, Dankwart A. Rustow, "The Habsburg and Ottoman Empires and Their Aftermaths," in *End of Empire?* ed. Dawisha and Parrott; Serif Mardin, "The Ottoman Empire," in *After Empire*, ed. Barkey and von Hagen; C. Ernest Dawn, *From Ottomanism to Arabism: Essays on the Origin of Arab Nationalism* (Urbana: University of Illinois Press, 1973); and L. Carl Brown, ed., *Imperial Legacy: The Ottoman Imprint on the Balkans and the Middle East* (New York: Columbia University Press, 1996).

for reassembly. As a result, both sets of postimperial politics presented issues of *regional* cooperation and discord, reintegration and disintegration—issues that the postimperial politics of the overseas colonial empires did not face in quite the same way.

The Habsburg economy, like the Soviet, had been autarkic and self-sufficient; both were organized to take advantage of regional divisions of labor. Therefore, because they had been constituent parts of a single economy, the Habsburg and Soviet successor states faced levels of economic interdependence much higher than commonly occur in international relations. But the very collapse of political authority politicized societal identities in the successor states. Nationalist mobilizations preceded both moments of imperial dissolution, and the governments of the successor states legitimated their statehood with concomitant claims to specific interpretations of their nationhood. This historical comparison offers insight into economic nationalism by presenting broader and more historically informed generalizations about the relationships among nationalism, national identities, and international political economy.

Cooperation and Discord in the Post-Habsburg Regional Economy

The collapse of the Habsburg empire also caused the dissolution of its economic union, which caused in turn the decline of intraregional trade, the central economic problem of interwar eastern Europe.[12] What resulted, according to Carr, was a "dislocation of economic life from which the Danubian countries never fully recovered."[13]

Liberal economists in interwar Europe urged the Danubian states to cooperate. John Maynard Keynes, for example, argued that the successor states "should be compelled to adhere" to a free trade union for at least ten years.[14] As noted in chapter 3, many economists during the early 1990s made similar recommendations of free trade, or at least a preferential trade agreement, for post-Soviet states. To many economists, in both contexts, cooperation among such interdependent states seemed an obvious necessity, and the disintegrative economic policies that followed irrational.

Those with an economistic perspective on the dissolution thus were surprised by the collapse of economic cooperation. Joseph Schumpeter, who

[12] See E. A. Radice, "General Characteristics of the Region between the Wars," in *Economic Structure and Performance between the Two Wars*, ed. M. C. Kaser and E. A. Radice, vol. 1 of *The Economic History of Eastern Europe*, ed. Kaser (Oxford: Clarendon, 1985), 35.

[13] E. H. Carr, *International Relations between the Two World Wars, 1919–1939* (London: Macmillan, 1947), 61.

[14] John Maynard Keynes, *The Economic Consequences of the Peace* (London: Macmillan, 1920), 265.

was then Austria's finance minister, analyzed the post-Habsburg economic situation at a press conference in 1919 with optimism:

> Nationalizing an economy may be a very fine thing. The Czechs worked at it for years, but often enough to their own detriment and only for the sake of a national ideal. . . . Becoming independent is far easier politically than economically. In the end we shall have to find a modus vivendi. The frontiers of future development can be recognized even today with great clarity. In this new organism Vienna will have to continue as the financial center, and the political separation will affect only marginally the purely economic relations.[15]

What became clear during the 1920s, however, was that there were no "purely economic" relations in interwar eastern Europe. The societies and governments of the successor states interpreted their foreign economic relations as inescapably political.

The peace treaties of Versailles (1919), St. Germain (1919), and Trianon (1920) divided the autarkic imperial economy into five new economies demarcated by the state boundaries of Austria, Hungary, Czechoslovakia, Yugoslavia, and Romania. Austria and Hungary, which had been the two institutional halves of the dual monarchy, were drastically reduced, and their territories and populations were divided among the other three states.[16] The empire's customs and currency union of sixty-eight years was dissolved.[17] The Habsburg economy had been geographically specialized; production processes were dependent on raw

---

[15] Schumpeter is quoted in Eduard März, *Austrian Banking and Financial Policy: Creditanstalt at a Turning Point, 1913–1923*, trans. Charles Kessler (New York: St. Martin's, 1984), 330. Shortly thereafter Schumpeter addressed the Vienna Industrial and Trade Association, to which he explained that the "states of the Danube basin are undoubtedly dependent on close economic cooperation, whether they like it or not. . . . We must undoubtedly arrive, if not at free trade, at least at a customs agreement with the successor states and, if not at a monetary union, at least at a monetary convention." See 331–32.

[16] Only Austria, Hungary, and Czechoslovakia, having been carved solely out of the empire's territories, were truly post-Habsburg. Interwar Yugoslavia and Romania were dramatic expansions of the small prewar kingdoms of Serbia and Romania, primarily with former Habsburg territories. Serbia and Romania had been part of the Ottoman empire until the Congress of Berlin in 1879. Nevertheless, their incorporation of large parts of the empire's territory and economy made Yugoslavia's and Romania's foreign economic policies crucial to the reorganization of the post-Habsburg economic area. For convenience, in this chapter I call all five states post-Habsburg. On the empire's collapse and the region's international relations afterward, see István Deák, "The Habsburg Empire," in *After Empire*, ed. Barkey and von Hagen; Leo Valiani, *The End of Austria-Hungary* (New York: Knopf, 1973); Oscar Jaszi, *The Dissolution of the Habsburg Monarchy* (Chicago: University of Chicago Press, 1961); and Alan Sked, *The Decline and Fall of the Habsburg Empire* (New York: Longman, 1989).

[17] The currency and customs union dated to 1850–51, and the political union of the Austrian Habsburg empire with the Hungarian monarchy to the Compromise of 1867. The Austro-Hungarian Bank, under a charter from the governments of Austria and Hungary, was the central bank for the Dual Monarchy. See John Komlos, *The Habsburg Monarchy as a Customs*

materials from other regions of the empire. Textile weaving in Czech lands, for example, depended on spinning mills located in Austria. Almost all industrial and agricultural production had been for the home market. Despite the collapse of the empire, the post-Habsburg economies remained tightly linked throughout the interwar years.[18] They traded more with one another than with other states for some time after the fall of the Habsburgs.

As a result of this interdependence, proposals for Danubian economic and political unity were abundant during the 1920s. Representatives of the states met in Portorose, Italy, to reorganize political-economic relations among themselves and agreed in November 1921 to free trade.[19] Regional cooperation promised economic renewal after the long war. The Portorose conference was the promise of liberal multilateralism.

But the post-Habsburg governments refused to ratify the Portorose protocols.[20] The problem, according to Frederick Hertz, was that the Danubian governments "regarded the formation of an economic union, or any other cooperation, far too much from the point of view of power politics and not from that of economic interests."[21] Instead of implementing the free trade promised at Portorose, they protected their agriculture and industry, primarily from one another. Monetary cooperation had already collapsed, and all the states introduced their own national currencies, most of which suffered from hyperinflation during the first few years of independent statehood. The new governments rejected multilateral economic cooperation and the reintegration of the Habsburg economic area. Trade among them fell by 1924 to less than half their prewar levels.[22] The failure

---

Union (Princeton: Princeton University Press, 1983); and David F. Good, *Economic Rise of the Habsburg Empire, 1750–1914* (Berkeley: University of California Press, 1984).

[18] See Jürgen Nautz, "Between Political Disintegration and Economic Reintegration: Austrian Trade Relations with the Successor States after World War I," in *Economic Transformations in East Central Europe: Legacies from the Past and Policies for the Future,* ed. David F. Good (London: Routledge, 1994); and Georges de Menil and Mathilde Maurel, "Breaking Up a Customs Union: The Case of the Austro-Hungarian Empire in 1919," *Weltwirtschaftliches Archiv* 130, 3 (1994): 553–75.

[19] "Protocols and Agreements Concluded at the Portorose Conference, November, 1921," *International Conciliation* 176 (1922): 252–312. The agenda of the Portorose conference is discussed on 252–53, the trade accords on 256–61. At the time, the city was Portorosa, in Italy; after 1945 it was Portoroz in Yugoslavia.

[20] See Radice's argument in "General Characteristics," 35, that the "fear of economic and financial domination by Vienna and Budapest" led post-Habsburg governments not to ratify the Portorose protocols.

[21] Frederick Hertz, *The Economic Problem of the Danubian States: A Study in Economic Nationalism* (London: Victor Gollancz, 1947), 68.

[22] W. T. Layton and Charles Rist, *The Economic Situation of Austria: A Report Presented to the Council of the League of Nations* (Geneva: League of Nations, 1925), 23–29.

of the Portorose conference was, according to Z. Drabek, the most costly failure of trade cooperation in interwar eastern Europe.[23]

Monetary Dissolution. Even after the dismemberment of the empire, the Austrian crown was the primary currency in use in the five states. The central bank was located in Vienna, where monetary decisions for the region therefore were still being made. The monetary union did not last long, however. Despite the efforts of Austria to include Czechoslovak members on the board of the Austro-Hungarian bank, as a compromise to maintain a common currency, Czechoslovakia effected its currency separation by calling in all Austrian crowns and stamping them with the new national emblem, something that Yugoslavia had done in January. Hungary was the last to withdraw from the Austrian monetary union, in March 1920.[24] Monetary separation in each case was an assertion of sovereignty and state building, and the five governments made no further attempts to organize their new currencies with regional cooperation, though Austria certainly would have been interested. In sum, currencies in post-Habsburg eastern Europe were wholly disorganized, even chaotic.[25]

Trade Discord. The same conflictual story can be told for trade, at least for the first several years after the dissolution. The average tariff levels of the Danubian states in 1927 reflected their varying levels of commitment to regional cooperation. Although Austria's average tariff was, at 17.5 percent, by far the lowest in central and eastern Europe, Hungary's (30 percent), Czechoslovakia's (31 percent), Romania's (42 percent), and Yugoslavia's (32 percent) were all among the most protectionist.[26]

Even these average levels do not reveal how protectionist these states were specifically toward one another. Each of the states had complex tariff schedules that were designed expressly to exclude products from the states they perceived to be their industrial competitors. Also, because

---

[23] Z. Drabek, "Foreign Trade Performance and Policy," in *Economic Structure and Performance*, ed. Kaser and Radice, 408–9.

[24] See Garber and Spencer, *Dissolution of the Austro-Hungarian Empire;* Dornbusch, "Monetary Problems," 396–400; and Brendan Brown, *Monetary Chaos in Europe* (London: Croom Helm, 1988), chap. 3.

[25] Czechoslovakia managed to stabilize its new currency. See Alice Teichova, "A Comparative View of the Inflation of the 1920s in Austria and Czechoslovakia," in *Inflation through the Ages*, ed. Nathan Schmukler and Edward Marcus (New York: Columbia University Press, 1983); and Alois Rasin, *Financial Policy of Czechoslovakia during the First Year of Its History* (Oxford: Clarendon, 1923).

[26] Heinrich Liepmann, *Tariff Levels and the Unity of Europe* (London: Allen and Unwin, 1938), 382–400.

industry and agriculture in the successor states in eastern Europe were not as competitive as in western Europe, the tariffs were an even larger barrier for neighbors' products.[27]

Ultimately, the failure of post-Habsburg economic cooperation severely limited the export markets of the states of the region. They were thus particularly vulnerable to the German trade drive of the 1930s. German trade policies focused specifically on these states, which were by then desperate for markets for their agricultural surpluses.[28]

Economic Nationalism as an Explanation

The disaster of international political economy in interwar eastern Europe was caused by nationalism.[29] That is, nationalism in Czechoslovakia, Romania, and Yugoslavia caused their governments to interpret economic dependence on Austria and Hungary as a security threat. Czechoslovakia, Romania, and Yugoslavia considered Hungarian irredentism a serious threat to the postwar settlement. And the still considerable financial power of Vienna was viewed as equally pernicious, even by the Hungarian government.[30] Economic relations were politicized by concerns for power, security, and autonomy. It was the nationalists in each state who articulated those concerns.

This is the conventional explanation for the failure of post-Habsburg economic cooperation, but perhaps it should be revised somewhat.[31] Most

[27] Ivan Berend and György Ránki, "Economic Problems of the Danube Region after the Breakup of the Austro-Hungarian Monarchy," *Journal of Contemporary History* 4, 3 (1969): 169–85, at 177.

[28] See Albert O. Hirschman, *National Power and the Structure of Foreign Trade* (Berkeley: University of California Press, [1945] 1980), 34–40 and chaps. 5–7. On Germany's cultivation of monetary dependence in the region, see Jonathan Kirshner, *Currency and Coercion: The Political Economy of International Monetary Power* (Princeton: Princeton University Press, 1995), 121–40.

[29] This is the scholarly consensus on the interwar political economy of the region. See, for example, Leo Pasvolsky, *Economic Nationalism of the Danubian States* (New York: Macmillan, 1928); Hertz, *Economic Problem*; Berend and Ránki, "Economic Problems"; Jan Kofman, "Economic Nationalism in East-Central Europe in the Interwar Period," in *Economic Nationalism in East-Central Europe and South America, 1918–1939*, ed. Henryk Szlajfer, trans. Maria Chmielewska-Szlajfer and Piotr Goc (Geneva: Librairie Droz, 1990); Kofman, *Economic Nationalism and Development: Central and Eastern Europe between the Two World Wars* (Boulder, Colo.: Westview, 1997); Ivan Berend, *Decades of Crisis: Central and Eastern Europe before World War II* (Berkeley: University of California Press, 1998), chap. 9; and Dornbusch, "Monetary Problems." Because east European international relations were so politicized by nationalism after the Habsburg empire collapsed, the expression *economic nationalism* was in fact closely tied to nationalism rather than to mercantilism. On this issue, see chapter 2 of this book. The tradition of thought that identifies economic nationalism with the economic policies that result from nationalism dates to this interwar period.

[30] Pasvolsky, *Economic Nationalism*, 562–64.

[31] These revisions are partly terminological and partly analytical. In the discussion that follows I reinterpret accounts of economic nationalism in 1920s eastern Europe in light of the

important is the fact that the nationalisms of several of the successor states were related to their statehood in complex ways. Yugoslavia and Czechoslovakia were not conceived, even by their governments and despite their official ideologies, purely as national states; they were, respectively, multinational and binational. Although Czechoslovak and Yugoslav governments attempted to create Czechoslovak and Yugoslav national identities, in practice everyone acknowledged that Czechs dominated a state composed also of Slovaks, and that Serbs dominated a state composed also of Croats and Slovenes.[32] Czechs and Serbs consistently rejected the demands of Slovaks and Croats for a federal system.[33] The Slovaks, Croats, and Slovenes resented their governments' equation of Czechoslovakism with Czech nationalism and Yugoslavism with Serbian nationalism.

Therefore, the economic policies that tore apart the Habsburg economic space did not result from Czechoslovak or Yugoslav nationalisms. Rather, Czech and Serbian nationalists were making foreign policy for the Czechoslovak and Yugoslav states. Slovak, Croatian, and Slovenian nationalists contested the internal goals of Czech and Serbian nationalists, but they all agreed about the necessity of autonomy from Austria and Hungary. Czechs and Slovaks did not agree that they constituted a single nation, but they insisted that together they belonged in a state autonomous from Germans and Magyars. In other words, Czechoslovaks and Yugoslavs were not sure who they were, but they were very sure who they were not.

Because Czech and Slovak nationalists agreed on the external purpose of the Czechoslovak state, and Serbian and Croatian nationalists shared the same ideas about the external purpose of the Yugoslav state, the leaders of those countries made foreign economic policies that were coherent, purposeful, and directional. Nationalists within Czechoslovakia and Yugoslavia articulated the reasons for their economic nationalisms. In contrast, the societies of Romania and Hungary, both conceived as national states, produced their own coherent national identities and nationalisms, from which their own largely uncooperative economic policies followed.

---

theoretical arguments about nationalism and international political economy in chapters 1 and 2 of this book. In most respects, however, existing accounts of nationalism's influence on the regional economy are excellent.

[32] It is common practice to call the interwar South Slav state Yugoslavia, but in fact the name of the state itself reflected its multinational character. Until 1929, when King Aleksandar renamed the state Yugoslavia, it was the Kingdom of Serbs, Croats, and Slovenes. The 1918 name reflected the contestation of a single Yugoslav national identity, and the 1929 change was indicative of the effort to create such an identity.

[33] The reasons for this rejection of federalism were, in both cases, complex. In the Czechoslovak case one crucial issue was the very large German minority, which actually outnumbered Slovaks. Federal autonomy for Slovaks obviously would have complicated the internal German problem substantially.

And in the case of Hungary, the dramatic contraction of its territory, leaving millions of ethnic Magyars abroad (of which more later), caused the national question to be its most important in the reconstruction of political and economic relations with neighboring states. Thus, it was Romanian, Hungarian, Czech, and Serbian nationalists who were primarily responsible for framing the economic policy debates of the interwar period.

The second and even more interesting reason that the standard story about interwar economic nationalism needs to be qualified is the Austrian case. Austrians sought neither to dissolve the common economic space nor to reconstruct it aggressively, as Hungarians did and as one might expect from its previously hegemonic role in the empire. Properly speaking, there was little specifically Austrian nationalism at all; much more powerful were pan-Germanists in interwar Austria. So although Austrian identity also was politicized by the collapse of the empire, it was politicized in a way drastically different from elsewhere in the region. Austrian national identity was seriously contested and ambiguous throughout the 1920s, as Austrian society could not agree on the proper role of the state in the region or even whether Austria should exist as an independent state.

Nationalism and the Foreign Economic
Policies of the Habsburg Successor States in Comparison

Three types of foreign economic policies existed in the former Soviet Union. First were those states, such as Lithuania, that sought autonomy from Russia. Second were those, such as Ukraine, that were ambivalent. And third were those, such as Belarus, that were acquiescent and sought regional reintegration. These patterns reflected the success of nationalists in getting their preferred economic policies—in Lithuania the nationalists got what they wanted, in Ukraine less so, and in Belarus not at all.

In post-Habsburg eastern Europe only two of these patterns existed. Significantly, there was no ambivalence and therefore no middle pattern similar to Ukraine's. Four post-Habsburg states—Czechoslovakia, Romania, Yugoslavia, and Hungary—sought autonomy and rejected regional economic reintegration. In all four the nationalists dominated policy making and achieved their economic goals.

In only one state, Austria, did the government prefer economic reintegration with the rest of the post-Habsburg economy. Many Austrians also sought political-economic integration with Germany, particularly when the other successor states rejected Austria's preferred Danubian option of reintegration among the successor states. As was the case in Belarus, Austria's acquiescence and interest in economic integration into some larger political-economic area resulted directly from the incoherence and ambiguity of its national identity.

Austria: Preference for Reintegration. Austria did not reassert its hegemony, financial or otherwise, in the region. Leaders of the new Austrian state were obsessed with the idea that it was too small to survive, and their most pressing concern was that Austria's economy was not viable.[34] Austria's government therefore sought to integrate its economy into a larger one, either the German or the Danubian. As the Austrian Chamber for Workers and Employees explained, "Reconstruction of the economic life of Austria can only be *effected in conjunction with some larger economic unit.*" Although economic unification with the Danubian states made more sense economically, the poor condition of the region's politics, the chamber argued, led directly to "the necessity of union with the German economic system."[35] As the 1920s progressed, Austria's supplication led the governments of Czechoslovakia, Romania, and Yugoslavia to moderate their noncooperative economic policy stance somewhat.[36]

Austrian politics of the 1920s were an experiment in both state building and nation making. But it was clear that most Austrians did not want statehood in the form set out by the peace treaties. Karl Renner, a founding father of the Republic of Austria, complained in 1919 that Austria's intention to join some larger economic unit, particularly Germany, resulted from its economic unviability. "We shall become dependent on all our neighbors," Renner explained; "on the Poles and Czechoslovakians for coal, on the Poles and Romanians for petroleum, on the Hungarians for grain, on the Southern Slavs for cattle, and on the Italians for access to the sea."[37]

Austrian national identity was highly contested during the interwar years. Many Austrians insisted on the primacy of their pan-German identity,

[34] See Stefan Karner, "From Empire to Republic: Economic Problems in a Period of Collapse, Reorientation, and Reconstruction," in *Economic Development in the Habsburg Monarchy and the Successor States,* ed. John Komlos (New York: Columbia University Press, 1990); and Edward P. Keleher, "Austria's Lebensfähigkeit and the Anschluss Question, 1918–1922," *East European Quarterly* 23, 1 (1989): 71–83. For an economic assessment of the issue, see Kurt W. Rothschild, "Size and Viability: The Lesson of Austria," in *Economic Consequences of the Size of Nations,* ed. E. A. G. Robinson (London: Macmillan, 1963).

[35] Memorandum included in the report of Layton and Rist, *Economic Situation of Austria,* 201–13, at 213, emphasis in original.

[36] See, for example, Peter Burian, "Politische Probleme zwischen Österreich und den Nachfolgestaaten," in *Die Auflösung des Habsburgerreiches: Zusammenbruch und Neuorientierung im Donauraum,* ed. Richard Georg Plaschka and Karlheinz Mack (Vienna: Verlag für Geschichte und Politik, 1970).

[37] Quoted in Gottfried-Karl Kinderman, *Hitler's Defeat in Austria, 1933–1934,* trans. Sonia Brough and David Taylor (Boulder, Colo.: Westview, 1988), 7.

which caused them to prefer economic integration with Germany rather than with the Danubian states with which the Austrian economy was still much more tightly linked.[38] At the same time, because of those tight links, organized economic interests in Austria preferred the Danubian option.[39] The political contest in 1920s Austria between those who wanted *Anschluss* and those who did not was intense, and as discussed later, other states decisively influenced the outcome.

Briefly, Austria's politics reflected the society's ambivalence about its identity. Three political and ideological groups dominated 1920s Austria: the socialists (represented by the Social Democratic Party), the conservative Christian Social Party, and the pan-Germanists (represented by several parties, including the Great-German Party). The socialists, Christian Socials, and pan-Germanists competed to define the external economic and political orientation of the state, but none of them ever won a parliamentary majority during the decade and therefore could not choose alone. The socialists and pan-Germanists, political enemies in almost every respect, both sought *Anschluss*, though for very different reasons—the socialists believed unification with Germany would bring them to power whereas the pan-Germanists obviously identified with a German nationality that spanned the Austrian-German border. Thus, essentially two-thirds of Austria's political power was geared toward unification with Germany.

The Christian Socials, however, the only political party in interwar Austria to oppose *Anschluss*, maintained control over the Austrian government and foreign policy making during the 1920s. This control was possible because of the financial diplomacy of Czechoslovakia and France in the early 1920s.[40] The central point here is the enormous range of political-economic debate.

[38] The Austrian government in 1918–19 had actually proclaimed its state to be a constituent part of Germany. France prevented the union of Austria and Germany from taking place, and Austria's commitment not to give up its own sovereignty was codified in the peace treaties.

[39] Thus, the impetus toward Berlin was not primarily material; it was cultural and political. See especially Peter J. Katzenstein, *Disjoined Partners: Austria and Germany since 1815* (Berkeley: University of California Press, 1976), chap. 6. Also see Stanley Suval, *The Anschluss Question in the Weimar Era: A Study of Nationalism in Germany and Austria, 1918–1932* (Baltimore: Johns Hopkins University Press, 1974), 190–200. On the orientation of Austrian industry toward the Danube basin, see Jürgen Nautz, "Die österreichische Wirtschaft und der Anschluss," in *Tirol und der Anschluss*, ed. Thomas Albrich, Klaus Eisterer, and Rolf Steninger (Innsbruck: Haymon, 1988); and Karl H. Werner, "Österreichs Industrie- und Aussenhandelspolitik, 1848 bis 1948," in *Hundert Jahre Österreichischer Wirtschaftswicklung, 1848–1948*, ed. Hans Meyer (Vienna: Springer, 1949). And on Austrian finance's Danubian orientation, see F. L. Carsten, *The First Austrian Republic, 1918–1938* (Aldershot and Brookfield, Vt.: Gower, 1986), 160; and Hans Kernbauer and Fritz Weber, "Multinational Banking in the Danube Basin: The Business Strategy of Viennese Banks after the Collapse of the Habsburg Monarchy," in *Multinational Enterprise in Historical Perspective*, ed. Alice Teichova, Maurice Lévy-Leboyer, and Helga Nussbaum (Cambridge: Cambridge University Press; Paris: Éditions de la Maison des Sciences de l'Homme, 1986).

[40] See Rawi Abdelal and Jonathan Kirshner, "Strategy, Economic Relations, and the Definition of National Interests," *Security Studies* 9, 1–2 (1999–2000): 119–56. Also see Katzenstein,

The ambiguity and contestation of Austrian national identity thus affected its domestic politics and economic relations with other states during the interwar years.[41] Austria's interwar political struggles were over the direction of the state's political-economic integration. Most Austrians preferred free trade and economic integration with *someone* at least; the costs of going it alone seemed too high to bear. There was no coherent nationalist movement (or for that matter, a coherently *Austrian* nationalist movement) in 1920s Austria, and thus Austrian nationalism did not affect its economic relations with the other Habsburg successor states.

Economic Nationalism: Hungary, Czechoslovakia, Romania, and Yugoslavia. In contrast, the foreign economic policy debates in the four other post-Habsburg states were framed by nationalists. In particular, Hungarian, Czech, Romanian, and Serb nationalists defined the economic goals for their states, and those goals invariably included economic autonomy from Austria. Hungarian, Czechoslovak, Romanian, and Yugoslav governments rejected free trade, multilateral economic cooperation, and Danubian economic union.

Moreover, Hungarian nationalists completely rejected the peace settlements and insisted on their revision throughout the interwar period. Because of the territorial losses imposed by the victors of the war, the Treaty of Trianon became, in Tibor Frank's words, the "watershed moment in the history of Hungarian nationalism."[42] Hungarian nationalism had traditionally been oriented against Austria. Interwar Hungarian nationalists politically linked issues of national pride and the unity of the nation (since millions of Magyars now lived in neighboring states) with the idea that Hungary had been treated unfairly by the great powers and the other post-Habsburg states, which had taken advantage of Hungarian weakness and dismembered the state. Virtually all political parties agreed, and these ideas and goals became the central influence on government foreign policy preferences. These political concerns of successive Hungarian governments therefore led to several specific policies regarding the Danubian region. Most important, the government demanded that the peace settlement be revised

---

Disjoined Partners, 159–60; Zygmunt J. Gasiorowski, "Czechoslovakia and the Austrian Question, 1918–1928," *Südost-Forschungen* 16, 1 (1957): 87–122; and F. Gregory Campbell, *Confrontation in Central Europe* (Chicago: University of Chicago Press, 1975), 114–15.

[41] Interwar Austrians contested more than their national identity. They also contested ideology, the regime, and statehood. The question of national identity divided Austrian political parties in two: Pan-Germanists and socialists against Christian Socials. But the other issues divided them differently since, for example, Pan-Germanists and socialists disagreed about both ideology and regime.

[42] Tibor Frank, "Nation, National Minorities, and Nationalism in Twentieth-Century Hungary," in *Eastern European Nationalism in the Twentieth Century*, ed. Peter F. Sugar (Washington, D.C.: American University Press, 1995), 222, 227–29.

and borders redrawn.[43] Second, Hungary consistently and emphatically rejected Danubian economic union.[44] Instead, Hungary's "intense economic nationalism" sought to create both autonomy from Austria and more rapid industrial development than the other post-Habsburg states.[45]

Hungarian policy alarmed those states that benefited from the peace settlements: Czechoslovakia, Romania, and Yugoslavia. The Czechoslovak, Romanian, and Yugoslavian governments had a direction for their concerns about economic dependence and state security—against both Austria and Hungary. Although each of the three governments rejected a Danubian federation that included Austria and Hungary, each embraced their own regional alliance, the Little Entente. The Little Entente governments sought to deny Vienna and Budapest financial influence in their affairs and transferred ownership of multinational firms and especially banks operating within their borders, the so-called policies of nostrification.[46] Nevertheless, whereas capital in both Austria and Hungary was heavily regulated by the governments of the successor states, Czechoslovakia, Romania, and Yugoslavia remained open to west European and U.S. capital.[47] Also important was the fact that domestic distribution was a fundamental component of their economic nationalisms—in all three states governments sought to redistribute both land and capital from Austrians and Hungarians to nationals.[48]

---

[43] See especially C. A. Macartney, *Hungary and Her Successors: The Treaty of Trianon and Its Consequences, 1919–1937* (London: Oxford University Press, 1937). According to Joseph Rothschild, "Passionate revisionism was the general—indeed, the virtually universal—response of Hungarian society to Trianon." See his *East Central Europe between the Two World Wars* (Seattle: University of Washington Press, 1974), 157.

[44] Pasvolsky, *Economic Nationalism*, 375–78; and Gyula Juhasz, *Hungarian Foreign Policy, 1919–1945* (Budapest: Akademiai Kiado, 1979). See also István Deák, "Historical Foundations: The Development of Hungary from 1918 until 1945," in *Ungarn*, ed. Klaus-Detlev Grothusen (Göttingen: Vandenhoeck und Ruprecht, 1987), 49–53; and George Barany, "Hungary: From Aristocratic to Proletarian Nationalism," in *Nationalism in Eastern Europe*, ed. Peter F. Sugar and Ivo J. Lederer (Seattle: University of Washington Press, 1969), 287–89.

[45] Pasvolsky, *Economic Nationalism*, 361. On the concern for economic autonomy from Austria, see especially Ivan Berend and György Ránki, "Economic Development in Hungary between the Two World Wars," in their *Underdevelopment and Economic Growth: Studies in Hungarian Social and Economic History* (Budapest: Akademiai Kiado, 1979), 174–76; C. A. Macartney, *Problems of the Danube Basin* (London: Cambridge University Press, 1942), 132–33; and Macartney, *Hungary and Her Successors*, 468. For a historical reflection on this issue, see Berend and Ránki, "Economic Factors in Nationalism: A Case Study of Hungary at the Turn of the Century," in their *Underdevelopment and Economic Growth*. On protectionism and relative industrial development goals, see Andrew C. Janos, *The Politics of Backwardness in Hungary, 1825–1945* (Princeton: Princeton University Press, 1982), 218–22; Ivan Berend and György Ránki, *The Hungarian Economy in the Twentieth Century* (New York: St. Martin's, 1985), 42–44; and Rothschild, *East Central Europe*, 166.

[46] Pasvolsky, *Economic Nationalism*, 73.

[47] Kofman, "Economic Nationalism," 222.

[48] See Rothschild, *East Central Europe*, 15, 268, 290–92.

The Little Entente led ultimately neither to intensive trade cooperation nor to economic cohesion among the states that composed it. These states' rejection of Danubian economic union was coincident with an inward turn of their economic policies.[49] And even the Little Entente was averse to multilateralism among the member states themselves during the 1920s. Organized in 1920–21, the entente was an informal alliance established by a series of bilateral treaties among the three states. Only in 1933 did the entente become a multilateral, formal diplomatic federation.[50]

Nationalism in Czechoslovakia was the central influence on its foreign economic policy, leading the government to introduce its own currency, to seek economic autonomy, and ultimately also to seek regional hegemony. But it was primarily Czech nationalism that articulated those goals. Czechoslovak identity was vaguely defined during the 1920s and, as the decade progressed, increasingly contested by Slovak nationalists.[51] The government, dominated by Czech nationalists, interpreted Czech national goals to be largely synonymous with Czechoslovak state goals.[52] When it came to questions of foreign policy, Slovaks were completely in agreement.[53] In fact, the anti-Magyar basis of Slovak nationalism intensified Czechoslovakia's economic orientation away from Hungary. Because Czech nationalism had developed in opposition to German-Austrian identity, and Slovak nationalism had developed in opposition to Magyar identity, Czechoslovak citizens managed to share a political-economic orientation against both.[54]

Czechoslovakia had the most powerful industrial economy in the region because it inherited over two-thirds of the industrial potential of the Austro-Hungarian empire and only one-quarter of its population living in one-fifth

---

[49] See especially Magda Adam, *The Little Entente and Europe, 1920–1929* (Budapest: Akademiai Kiado, 1993), chap. 3, 183–92. See also Keith Hitchins, *Rumania, 1866–1947* (Oxford: Clarendon, 1994), 432–33; and Radice, "General Characteristics," 59.

[50] See Robert Machray, *The Little Entente* (London: Allen and Unwin, 1929); Harry N. Howard, "The Little Entente and the Balkan Entente," in *Czechoslovakia: Twenty Years of Independence*, ed. Robert J. Kerner (Berkeley: University of California Press, 1940); and John O. Crane, *The Little Entente* (New York: Macmillan, 1931).

[51] See Carol Skalnik Leff, *National Conflict in Czechoslovakia* (Princeton: Princeton University Press, 1988), chap. 1; and Hugh Seton-Watson, *Eastern Europe between the Wars, 1918–1941*, 3d ed. (Hamden, Conn.: Archon, 1962), 175–77.

[52] See, for example, Carol Skalnik Leff, "Czech and Slovak Nationalism in the Twentieth Century," in *Eastern European Nationalism*, ed. Sugar, 134–35; and Joseph F. Zacek, "Nationalism in Czechoslovakia," in *Nationalism in Eastern Europe*, ed. Sugar and Lederer, 193. Also see Zdenek Suda, "Slovakia in Czech National Consciousness," in *The End of Czechoslovakia*, ed. Jiri Musil (Budapest: Central European University Press, 1995), 111–14; and István Deák, "The Fall of Austria-Hungary," in *Fall of Great Powers*, ed. Lundestad, 98.

[53] For more on how the promotion of a unified Czechoslovak identity related to the state's international relations, see Leff, *National Conflict*, 134–38.

[54] See Felix John Vondracek, *The Foreign Policy of Czechoslovakia, 1918–1935* (New York: Columbia University Press, 1937), 60–62, 78–79; Leff, *National Conflict*, 26–32; and Macartney, *Danube Basin*, 132.

of its area.[55] Still, Czechoslovak foreign minister Eduard Benes contended in 1920 that the "Czechs had fought not for political freedom—for this they had enjoyed to a certain extent before the war—but for their economic independence, and therefore the scheme for a confederation of the Danubian states, or even of a 'Customs Union,' is out of the question for the Czechoslovak Republic."[56] The government sought to create economic autonomy from Hungary and Austria but chose a "western orientation as one of the means of safeguarding her independence."[57] Czechoslovakia therefore in the early 1920s consistently rejected the possibility of a Danubian economic union. Instead, economic policy was "directed toward the preservation of her economic, as well as political, identity."[58]

Similarly, nationalism determined the foreign economic policy of Romania, leading the government, according to Leo Pasvolsky, toward an "uncompromising assertion of economic sovereignty" and a fear of "economic colonization."[59] These security concerns of economic dependence led Romania to reject Danubian economic union, as did Czechoslovakia and Yugoslavia. Romania in the 1920s was ruled by the Liberal Party, composed primarily of Romanian nationalists. The motto for Romania's interwar economic development was, literally, "By ourselves alone." The government consequently sought what it called "economic emancipation,"[60] cultivating new industries, passing laws that severely limited foreign ownership in Romanian firms, and adopting highly protective tariffs between 1924 and 1927.[61] The 1923 constitution declared that natural resources were the property of the state and restricted landownership to Romanian citizens; concerns for internal redistribution were central to Romanian nationalist ideology.[62] The continuity of Romanian

[55] See, for example, Alice Teichova, *The Czechoslovak Economy, 1918–1980* (London: Routledge, 1988), 3, 17–18; Pasvolsky, *Economic Nationalism*, 201–2; and Rothschild, *East Central Europe*, 86.

[56] Quoted in Hertz, *Economic Problem*, 65. Benes also argued that Czechoslovakia was aware "of the fact that the present day economic policy of all [central European states] is characterized by an extreme nationalism—a protectionism, in fact, dictated by the nationalists," at 74.

[57] Pasvolsky, *Economic Nationalism*, 265–67. On the policy of "western orientation," see Vondracek, *Foreign Policy of Czechoslovakia*, 82, 98, 113. On economic policy and the direction of Czechoslovak foreign trade, see Doreen Warriner, "Czechoslovakia and Central European Tariffs, I and II," *Slavonic and East European Review* 11, 32 and 33 (1933): 314–27 and 543–55, at 549–50.

[58] Pasvolsky, *Economic Nationalism*, 282. According to M. L. Flaningam, "one of the best examples of nationalism as a motivating factor in economic policy is to be found in the tariff and commercial treaty relations of Czechoslovakia and Austria." See her "Survey of Czechoslovak-Austrian Tariff and Commercial Treaty Relations, 1919–1937," *Journal of Central European Affairs* 6, 1 (1946): 30–42, at 30.

[59] Pasvolsky, *Economic Nationalism*, 439, 459–63.

[60] Rothschild, *East Central Europe*, 293.

[61] See Berend, *Decades of Crisis*, 234.

foreign economic policy during the 1920s also indicated consensus on the necessity of economic autonomy. In 1928, when the National-Peasant Party supplanted the Liberals, the new government, motivated apparently by the same concerns, continued the policies of economic autonomy.[63] As was the case elsewhere in the region, political parties disagreed over domestic politics, but everyone agreed that the Romanian economy should be autonomous from Austria and Hungary and shared the "commitment to economic nationalism."[64]

Finally, like Romanian and Czechoslovak economic policy, Yugoslav economic policy during the interwar years sought to "reinforce the newly acquired political independence by strengthening the economy of the country," as Jozo Tomasevich notes. For this purpose, the government sought to reduce and control industrial imports and financial flows from Austria and Hungary, and it nationalized Austrian and Hungarian enterprises on Yugoslav territory to lessen dependence on both states.[65] The 1925 tariff set dual rates whose maximum, faced by countries with which the government had not concluded a trade agreement, were so high that importing many products simply was impossible.[66] And the Yugoslav government, like those of the other Danubian states, rejected the Portorose protocols for free trade.[67]

As was the case with Czechoslovakia, the Yugoslav state was established in the absence of a widely shared Yugoslav national identity. Serbian and Croatian nationalists, in particular, had contrasting interpretations of Yugoslav societal unity both before and after the establishment of the state.[68] Indeed, at the turn of the century Serbs, Croats, and Slovenes each had

[62] Rothschild, *East Central Europe*, 297. See also James P. Niessen, "Romanian Nationalism: An Ideology of Integration and Mobilization," in *Eastern European Nationalism*, ed. Sugar, 285–86.

[63] Hitchins, *Rumania*, 364–66. On the continuity of Romania's foreign economic policy between the wars, see David Turnock, *The Romanian Economy in the Twentieth Century* (New York: St. Martin's 1986), 53–54.

[64] Rothschild, *East Central Europe*, 297.

[65] Jozo Tomasevich, "Foreign Economic Relations, 1918–1941," in *Yugoslavia*, ed. Robert J. Kerner (Berkeley: University of California Press, 1949), 185–86, 197–98.

[66] Tomasevich, "Foreign Economic Relations," 198–99. Also see John R. Lampe and Marvin R. Jackson, *Balkan Economic History, 1550–1950* (Bloomington: Indiana University Press, 1982), 402–15; and Lampe, *Yugoslavia as History: Twice There Was a Country* (Cambridge: Cambridge University Press, 1996), chap. 5.

[67] Yugoslavia's failure to ratify the Portorose agreement was indicative of its own "economic nationalism," according to Fred Singleton and Bernard Carter, *The Economy of Yugoslavia* (New York: St. Martin's 1982), 62 and chaps. 3 and 4 more generally.

[68] See Charles Jelavich, *South Slav Nationalisms* (Columbus: Ohio State University Press, 1990), chap. 1, especially 30–31; and Ivo Banac, *The National Question in Yugoslavia: Origins, History, Politics* (Ithaca: Cornell University Press, 1984).

widely shared national identities and coherent nationalist ideologies.[69] And like the Czechs, Serb nationalists largely controlled their state and imposed their understanding of Yugoslav unity on the rest of society.[70] Their interpretation equated the identity of the Yugoslav state with the historical destiny of a Greater Serbia and the liberation of all the South Slavs from the foreign rule of Austria and Hungary.[71] Prewar Serbian nationalism, which had guided policy in the kingdom before 1914, was even more assertive in the economic debates of interwar Yugoslavia.[72] With regard to foreign economic policy (though not much else) Serbs, Croats, and Slovenes tended to agree, and policy followed the Serb national purpose without contradicting the preferences of the other nationalities.

In sum, the nationalisms within Czechoslovakia, Romania, Yugoslavia, and Hungary led their governments not to cooperate with one another in economic affairs. They sought either to reorient their economies to other states or to seek self-sufficiency, primarily for reasons of state security.[73] As Ivan Berend argues, the new governments of the region "sought to establish national identities in a form that included economic independence."[74] Nationalists framed the economic policy debate in each of these four cases and successfully implemented their preferred policies.

The same was not true for Austria. The contested and ambiguous national identity of Austrians led political elites to debate bitterly whether the country should stay economically integrated with the Danubian states or reorient its economy toward Germany. Austria was thus alone in its openness to regional economic reintegration in post-Habsburg eastern Europe.

INDONESIA AFTER EMPIRE, 1949–1965

The next moment of imperial collapse and new state formation came at the end of World War II. Southeast Asia was a central location of nationalist movements and newly independent states. The formation of Indonesia was one of the region's most important events.

[69] Rothschild, *East Central Europe*, 206; Seton-Watson, *Eastern Europe*, 217, 226–27; and Dennison Rusinow, "The Yugoslav Peoples," in *Eastern European Nationalism*, ed. Sugar, 355, 357–63.

[70] See, for example, Aleksa Djilas, *The Contested Country* (Cambridge: Harvard University Press, 1991), 12–13; and Rothschild, *East Central Europe*, 206–7. According to Deák, "interwar Czechoslovakia was dominated by the Czech intelligentsia and interwar Yugoslavia by the Serbian military and bureaucratic establishments." "Fall of Austria-Hungary," 98.

[71] See Ivo J. Lederer, "Nationalism and the Yugoslavs," in *Nationalism in Eastern Europe*, ed. Sugar and Lederer, 425.

[72] Pasvolsky, *Economic Nationalism*, 522.

[73] Macartney, *Problems of the Danube Basin*, 133.

[74] Berend, *Decades of Crisis*, 234.

President Sukarno addressed the Indonesian people on 17 August, Independence Day, every year of his tenure, which lasted from 1949 to 1965. In his 1963 Independence Day speech Sukarno hoped to rally Indonesians to continue their sacrifice for the sake of economic autonomy from the Dutch. Inflation was rampant and production had declined, but at least the economy was theirs, a "national" economy, not the "colonial" economy they had inherited in December 1949. The government had done everything it could to make economic activity within its borders more independent and more Indonesian. Eventually, Indonesianization came to include the nationalization of all Dutch capital and enterprises in 1957. There were costs to such a policy, and everyone knew them. But Sukarno exhorted Indonesians to "economic patriotism" and, in the nationalist's familiar trope, insisted, "Better to eat poverty rations of cassava and be independent than eat beefsteak and be enslaved."[75] In Sukarno's Indonesia, nationalist ideology, articulated most forcefully by Sukarno himself, both defined the social purposes of the new state and urged society's sacrifice for those goals.

Nationalism and Revolution in Indonesia

From 1945, when Sukarno proclaimed the independence of the Republic of Indonesia, until 1949, when the Dutch transferred sovereignty, the military of the incipient republic intermittently fought against Netherlands armed forces determined to maintain power over the archipelago. Meanwhile, the government of the republic negotiated with the Dutch over the transfer of sovereignty.[76]

The East Indies had been occupied by the Japanese from 1942 to 1945, during which time Indonesian nationalists, including Sukarno, were encouraged by Japan to mobilize against Western colonialism; at the same time, they were hindered by the Japanese themselves. With Sukarno's declaration of independence coming only two days after the Japanese surrender, the Netherlands considered the republic a Japanese creation, not to say conspiracy. Dutch soldiers established and maintained control over a number of territories over which the republic also claimed sovereignty, and there were, in effect, two states on the archipelago. In 1947, with more than one hundred fifty thousand soldiers on the islands, the Dutch intensified their efforts to retain control over the East Indies and advanced aggressively into territories controlled by the republic. In late 1948 the

[75] Sukarno, "The Economics of a Nation in Revolution," in *Indonesian Political Thinking, 1945–1965*, ed. Herbert Feith and Lance Castles (Ithaca: Cornell University Press, 1970), 395.
[76] On the politics of this period, the classic text is George McT. Kahin, *Nationalism and Revolution in Indonesia* (Ithaca: Cornell University Press, 1952). See also Benedict R. O'G. Anderson, *Java in a Time of Revolution* (Ithaca: Cornell University Press, 1972).

Dutch captured Jogjakarta, the republic's capital, and took its leaders, including Sukarno, into custody. The United States and the United Nations Security Council reacted quickly and negatively to the Dutch action, however, and faced with growing international pressure and the suspension of Marshall Plan aid, the Netherlands finally relented in December 1949.

Economic Strategy, 1949–1965: Indonesianisasi

The first fifteen years of Indonesia's independent statehood were dominated by its first president, Sukarno. The Sukarno period has two halves. The first half began in 1949, at the moment of independence, and ended around 1957. In this period Indonesia enjoyed what was officially called "Liberal Democracy," during which power was shared by president and parliament. Under Liberal Democracy, the government's attempts to Indonesianize the economy were pragmatic and relatively restrained.

Restrained, that is, relative to the economic nationalism that came after 1957. The break came in 1957–58, when a regional crisis threatened the unity of the state, and the government responded with the imposition of martial law. At around the same time, the Indonesian government nationalized all existing Dutch firms and capital, as its strategy for national economic autonomy became more radical. This period, from 1957 until 1965, was Sukarno's "Guided Democracy" and "Guided Economy." It lasted until the military and General Suharto ousted Sukarno and initiated the "New Order," which, among its many other dramas, opened Indonesia to Western finance and commerce and transformed the development strategy of the state.

Here I am concerned with politics under Sukarno, who presided over Indonesia's postimperial moment, when nearly every policy was a response to the colonial past. It is also, according to Richard Robison, "the period in which the Dutch colonial economy was dismantled."[77] Moreover, compared with the New Order, politics under Sukarno were influenced overwhelmingly by nationalism and debates about national identity. Even if the New Order was not normal politics, Suharto normalized Indonesia's foreign economic relations, in the sense that policy became motivated by the usual concerns of strategy and development rather than exclusively by the nationalists' interpretation of their revolutionary break from the Netherlands. If nationalism was the motive of economic strategy before 1965, statism—"the maximal expression of state interests," according to Benedict Anderson—defined politics under Suharto. As Anderson has argued, the

---

[77] Richard Robison, *Indonesia: The Rise of Capital* (Sydney and Winchester, Mass.: Allen and Unwin, 1986), 36.

New Order is "best understood as the resurrection of the state and its tri-umph vis-à-vis society and nation."[78] This episode, then, is about Indonesia's economic strategy as created by society and nation—Indonesia's economic nationalism, as distinct from the economic statism that came later.

During both Liberal and Guided Democracy, Indonesian political elites, including Sukarno, the nationalist party, and the Communist Party, enjoyed a remarkable consensus on their economic goals.[79] According to Herbert Feith, writing in 1964, "all political parties in Indonesia are agreed on 'con-verting the colonial economy into a national economy.' A 'national' econ-omy does not mean 'nationalized,' but 'Indonesianized.'"[80] Thus, the In-donesian government consistently sought to make the economy and its institutions more national and achieve economic autonomy from the Netherlands, first, and eventually from Western capital in general. Foreign investment, and most centrally Dutch capital, was the most politicized as-pect of the Indonesian economy in the 1950s and 1960s; all political elites, and virtually everyone else, considered it a problem to be solved.[81] This consensus and consistency of purpose resulted from Indonesian national identity, certainly as it was defined and shared by those in power under Sukarno, as well as by his primary political rivals.[82] The only debate about

---

[78] Benedict R. O'G. Anderson, "Old State, New Society: Indonesia's New Order in Com-parative Perspective," *Journal of Asian Studies* 42, 3 (1983): 477–96, at 477, 487.

[79] Five major Indonesian parties held influence during Liberal Democracy, including the relatively conservative Islamic party, Masjumi, which shared the goals of Indonesianization and economic autonomy but opposed radical moves such as nationalization. The other four, the Communist Party (PKI), the Socialist Party (PSI), the Nationalist Party (PNI), and the Is-lamic Nahdatal Ulama (NU), all shared a relatively coherent interpretation of the economic goals that were fundamental to Indonesia after empire, at least in terms of foreign economic relations and the necessity of autonomy.

[80] Herbert Feith, "Indonesia," in *Governments and Politics of Southeast Asia*, 2d ed., ed. George McT. Kahin (Ithaca: Cornell University Press, 1964), 105. See also Everett D. Hawkins, "Prospects for Economic Development in Indonesia," *World Politics* 8, 1 (1955): 91–111, espe-cially at 91: "Like many other new countries in Asia, Africa, and Latin America, Indonesia is striving for a 'national,' not a 'colonial,' economy"; and Sharon Siddique and Leo Suryadinata, "Bumiputra and Pribumi: Economic Nationalism (Indigenism) in Malaysia and Indonesia," *Pa-cific Affairs* 54, 4 (1981–82): 662–87. On colonial continuity, see Harry J. Benda, "Decolo-nization in Indonesia: The Problem of Continuity and Change," *American Historical Review* 70, 4 (1965): 1058–73.

[81] Thee Kian Wie, "Economic Policies in Indonesia during the Period 1950–1965," in *His-torical Foundations of a National Economy in Indonesia*, ed. J. Th. Lindblad (Amsterdam: North-Holland, 1996), especially 325.

[82] For this conclusion, see also, for example, John O. Sutter, *Sovereign Indonesia Strives for a National Economy: Political Attitudes towards the Economy, Foreign Investment, and Nationalization*, vol. 4 of his *Indonesianisasi: Politics in a Changing Economy, 1940–1955* (Ithaca: Cornell Uni-versity Southeast Asia Program, 1959), chap. 27; and Wie, "Economic Policies in Indonesia," 316–17. On this consensus even between Indonesia's nationalists and Communists, see Benjamin Higgins, *Indonesia's Economic Stabilization and Development* (New York: Institute of Pacific Relations, 1957), 96–99.

the creation of the national economy was the speed of change, how radical it should be.[83] In sum, although Indonesia's Nationalist Party itself never held power during Liberal Democracy, nationalist ideology so thoroughly framed the terms of debate that almost all Indonesian elites agreed with the fundamental economic policy goals of the nationalists.

Indonesia's first independent government outlined four clear economic goals: establishing Indonesian control over economic activity, encouraging the redistribution of output to Indonesian nationals, promoting development, and maintaining economic stability. By the late 1950s, however, the government had shown that it would always privilege the first two at the expense of the latter.[84] The trade-off between the two sets of goals was quite real. The First Five-Year Plan of 1956 placed enormous emphasis on the "willingness of the people to accept a period of special effort of a particular strain for the sake of the coming generation."[85] As I argued in chapters 1 and 2, this was precisely List's understanding of the sacrifice engendered by nationalism—sacrifice of the present for the sake of the future, especially the nation's future.

There was no question among political elites that the government would create a central bank and independent currency. But the Dutch hoped to maintain control of the Java Bank, a large commercial bank that handled the colony's major central banking functions. So when in 1949 the Netherlands and the nascent republic negotiated the Roundtable Conference Agreement to regulate economic relations between them, the Dutch government insisted it had the right to preapprove any changes in monetary policy or personnel. The latter condition was crucial since the staff of Java Bank was almost exclusively Dutch. In 1950–51 the Indonesian government was still several years away from the formal abrogation of the Roundtable agreement. Nevertheless, Finance Minister Wibisono announced that Indonesia would nationalize the Java Bank, and thus began the rapid establishment of the Bank Indonesia. The new central bank was Indonesianized in every sense, including its staff.[86]

[83] Douglas S. Pauuw, "From Colonial to Guided Economy," in *Indonesia*, ed. Ruth McVey (New Haven: Yale University Southeast Asian Studies, 1963), 207–9.

[84] Pauuw, "From Colonial to Guided Economy," 231–32. As Feith argued, "The government's leaders usually put the nation's strength and prestige and its cultural identity first and the maximization of production second." "Indonesia," 258.

[85] National Planning Bureau, "A Study of the Indonesian Development Scheme," *Ekonomi dan Keuangan Indonesia* 10, 7 (1957): 600–642, at 642.

[86] See Ralph Anspach, "Indonesia," in Frank H. Golay, Ralph Anspach, M. Ruth Pfanner, and Eliezer B. Ayal, *Underdevelopment and Economic Nationalism in Southeast Asia* (Ithaca: Cornell University Press, 1969), 137–40. See also Ali Wardhana, "The Indonesian Banking System: The Central Bank," in *The Economy of Indonesia*, ed. Bruce Glassburner (Ithaca: Cornell University Press, 1971); and Benjamin Higgins and William C. Hollingen, "Central Banking in Indonesia," in *Central Banking in South and East Asia*, ed. S. Gethyn Davies (London: Oxford University Press; Aberdeen: Hong Kong University Press, 1960).

Then, as throughout postcolonial southeast Asia, the Indonesian government concentrated its Indonesianization efforts on commerce, and particularly the import trade. In April 1950 Prosperity Minister Djuanda initiated what became known as the Benteng program.[87] Under Benteng, or Fortress, the government reserved a range of consumer goods to national, meaning native Indonesian, importers. Within the same framework the government also financed the emergence and activities of Indonesians entering the import sector. Most Indonesians considered Benteng important because the import sector was so visible and had been dominated for so long by the Chinese-speaking population in the cities and by the "Big Five" Dutch firms (Borsumij, Jacobsen van den Berg, George Wehry, Inernatio, and Lindeteves). Thus, Benteng began as a relatively modest but politically salient initiative to alter the structure of Indonesian commerce by fostering the development of an Indonesian business class. Over time the government expanded the role of Benteng so that by 1953 40 percent of all imports were reserved for native Indonesians. Ultimately, the policy did not dramatically alter the practice of Indonesian commerce, and public frustration with the lack of progress in the Indonesianization of economic activity grew during the early and mid-1950s.

Another perceived failure was the government's effort to create Indonesian-owned industrial capacity with the 1951 Economic Urgency Plan,[88] which was intended to foster the development of large-scale industrial enterprises, such as in rubber remilling, printing, cotton spinning, and cement.[89] The most important aspect of the plan, for the purposes of this argument, is that it demanded that the Department of Industries favor the development of "national capital" in the industrialization drive. Like Benteng, the industrialization efforts created by the Urgency Plan did not satisfy either the government or the Indonesian public. But also like Benteng, it was through the development of specifically Indonesian capital that the government sought to displace both Dutch and Chinese business within the borders of the new state.

[87] On Benteng, see Wie, "Economic Policies in Indonesia," 167–69; John O. Sutter, *Sovereign Indonesia Strives for a National Economy: The Sectors of the Economy*, vol. 3 of his *Indonesianisasi*, chap. 24, especially 1017–21; and Robison, *Indonesia*, 44–46. Also see Bruce Glassburner, "Economic Policy-Making in Indonesia, 1950–1957," *Economic Development and Cultural Change* 10, 2 (1962): 113–33.

[88] See especially Sumitro Djojohadikusumo, "The Government's Program on Industries," *Ekonomi dan Keuangan Indonesia* 7, 11 (1954): 702–36. Bruce Glassburner called the plan a "highly nationalistic attempt to diminish the nation's dependence on foreign trade by developing small, national (i.e., indigenous) industry to produce import substitutes by means of capital assistance and restriction of certain markets to indigenous sellers." See his "Problems of Economic Policy in Indonesia, 1950–1957," *Ekonomi dan Keuangan Indonesia* 13, 7–8 (1960): 302–21, at 311.

[89] Anspach, "Indonesia," 161–67.

The Urgency Plan was replaced in 1956 by the First Five-Year Plan, designed to coordinate all the government's efforts to Indonesianize the economy.[90] And the government then formally abrogated the Roundtable Conference Agreement, which had ensured the protection of Dutch financial and business interests.[91] In addition, by this time international and domestic political changes had begun that would transform economic policy making even more dramatically.

Most important, the government recognized that its relatively limited efforts to displace the so-called alien capital from the Indonesian economy would not achieve its dramatic goal: the creation of an Indonesian national economy out of the foreign-controlled economic space the state inherited from the Netherlands East Indies. The increasing radicalization of the government during the mid-1950s led to Sukarno's single most important political and conceptual initiative: the creation of Guided Democracy and Guided Economy.

Two crises framed the transition to Guided Economy. First, in December 1956 bloodless coups in the three provinces of the island of Sumatra brought army-led regional councils to power, and the councils refused to recognize the authority of the cabinet of ministers. Then, in March 1957, another coup in East Indonesia empowered another army-led council with a similar critique of the government. In the face of the regional crisis the cabinet resigned in March 1957, and President Sukarno declared martial law to restore order. Thus began his experiment suspending "Liberal" democracy in favor of one more "Guided," organized by Sukarno and directed from Java. It was, in the words of Sukarno, a "democracy that accords with our national identity."[92]

The second crisis was international and of the government's making. The Indonesian government had throughout the 1950s claimed authority over West New Guinea (West Irian) and in the mid-1950s launched the "West Irian Action," designed to put pressure on the Netherlands to relinquish sovereignty over the region. In November 1957 the government orchestrated a motion in the UN General Assembly that urged the Indonesians and Dutch to negotiate with each other about the Indonesian claim to West Irian. At the same time, Sukarno threatened the Dutch with more radical action if the motion failed to pass in the General Assembly. When the West Irian Action failed at the UN, the government both initiated and tacitly encouraged a whole range of activities against Dutch political and commercial interests in Indonesia, including the expulsion of Dutch nationals and

[90] National Planning Bureau, "Indonesian Development Scheme."

[91] See Herbert Feith, *The Decline of Constitutional Democracy in Indonesia* (Ithaca: Cornell University Press, 1962), 456.

[92] Quoted in Feith, "Indonesia," 213.

sporadic takeovers of Dutch concerns by Indonesian workers. This context provided the ideal moment for the Indonesian government to undertake what it had been planning for some time: in December 1957 the cabinet ordered all Dutch property to be placed under military control. A year later the parliament unanimously formalized the expropriation.[93]

The nationalization of Dutch capital was the culmination of Indonesian economic nationalism. It ushered in the period of Guided Economy, under which the state's role in the economy expanded, and the continuing "colonial" bonds between the Netherlands and the Indonesian economy were thus decisively severed. The effects were striking: the nationalization transferred ownership of 90 percent of plantation output, 60 percent of trade, and more than 246 factories and mining enterprises.[94] Economic autonomy from the Netherlands, and later from Western capital in general, remained the central goal of the Indonesian government throughout the era of Guided Economy.

In the Political Manifesto of 1959 Sukarno outlined the goals of "Socialism à la Indonesia" and "Guided Economy." Guided Economy had three principles: coordination by the state of all sectors of the economy; destruction of imperialism and subordination of foreign capital to national social and economic goals; and replacement of the colonial import / export economy with a more self-sufficient and industrialized economy.[95]

The increasing radicalization of the government's development plans was reflected in the 1961 Eight-Year Overall Development Plan. If earlier plans were to create an independent Indonesian capitalist class eventually to supplant the Dutch and Chinese, the new plan revealed the government's willingness to take on the task of Indonesianization through increased state control and ownership. The rhetoric of nationalism and socialism were combined everywhere in the plan: "The socialist society at which we aim must carry our own national identity."[96] By August 1962 Sukarno announced that foreign direct investment with profit transfers abroad was simply no longer welcome in the Indonesian economy.[97]

Ultimately, however, Sukarno's economic policies turned out to be unsustainable, not least because of the rapid inflation that the government's

[93] On these events and their politics, see Justus M. van der Kroef, "Indonesia's Economic Future," *Pacific Affairs* 32, 1 (1959): 46–72.

[94] See Robison, *Indonesia*, 72–73; and Anspach, "Indonesia," 184–91. Also see J. A. C. Mackie, "Indonesian's Government Estates and Their Masters," *Pacific Affairs* 34, 4 (1961–62): 337–60.

[95] Robison, *Indonesia*, 71–72; and Feith, "Indonesia," 235–36.

[96] Quoted in Guy Pauker, "Indonesia's Eight-Year Development Plan," *Pacific Affairs* 34, 2 (1961): 115-30, at 118. On the plan's discussion of national determination, national will, and national ideals, see J. A. C. Mackie, "The Indonesian Economy, 1950–1963," in *Economy of Indonesia*, ed. Glassburner, 52–53. Also see Don D. Humphrey, "Indonesia's National Plan for Economic Development," *Asian Survey* 2, 10 (1962): 12–21.

[97] Anspach, "Indonesia," 197.

money printing let loose.[98] One cause was the August 1959 devaluation of the Indonesian rupiah relative to the dollar from 11.4 to 45. Another was the enormity since 1950 of government deficits, which mushroomed after the transition to Guided Economy. The military and General Suharto ended Sukarno's experiment in Guided Economy in 1965.

Socialism and Nationalist Ideology in Sukarno's Indonesia

Nationalism was ideologically linked to socialism in Sukarno's Indonesia, with social (and socialist) purpose understood as equity and independence from Dutch capital and Western capitalism in general. As throughout the region, capitalism was equated with colonialism because, under Dutch rule, both were what came before. The argument seemed to be that if capitalism is equivalent to colonialism, nationalism must be equivalent to socialism.[99] Thee Kian Wie claims: "To the extent that socialism was equated with 'Indonesianization,' this brand of socialism was actually the same as economic nationalism. To the extent that economic nationalism attaches great importance to having property owned by nationals and having economic functions performed by nationals and taking over national control of productive functions . . . economic nationalism coincided with this interpretation of 'socialism.'"[100] As Bruce Glassburner argued in his assessment of Indonesian economic policy making, "Any successful Indonesian politician is, first of all, a nationalist, and secondly, a socialist."[101]

Perhaps the most telling indicator both that Indonesian nationalism was malleable enough to accommodate socialist rhetoric and that the socialist content of national identity was quite vague was that during the Liberal period the method of indigenization and autonomy was the creation of an independent Indonesian capitalist class. Even the Communist Party supported this goal.[102]

Thus, nationalism and debates about national identity were the most important influence on Indonesian foreign policy making in general during

---

[98] See Anderson, "Old State, New Society," 486. Also see Douglas S. Pauuw, "The High Cost of Political Instability in Indonesia, 1957–1958," in *Indonesia's Struggle, 1957–1958,* ed. B. H. M. Vlekke (The Hague: Netherlands Institute of International Affairs, 1959); and Ralph Anspach, "Monetary Aspects of Indonesia's Economic Reorganization in 1959," *Ekonomi dan Keuangan Indonesia* 13, 1–2 (1960): 2–47.

[99] See Benjamin Higgins, "Thought and Action: Indonesian Economic Studies and Policies in the 1950s," *Bulletin of Indonesian Economic Studies* 26, 1 (1990): 37–47, especially 45.

[100] Wie, "Economic Policies in Indonesia," 320.

[101] Glassburner, "Economic Policy-Making in Indonesia," 120.

[102] See, for example, Benedict R. O'G. Anderson, "Indonesia: United against Progress," *Current History* 48, 282 (1965): 75–81. Also see Anspach, "Indonesia," 121.

the 1950s and early 1960s.[103] Under Sukarno independence in the economy and foreign policy was understood not as nominal sovereignty but as avoiding dependence on the Dutch in defense of the national identity.[104] In sum, party competition in 1950s Indonesia was intense, but there was widespread agreement about the necessity and desirability of wresting "national" control over economic activity in Indonesia from "colonial" control. After Guided Democracy began in 1957, Sukarno himself was the most important locus for the production and interpretation of Indonesian nationalist ideology, and political parties' consensus, such as it was, became less important.

Indonesia and Southeast Asia

"Commercial policy in postwar Southeast Asia is intelligible not in terms of efforts to accelerate economic growth," argued Frank Golay, "but in terms of the economic content of nationalism. The economic counterpart of political nationalism in newly sovereign Southeast Asia is best understood as a determination to 'de-alienize' the economies inherited from the period of colonialism."[105]

Indonesia was the classic case of economic nationalism in postcolonial southeast Asia.[106] According to Douglas Pauuw, "among Southeast Asia's newly independent countries, Indonesia stands out for the rapidity with which it has destroyed Western social and economic institutions implanted by colonialism: Dutch enterprise there virtually ceased to exist less than ten years after sovereignty was transferred."[107] Of course, Indonesia was the only Dutch postcolonial state in the region, so comparison across cases is

[103] See Franklin B. Weinstein, "The Uses of Foreign Policy in Indonesia," *World Politics* 24, 3 (1972): 356–81; Jon M. Reinhardt, *Foreign Policy and National Integration: The Case of Indonesia* (New Haven: Yale University Southeast Asia Studies, 1971), especially chaps. 2, 3, and 6; and Norman G. Owen, "Economic and Social Change," in *The Nineteenth and Twentieth Centuries*, vol. 2 of *The Cambridge History of Southeast Asia*, ed. Nicholas Tarling (Cambridge: Cambridge University Press, 1992), 489–90. On the debates themselves, see, for example, Justus M. van der Kroef, "Indonesia's 'Identity Revolution,'" *Topic* 6, 1 (1963): 5–18; Guy J. Pauker, "Indonesian Images of Their National Self," *Public Opinion Quarterly* 22, 3 (1958): 305–24; and J. Eliseo Rocamora, *Nationalism in Search of Ideology: The Indonesian Nationalist Party, 1946–1965* (Quezon City: Philippine Center for Advanced Studies, 1975), especially chaps. 2 and 3.

[104] Franklin B. Weinstein, *Indonesian Foreign Policy and the Dilemma of Dependence: From Sukarno to Soeharto* (Ithaca: Cornell University Press, 1976), 30.

[105] Frank H. Golay, "Commercial Policy and Economic Nationalism," *Quarterly Journal of Economics* 72, 4 (1958): 574–87, at 579.

[106] The literature on economic nationalism in the rest of postcolonial southeast Asia is quite large. For an overview, see Norman G. Owen, "Economic and Social Change," in *The Nineteenth and Twentieth Centuries*, vol. 2 of *Cambridge History of Southeast Asia*, ed. Tarling. Owen describes economic nationalism as the attempt "to indigenize wealth and production, reduce foreign influence, and establish self-sufficiency," at 471.

[107] Pauuw, "From Colonial to Guided Economy," 155.

difficult. The difficulty of comparison is compounded because the history of imperialism in the region is so varied: nearly every European colonial state held territory there, including Britain (in Burma, Malaya, Singapore, and northern Borneo), France (in Laos, Cambodia, and Vietnam), Portugal (in eastern Timor), and Spain and the United States (in the Philippines).[108] In every state throughout the region, however, national identity was the central axis of debate about economic policy. In the states where nationalists' ideas and goals achieved widespread support and powerfully influenced economic policy making, such as Indonesia and Burma, economic nationalism was coherent and purposive.[109]

In sum, the two most common themes of postcolonial political economy in southeast Asia were the necessity of transforming the "colonial economy" into a "national economy" at whatever cost, even slow growth, and the equation of capitalism with imperialism. Wherever nationalism was powerful, therefore, so was some (at least vaguely) socialist ideology. In other states, however, such as the Philippines, where the nationalists were unable to eliminate the entrenched coalitions that benefited from continued and tight economic links between the former colony and the metropole, economic nationalism was compromised. Finally, in several cases— the postcolonial states of French Indochina—economic policy making inspired by nationalism never had much of a chance because of outright war that continued throughout the 1950s. Other former French colonies, as described in the next section, were not as universally assertive.

FRENCH WEST AFRICA AFTER EMPIRE

Throughout postcolonial Asia and Africa many national elites were concerned with "neocolonialism" and the possibility that the former metropole's position of political, cultural, and economic dominance would remain well past the moment of independent statehood.[110] The quintessential neocolonial relationship, which worried the leaders of new states throughout the world, was that between France and francophone Africa. It is true that France actively sought to maintain its political and cultural influence in Africa, and

[108] On the "strange history of mottled imperialism" in southeast Asia, see Benedict R. O'G. Anderson, introduction to *Spectre of Comparisons: Nationalism, Southeast Asia, and the World* (London: Verso, 1998).

[109] On Burma and "Burmanization," see especially M. Ruth Pfanner, "Burma," in Golay, Anspach, Pfanner, and Ayal, *Underdevelopment and Economic Nationalism*; Josef Silverstein, "Burma," in *Southeast Asia*, ed. Kahin; and Louis J. Walinsky, *Economic Development in Burma, 1951–1960* (New York: Twentieth Century Fund, 1962), 23–30, 491–95, and 580–81.

[110] See, for example, Samir Amin, *Neo-Colonialism in West Africa* (Harmondsworth, Middlesex: Penguin, 1973).

the French government was willing to pay for its influence with subsidies, artificially high prices for imports from its former colonies, and financial aid. France's former colonies did not have to do much in exchange for this bounty; they simply were expected to follow France, voting with it in the UN, offering a hospitable climate for French investment, and accepting the idea of a Franco-African identity, of a Eurafrican community of peoples. French policy toward its former colonies in sub-Saharan Africa was essentially invariant: the government made its offer, implicitly and explicitly, and the African societies could choose.

There were two clear moments of choice for French Africa. The first was in 1958, when French president Charles de Gaulle offered to redefine France's relationship with its African territories. The Algerian war had led to a profound political crisis in France, and de Gaulle reentered politics, ultimately creating a new constitution and the Fifth Republic. The constitution of the Fifth Republic reorganized political power in France. In Africa the colonies were presented with a referendum on whether to adopt the constitution or not: adopting it meant remaining in a redefined French community as republics; rejecting it meant outright and immediate independence. Every colony, save one, voted to stay in the French community. In Guinea, a small, west African colony of three million people, 94 percent of the population voted against the French constitution and for independence. De Gaulle had warned the Guineans of the consequences of independence, including the suspension of aid and the decay of economic ties, in Guinea's capital, Conakry, shortly before the referendum. Still, Guinea alone chose independence. As a result, and as both the Guineans and the French knew, their political relations became extremely strained and their economic relations collapsed.

Ultimately, full decolonization came to the rest of francophone Africa only two years later, though France continued to punish Guinea economically for its insubordination well into the mid-1960s. In the place of a clearly defined political relationship with its former African territories, France offered a vaguely defined economic relationship, which included a kind of monetary union. The franc zone was a currency union between France and many of its former African colonies. Under the arrangement the former colonies shared a single currency, the CFA franc, pegged to the French franc at a rate of 50 to 1. The franc zone was divided into two halves, West and East, which reflected administrative boundaries from the colonial period. As with the Fifth Republic constitution, the French government made it clear that it valued Africans' membership in the monetary union and was willing to offer substantial economic benefits to its members. The benefits, which included waived import duties, high prices for imports from the former colonies, and direct financial aid, were part of

France's attempt to cultivate monetary dependence in exchange for political influence.[111]

For most former French colonies, which inherited struggling, monoculture economies and weak state institutions, the French deal for franc zone membership was much too sweet to pass up. Although even Guinea continued to use the CFA franc until 1960, and promised to continue to do so, the Guinean government, not surprisingly, introduced its own currency with much celebration of its national identity and sovereignty. Then, in a surprise move, another new state in French West Africa, Mali, introduced its own currency and left the franc zone in 1962, with its own assertions of nationalism and statehood. Only five years later, however, Mali was forced by economic crisis back into the franc zone, its leaders and society apparently unwilling to bear the enormous costs associated with economic autonomy from France. Guinea, despite its own rather disastrous economic performance in the 1960s, remained outside the franc zone entirely. The remarkable thing about these two west African states was that everyone had understood that there would be profound material costs to a strategy of autonomy from France, and their governments chose it anyway—even if they had underestimated the costs, or overestimated their will, in Mali. From the perspective of Realist theories of IPE, the behavior of Guinea and Mali was not so remarkable, since states' choice of autonomy from the metropole seems an obvious necessity of power politics and state autonomy.

But what about the rest of the French colonies, which utterly acquiesced in French political, cultural, and economic hegemony? Ivory Coast and Senegal, two other French West African states, chose their neocolonial relationship with France willingly; France, after all, did not impose franc zone membership or the economic benefits associated with it.

The enormous range of economic policy variation in Guinea, Mali, Ivory Coast, and Senegal during the 1960s resulted from the ability of their respective nationalists to mobilize the population around issues of "complete decolonization," understood as economic, cultural, and political autonomy from France as well as the Africanization of the state and bureaucracy.[112]

---

[111] See Kirshner, *Currency and Coercion*, 148–56 and chap. 4 generally. On the material advantages and political complications of franc zone membership, see Aguibou Y. Yansané, "Some Problems of Monetary Dependency in French-Speaking West African States," *Journal of African Studies* 5, 4 (1978): 444–70. More generally, see International Monetary Fund, "The CFA Franc System," *IMF Staff Papers* 10, 3 (1963): 345–96. The best discussion of the politics of the franc zone is David Stasavage, "The Political Economy of Monetary Union: Evolution of the African Franc Zone, 1945–1994" (Ph.D. dissertation, Department of Government, Harvard University, 1995).

[112] On Africanization, see, for example, Prosser Gifford and Wm. Roger Louis, introduction to *Decolonization and African Independence: The Transfers of Power, 1960–1980*, ed. Gifford and Louis (New Haven: Yale University Press, 1988).

In each of the four newly independent states, nationalist groups, which had fought to reject the Fifth Republic constitution in 1958, argued that franc zone membership and economic dependence in general were unacceptable. The nationalists wanted utter transformation of the political-economic system, including the creation of "socialism," because capitalism was, by their account, the equivalent of imperialism, France, and the West. Also, in all four states a single party emerged hegemonic immediately after independence. In Guinea the nationalists controlled the party; in Mali the party was divided among nationalists and those more willing to compromise with French economic interests; and in Senegal and Ivory Coast the dominant political parties were bastions of moderation in the radicalized world of postcolonial African politics. Thus, as in the former Soviet Union, the nationalists' success in domestic politics, success that reflected underlying consensus or contestation of societal identity, determined the political-economic relationship between the newly independent states of western Africa and France.

Guinea: Economic Nationalism after Empire

Just days after Guinea's vote for independence and against de Gaulle's constitution, on 28 September 1958, its exports were no longer as welcome in France. This was true in several senses, the most obvious being de Gaulle's interpretation of Guinea's choice as a betrayal. Less sensational politically, though having more effect economically, was the fact that almost immediately Guinea's exports no longer received the price supports France offered Guinea's west African neighbors. Moreover, many of those neighbors produced the same things—bananas, coffee, peanuts, and palm oil, for example. Guinea's exports were priced out of the market instantly, and at the same time, all financial assistance and investment from the French government ceased, as Paris made an example of Guinea.[113]

This was a role Guinea was not unhappy to play. Postcolonial Guinea had one central foreign economic policy goal: autonomy from France.[114] The goal of autonomy permeated every aspect of Guinean politics, and the government relentlessly pursued total "decolonization." Guinea's political economy after empire reflected President Ahmed Sékou Touré's rebuttal

[113] See Victor D. du Bois, "The Guinean Vote for Independence," *AUFS Reports West Africa Series* 5, 7 (1962): 1–11, especially 11.

[114] See, for example, Victor D. du Bois, "Reorganization of the Guinean Economy: The Attempt to Remove the Economic Vestiges of Colonialism," *AUFS Reports West Africa Series* 6, 1 (1963): 1–21; Claude Riviere, *Guinea: The Mobilization of a People* (Ithaca: Cornell University Press, 1977), especially 110–12; and Guy de Lusignan, *French-Speaking Africa since Independence* (New York: Praeger, 1969), chap. 5, 183–88.

of de Gaulle and the Fifth Republic's constitution in 1958: "We prefer poverty in liberty to riches in slavery."[115] Unfortunately, Guinea under Sékou Touré got both: independence and economic disaster.

The government was under the control of the Democratic Party of Guinea (Parti démocratique de Guinée, or PDG), which had been the Guinean section of the African Democratic Assembly (Rassemblement démocratique africain, or RDA). The RDA, organized in October 1946 by representatives of nearly all French African colonies, became an increasingly anticolonial, anti-French organization during the 1940s and 1950s, demanding reform of the French-African relationship. Ultimately, the RDA became an expression of pan-Africanism. Its local sections were not equally radical in every French colony, however, and it was in Guinea that under the leadership of Sékou Touré, the RDA became most radical and assertive.[116]

By the time the PDG was organizing the campaign against the Fifth Republic constitution in 1958, it had rallied nearly the entire country behind its goals. Thus, when more than 90 percent of Guineans voted for independence in 1958, it represented a tremendously broad consensus on the basic goals of nation- and statehood, particularly in light of the fact that the largest "no" vote in any other colony was just over 30 percent, in Niger.

A large portion of the rupture of economic ties with France was caused by France itself in retaliation for Guinea's rejection of the Eurafrican community and identity. The rest Guinea did on its own. So although in January 1959 the government had agreed with Paris to remain in the franc zone, in February 1960 it left anyway, citing autonomy and sovereignty as the main reasons for its departure. Guinea nationalized the French-operated Central Bank of West Africa and its assets and changed its name to the Bank of the Republic of Guinea. The PDG declared: "The colonial franc is dead, pulling down with it in its fall the whole system of economic domination so minutely built up by colonization. Long live the Guinean franc!—Condition, instrument, and symbol of our economic liberation."[117] The government also sought to nationalize the banking sector and in August 1960 announced that banks would be required to hold half their assets in the Bank of the Republic of Guinea; if they did not do so within ten days, they would be taken over. In the end the government took over every bank.[118]

[115] See Victor D. du Bois, "Guinea," in *Political Parties and National Integration in Tropical Africa*, ed. James S. Coleman and Carl G. Rosberg (Berkeley: University of California Press, 1964), 194.

[116] See Victor D. du Bois, "Guinea's Prelude to Independence: Political Authority, 1945–1958," *AUFS Reports West Africa Series* 5, 6 (1962): 1–16.

[117] Quoted in du Bois, "Guinean Economy," 6–7. See also Aguibou Y. Yansané, "Monetary Independence and Transition to Socialism in Guinea," *Journal of African Studies* 6, 3 (1979): 132–43.

[118] See du Bois, "Guinean Economy," 10.

After its dramatic departure from the franc zone, the government turned its attention to the dominance of French firms and French markets in the production and commerce of the Guinean economy. While the rest of French West Africa was selling its products in France and the European Economic Community (EEC), Guinea's leaders denounced the EEC as an instrument of neo-imperialism. Because the country lacked foreign exchange (its exchange needs had been provided for by Paris during the colonial period), Guinea negotiated barter agreements with East Germany, Czechoslovakia, Poland, Hungary, and the Soviet Union—all thought to be less of a threat to autonomy than France because of their intentions and their state socialist economic structure.[119] To make the economy more responsive to the needs of the Guinean people, the government also decreed that business adopt a more "national character" by being headquartered in Conakry and financed by local capital. Then, during the 1960s, Guinea nationalized most manufacturing and commerce, including a large bauxite mining operation, until finally, in 1968, the government simply banned foreign businesspeople altogether.[120]

These efforts had been more organized, at least in principle, by the government when it introduced its Three-Year Plan in 1961. Among the plan's stated objectives were the replacement of the colonial economic structure with a more national, sovereign structure—"economic decolonization," as it was called; the nationalization of foreign and domestic trade; and the achievement of societal equity through socialist planning.[121] What was clear to the government, in the context of its plan making, was that there were costs to the policy, even if the long-term development of Guinea might ultimately legitimate the necessary current sacrifices.[122] For an explanation of how Guinea sustained its autonomy policy despite the enormous costs, Lansiné Kaba proposes the "reminder of the mass mobilization which had occurred for nationalism and independence."[123]

Mali: Economic Nationalism Compromised

Mali's economic strategy was not as dramatic as Guinea's, nor was it as coherent or sustained. First of all, Mali, unlike Guinea, voted to accept de

---

[119] Du Bois, "Guinean Economy," 1–2.

[120] See Leslie L. Rood, "Nationalization and Indigenization in Africa," *Journal of Modern African Studies* 14, 3 (1976): 427–47.

[121] See Riviere, *Guinea*, 110–12; and du Bois, "Guinean Economy," 15–20.

[122] See, for example, Arnold Rivkin, *Nation-Building in Africa: Problems and Prospects* (New Brunswick: Rutgers University Press, 1969), 159–61.

[123] Lansiné Kaba, "From Colonialism to Autocracy: Guinea under Sékou Touré, 1957–1984," in *Decolonization and African Independence*, ed. Gifford and Louis, 230. Also see Kaba, "Guinean Politics: A Critical Overview," *Journal of Modern African Studies* 15, 1 (1977): 25–45.

Gaulle and his constitution in 1958. The vote reflected Malians' relative ambivalence about their relationship to France. Also, Mali did not leave the franc zone in a huff of nationalist assertiveness. Instead, when Mali introduced its own currency in 1962, it insisted that it was in fact remaining in the franc zone and that there was no inconsistency in having an independent currency that would be guaranteed by France.[124]

Like Guinea, postcolonial Mali was a one-party state. The Union Soudanaise, similar to the PDG, sought to make Mali more autonomous from France and explicitly rejected the "neocolonialism" of Senegal. Under Modibo Keita, the Malian government chose "socialism," by which it meant primarily fundamental economic reorganization, especially "vigorous economic decolonization" and a challenge to the dominant position of France and French firms in the Malian economy.[125]

Also as in Guinea, policy makers were well aware that any breaking of economic ties with France would have serious costs, unquestionably large in the short run. The government asserted that Malians were willing to bear the costs of autonomy and to pay for the goals of nation making and state building.[126]

Autonomy, however, required an independent currency, not least because of persistent conflict with the West African central bank over the distribution of credit to Mali's banks: to stimulate the economy, the banking system needed a dramatic expansion of credit, and during 1961–62 the central bank was unwilling to give Mali more than its share. Thus, in order to achieve its domestic economic and social goals, the Malian government simply required an independent currency.[127] Note, however, that this is quite a different motivation from that which underlay the Guinean decision to leave the franc zone, since Guinea's leaders were committed on principle, for reasons of nation making and state building, to having their own currency. Although Mali's Union Soudanaise was committed to similar goals, it was assuredly less committed, and thus the decision to leave the franc zone was made more reluctantly and, in some senses, pragmatically.[128] As Victor du Bois reported, "Mali has gone neither as far as Guinea in its acceptance of radical economic and political orientation toward the East, nor as far as the Ivory Coast in its embrace of the orthodox Western counterpart."[129]

[124] See de Lusignan, *French-Speaking Africa*, 239.

[125] See Aristide R. Zolberg, "The Political Use of Economic Planning in Mali," in *Economic Nationalism in Old and New States*, ed. Harry G. Johnson (Chicago: University of Chicago Press, 1967), 109–10; and John N. Hazard, "Marxian Socialism in Africa: The Case of Mali," *Comparative Politics* 2, 1 (1969): 1–15.

[126] See especially Zolberg, "Economic Planning in Mali," 121. See also Rivkin, *Nation-Building in Africa*, 159–61.

[127] See Zolberg, "Economic Planning in Mali," 114.

[128] On the Union Soudanaise, see Victor D. du Bois, "Mali Five Years after the Referendum," *AUFS Reports West Africa Series* 6, 3 (1963): 1–17, especially 5.

[129] Du Bois, "Mali," 1.

In the broader perspective of the effects of politics on economic performance, Mali's decision to leave the franc zone was anything but pragmatic, however, because its public finances and export industries were utterly dependent on French support. When the government created the Bank of the Republic of Mali and the Malian franc on 1 July 1962, the economy immediately faced the problems that had wreaked havoc on the Guinean economy several years earlier when it left the franc zone: the loss of French price supports decimated exports, and rampant inflation led to economic instability and a decline in the real value of the Malian franc.

As a result of this economic crisis, Mali negotiated its reentry into the franc zone in February 1967, a move that substantially restricted its monetary autonomy.[130] The Malian franc, which remained in existence, was devalued by half; a new central bank subject to greater French influence was created; and the French treasury guaranteed the currency. As a result, of course, the economic autonomy of the Malian government, and certainly its penchant for printing money and offering loans, became quite constrained. Although President Modibo Keita continued to talk the language of nationalist autonomy, socialist change, and postcolonial transformation, Mali's policies were actually quite conservative. According to Jonathan Kirshner, "this uneasy mix satisfied no one," and the military overthrew him in November 1968. After 1968 the new military government, like Indonesia's under Suharto, cultivated a closer economic relationship with the former metropole and substantially liberalized its policies with regard to foreign capital.[131]

Senegal and Ivory Coast: Liberal, "Socialist," and "Miracle" Economies

While Guinea succeeded in achieving autonomy from France, and Mali recoiled at the enormous cost of its own bid for autonomy, the governments of postcolonial Senegal and Ivory Coast never considered autonomy a worthwhile goal—certainly not one worth suffering for. In the starkest of contrasts, as Aguibou Yansané notes, Ivory Coast and Senegal embarked on a "pragmatic path of development with a smooth continuity between the colonial and post-independence eras."[132]

---

[130] On Mali's exit from and reentry into the franc zone, see Kirshner, *Currency and Coercion*, 151–56; and Stasavage, "Monetary Union," 160.

[131] See Kirshner, *Currency and Coercion*, 153–54; and Francis G. Snyder, "An Era Ends in Mali," *Africa Report* 14, 1 (1969): 16–22.

[132] Aguibou Y. Yansané, *Decolonization in West African States with French Colonial Legacy* (Cambridge, Mass.: Schenkman, 1984), 210–11. Also see Yansané, "Decolonization, Dependency, and Development in Africa," in *Decolonization and Dependency: Problems of Development in African Societies*, ed. Yansané (Westport, Conn.: Greenwood, 1980), 27–28; and Michael O'Connor, "Guinea and the Ivory Coast: Contrasts in Economic Development," *Journal of Modern African Studies* 10, 3 (1972): 409–26.

Ivory Coast and Senegal did not seek to make their economies more "national" or more responsive to their societies. With the exception of part of Senegal's phosphate industry, neither nationalized any part of its economy.[133] Senegal passed extremely liberal foreign investment laws to attract French investors, and the French came.[134] Likewise, Ivory Coast enacted economic policy programs designed explicitly not for socioeconomic change or well-defined social objectives. Instead, Ivory Coast sought to create a welcoming investment climate, particularly for the purposes of protecting and encouraging French business. For example, Ivory Coast's 1959 foreign investment law offered foreign investors a five-year tax holiday, a ten-year exemption from import duties on capital goods, and unlimited repatriation of profits.[135] Senegal and Ivory Coast both sought the closest of economic, and political, ties with Paris. Not surprisingly, both staunchly supported the franc zone as well, "in view of the very real economic advantages."[136] The franc zone, for Senegal and Ivory Coast, was "an entire system of economic and financial assistance."[137] So while Guinean leaders were drawing up their radical first (1961–63) economic plan, the rest of French West Africa's new states' plans were being prepared by French experts.[138]

During the 1960s, then, the governments of Senegal and Ivory Coast primarily sought stability and continuity in their foreign economic relations, not dramatic change. The leaders of Ivory Coast believed fundamental continuity would lead to wealth. And economic success was what they got, as they achieved by far the best economic performance in postcolonial Africa. It was quite clear that Ivory Coast's "miracle" economy resulted from its close economic relationship with France and the massive amounts of French aid and investment that flowed in.[139] The Senegalese economy, despite strong

---

[133] See Rood, "Nationalization and Indigenization."

[134] Yansané, *Decolonization in West African States*, 332.

[135] See Bonnie Campbell, "Ivory Coast," in *West African States: Failure and Promise*, ed. John Dunn (Cambridge: Cambridge University Press, 1978); Yansané, *Decolonization in West African States*, chap. 4; and D. K. Fieldhouse, *Black Africa, 1945–1980: Economic Decolonization and Arrested Development* (London: Allen and Unwin, 1986), 191.

[136] De Lusignan, *French-Speaking Africa*, 329. See also Stasavage, "Monetary Union."

[137] De Lusignan, *French-Speaking Africa*, 331. See also Jean Coussy, "The Franc Zone," in *State and Society in Francophone Africa since Independence*, ed. Anthony Kirk-Greene and Daniel Bach (New York: St. Martin's, 1995). For an argument that France subsidized the former colonies that were submissive and accommodating to local capitalists, see G. D. de Bernis, "Some Aspects of the Economic Relationship between France and Its Ex-Colonies," in *Decolonization and After*, ed. W. H. Morris-Jones and Georges Fischer (London: Frank Cass, 1980), 121.

[138] See Catherine Coquery-Vidrovitch, "The Transfer of Economic Power in French-Speaking West Africa," in *Decolonization and African Independence*, ed. Gifford and Louis, 116.

[139] See Timothy C. Weiskell, "Independence and the *Longue Durée*: The Ivory Coast 'Miracle' Reconsidered," in *Decolonization and African Independence*, ed. Gifford and Louis; and Amin, *Neo-Colonialism in West Africa*, 49–75. Also see Marvin P. Miracle, "The Economy of the Ivory

French support, suffered during the 1960s, failing to grow nearly as quickly as the Ivorian economy, primarily because its essentially monoculture economy, based on groundnut production, failed—but not for lack of trying to use the French market to sustain its dependence.[140] Senegal's economy outperformed Guinea's and Mali's during the same period.

Interestingly, Senegal and Ivory Coast were, like both Guinea and Mali, one-party states.[141] The Democratic Party of the Ivory Coast (Parti Démocratique de Côte d'Ivoire, or PDCI), led by Felix Houphouët-Boigny, and the Senegalese Progressive Union (Union Progressiste Sénégalaise, or UPS), led by Leopold Senghor, controlled their respective states, just as in Guinea and Mali. But in contrast to the radicalism of Guinea's and Mali's dominant parties, the PDCI and UPS were conservative, moderate, and fiscally responsible.[142] One ostensible difference between Ivory Coast's and Senegal's powerful parties, a difference that might have changed their political economies substantially, was that Senegal's government was nominally socialist whereas Ivory Coast's was nominally, and actually, capitalist. This difference did not lead to any substantive differences in the two states' economic and political relations with France, however. Neither government sought to change the existing economic ties with France; they sought to benefit from them. In Senegal the UPS's ideology of socialism led the government only to establish a state monopoly in the primary agricultural sector; industry was left to the French, and trade links with France were given highest development priority.[143] The similarity of the foreign

---

Coast," in *The Economies of Africa*, ed. P. Robson and D. A. Lury (London: Allen and Unwin, 1969); and Victor D. du Bois, "The Quiet Revolution: The Ivory Coast in Transition," *AUFS Reports West Africa Series* 5, 1 (1962): 1–10, at 2–3.

[140] Fieldhouse argues that the social bases of the Senegalese state necessitated its economic orientation toward France and made changing the monoculture economy extremely difficult. In any case, Senegalese foreign economic policy was clearly a result of its domestic politics and was not somehow imposed by France. That domestic politics led to such a strategy simply shows that domestic consensus on economic sacrifice for the sake of change could have been legitimated only by some consensus about the national identity of the society. In other words, Senegal's choice for France resulted from its politics, which were different from those of Guinea, for example, in one crucial respect: the power and influence of the nationalists. See Fieldhouse, *Black Africa*, 226–28.

[141] See Aristide R. Zolberg, *Creating Political Order: The Party-States of West Africa* (Chicago: Rand McNally, 1966).

[142] Victor D. du Bois, "The Party and the Government: The Role of the PDCI in the Ivory Coast and African Affairs," *AUFS Reports West Africa Series* 5, 2 (1962): 1–10, 2; R. Mortimer, "From Federation to Francophonia: Senghor's African Policy," *African Studies Review* 15, 2 (1972): 283–306; and W. A. E. Skurnik, *The Foreign Policy of Senegal* (Evanston: Northwestern University Press, 1972).

[143] See Boubacar Barry, "Neocolonialism and Dependence in Senegal, 1960–1980," in *Decolonization and African Dependence*, ed. Gifford and Louis, 281. Also see William J. Foltz, "Senegal," in *Tropical Africa*, ed. Coleman and Rosberg; and Donal B. Cruise O'Brien, "Senegal," in *West African States*, ed. Dunn.

economic policies of Senegal and Ivory Coast was all the more remarkable because of the vastly different bases of support of their governments.[144]

Certainly compared with the radicalism of leaders in Guinea and Mali, as Aristide Zolberg notes, "the willingness of such leaders to cooperate with the colonial power after the first major victory might be interpreted as a sell-out that would cost them popular support." Instead, of course, "rather the opposite took place," which indicates that Houphouët and Senghor were actually fulfilling the mandate that Ivory Coast's and Senegal's societies had given them: to improve economic performance at whatever cost to autonomy.[145] That Ivory Coast was more successful than Senegal in creating and sustaining economic growth is irrelevant to the fact that both sets of leaders believed they had chosen the most rational, profitable path: economic cooperation with France.

Nationalism and Political Economy in Africa

Thus, postcolonial African governments chose one of two economic strategies: continued economic ties with the former metropole and the West or economic autonomy from the former metropole. For most of the 1960s nearly all African governments chose the first strategy, though eventually more demanded and sought increased autonomy, as did Kenya in 1967, Ghana in 1968, and Zambia in 1969. In the early 1960s, however, the moment of independence was economically inconsequential throughout most of Africa, and nowhere less consequential than in francophone Africa. If francophone Africa conceived the most accommodating postcolonial governments, it also gave birth to one of the most demanding: Guinea. French West Africa was a microcosm of the issues of political economy after empire, of the choice for autonomy, with all its costs, or dependence, with all its security.

As in the former Soviet Union, in former French Africa there was considerable variation in the economic strategies pursued by newly independent states. Guinea's strategy of autonomy at all costs during the 1960s resembles Lithuania's, Latvia's, and Estonia's strategies during the 1990s; Mali's hesitant and ultimately failed attempt to achieve autonomy from France resembles Ukraine's inability to sustain its economic autonomy program; and Senegal's and Ivory Coast's acceptance of dependence, with all its political and cultural consequences, was similar to Belarus's willingness to trade autonomy for economic gain.

[144] Stasavage, "Monetary Union," 127.
[145] Zolberg, *Creating Political Order*, 17–18. Also see du Bois, "Quiet Revolution," 9, which suggests that rather than appeal to nationalism, Houphouët hoped the loyalty of Ivorians would result from "general economic progress among the populace."

As in the former Soviet Union, the word *pragmatism* in postcolonial Africa was code for a newly independent state's willingness to maintain close ties with the former metropole, and any other motivation for policy—socialism, radicalism, decolonization, and nationalism—was the opposite of pragmatic: ideological, in other words. The most important source of an ideological approach to international political economy was the arguments of the nationalists, and this was true in Senegal and Ivory Coast as well.

Moreover, it was in Senegal and Ivory Coast that anticolonial nationalism in French West Africa first emerged. In Senegal, from 1958 to the early 1960s, the Democratic Assembly of Africa demanded that the country reject de Gaulle's 1958 constitution and that it break economically and politically from France. But unlike Sékou Touré's PDG in Guinea, the assembly failed to rally society behind the nationalist goals of political independence and economic autonomy.[146] The same was true in Ivory Coast, whose nationalists remained popular among Ivorian youth during the presidency of Houphouët.[147]

The success of the nationalists thus seems to be the most important variable in the four countries: if the Senegalese and Ivorian nationalists had been able to reject the 1958 constitution, choose independence, and break economic ties with France, they would have. According to Tony Smith, "the key variable to analyze in order to understand the colonial response to metropolitan policy is the local power position of the predominant nationalist elite." Nationalists demanding autonomy thus fought both "against the imperial power and against other local groups striving to replace it."[148]

The greater irony is that the president of Ivory Coast, Houphouët himself, had been both an Ivorian and a pan-African nationalist in the late 1940s. With Sékou Touré, he had helped found the RDA and led the Ivorian section of it. Ultimately, Houphouët altered the orientation of his party. According to Smith, Houphouët, a planter who benefited from the Franco-Ivorian economic relationship, must have decided that his, and his country's, future lay with France. Houphouët's stance led to the perception that he was the quintessential spokesman of the African bourgeoisie.[149] The source of his change of heart is uncertain, but by 1953 it was clearly complete, as Houphouët admonished his independence-minded compatriots in the rest of French West Africa that they should reconsider their demands: "If you don't want to vegetate in bamboo huts, concentrate your efforts on

---

[146] See Fieldhouse, *Black Africa*, 212; and Foltz, "Senegal."

[147] See Victor D. du Bois, "The Student-Government Conflict in the Ivory Coast," *AUFS Reports West Africa Series* 8, 1 (1965): 1–16.

[148] Tony Smith, *The Pattern of Imperialism* (Cambridge: Cambridge University Press, 1981), 120–21.

[149] Smith, *Pattern of Imperialism*, 118.

growing good cocoa and good coffee. They will fetch a good price and you will become rich."[150] Never mind, he seemed to argue, that the good price came at a cost: political and economic autonomy. Guinea's Sékou Touré's familiar nationalist proclamation that Guineans prefer liberty to riches is the opposite perspective on the choice. Sékou Touré called Ivory Coast's policy selling out, and Houphouët called it pragmatism: clearly, they perceived the same material incentives in radically different ways.

Recall from chapter 6 the pronouncement of Belarusian president Lukashenko that the national interest was subject to accounting. Houphouët certainly agreed, as indicated by his concern for efficiency and growth: "It is in the interest of the Ivory Coast systematically to turn its back on an Africanization [program] which considers diplomas rather than efficiency." Such thinking infuriated Ivory Coast's nationalist youth because it was the utter opposite of their conception of the national interest.[151] A nationalist does not calculate the national interest by attempting to maximize efficiency and current income. Houphouët, in contrast, insisted that nationalism was "outmoded" and needed to be "transcended" for a prosperous Ivorian future.[152]

It is true that Senegal and Ivory Coast traditionally had also been privileged French colonies, the largest beneficiaries of French development policies. Still, Guinea was among them in having the best economic prospects of French colonies in the 1950s, and it too had received enormous amounts of public and private investment channeled through Paris.[153] Mali, poorer and less developed than the other three, certainly had no economic rationale for leaving the franc zone and quite a lot to lose financially.

Monetary union in French West Africa, like monetary union in the former Soviet Union, represented much more than the costs and benefits of a common currency; it represented a whole package of economic and

[150] Quoted in Smith, *Pattern of Imperialism*, 118.

[151] Houphouët is quoted in du Bois, "Student-Government Conflict," 8. Du Bois also recounts the nationalists' reactions to Houphouët's analysis.

[152] See du Bois, "Party and the Government," 9.

[153] See, for example, the discussion in Elliot J. Berg, "The Economic Basis of Political Choice in French West Africa," *American Political Science Review* 54, 2 (1960): 391–405. Berg argues persuasively that economic differences among French West African colonies and, later, newly independent states conditioned their governments' preferences about federal relations among them. He also argues, much less persuasively, that the conditions of economic integration into the metropolitan economy, particularly the colonies' relative development, strongly discouraged the colonies from choosing independence in 1958. If the Ivory Coast were so advanced even during the 1950s, it should have been willing, according to Berg's logic, to risk independence, and Berg acknowledges the problem on 405. The bigger problem, of course, is Guinea, which clearly risked enormous economic sacrifice for choosing independence and, compared with Ivory Coast and Senegal on a number of material variables, including Berg's, should not have chosen so anomalous a path in 1958.

financial relations with France which, on balance, were extremely positive for the newly independent states. It was not the distribution of costs and benefits that explains franc-zone participation—why Guinea and Mali left while Senegal and Ivory Coast, among others, remained.

It was, rather, politics. As Robert Mundell concluded from his assessment of African monetary arrangements, "Monetary agreements have historically been one of the most reliable barometers of politics."[154] David Stasavage offers a compelling interpretation of these politics and argues that transnational contacts were the "central vehicle" for the continuity of the franc zone and therefore also for maintaining the ties created during the colonial period. Whereas elites in Senegal and Ivory Coast had been educated and had held political posts in France, elites in Guinea and Mali, for the most part, had not.[155]

These transnational ties also affected African elites' acceptance or rejection of the idea, and ideology, of Eurafrica, of a community of French and African peoples that was to have linked the colonies to the metropole.[156] Although transnational contacts certainly helped create such a Franco-African elite identity, it must have eventually become important in its own right. This identity clearly, as Stasavage shows, altered the way a number of African leaders, especially Senghor of Senegal and Houphouët of Ivory Coast, interpreted the economic interests of their new states.

The central difficulty with a purely elite-centered explanation, however, is that the Senegalese and Ivorian societies readily accepted and rewarded the "neocolonial" economic policies of their governments as well as those policies' cultural foundations. This is not to say that the societies of Senegal and Ivory Coast, or Senghor and Houphouët themselves, somehow longed to be French. Rather, the ambiguities of their identities prevented the arguments of the nationalists from winning the newly independent states' central political debate: to be with France or not. And the potential overlap of their identities with a broader identity of the transnational francophone community did not rule out close economic and cultural ties to France.[157] If France offered economic benefits in exchange for their political acquiescence, why should they not accept the deal? The nationalists had an answer to this question; most Senegalese and Ivorians did not.

[154] Robert A. Mundell, "African Trade, Politics, and Money," in *Africa and Monetary Integration*, ed. Rodrigue Tremblay (Montreal: Les Éditions HRW, 1972), 57.

[155] Stasavage, "Monetary Union," 143–44.

[156] Stasavage, "Monetary Union," 153–57 and 165. See also Guy Martin, "Africa and the Ideology of Eurafrica," *Journal of Modern African Studies* 20, 2 (1982): 221–38.

[157] Patrick Manning, *Francophone Sub-Saharan Africa, 1880–1995* (Cambridge: Cambridge University Press, 1998), 162–63.

There was one African twist to the political economy of nationalism after empire. Most nationalists in newly independent African states, and certainly in the former French colonies, associated the idea of their own nations with that of a pan-African nation—and, therefore, with a pan-African national-ism. This is further testament to the flexibility of nationalist ideologies. And it also shows yet again how easy it is for anticolonial nationalists to cooper-ate with one another in their attempts to bring down an empire, as hap-pened in the moments before imperial collapse throughout the twentieth century. In the case of Africa, this transnational cooperation among anti-colonial nationalists, institutionalized in the form of the Democratic As-sembly of Africa, persisted into the nationalist ideologies of the postcolo-nial period and led to a variety of halting, and ultimately unsuccessful, attempts at regional reintegration in defiance of French hegemony.[158] The pan-African nationalists did not reject the idea of a larger, natural com-munity of Africans, but they certainly rejected the idea of Eurafrica.

Finally, as in Indonesia, nationalists in postcolonial Africa equated West-ern capitalism and imperialism, a fact that led them to include aspects of socialist ideology within their nationalisms. Socialism, in this perspective, was understood to be the promotion of all of society, rather than the profit of a few, as well as the creation of an economy autonomous from the for-mer metropole.[159]

CONCLUSIONS OF A COMPARATIVE PERSPECTIVE

In the broadest sense, this chapter was about the variable strategies of newly independent states, the states carved from the ruins of empire. In postimperial political contexts state identities are necessarily in flux, am-biguous, and unformed. So are state institutions themselves since another commonality of imperial successor states has been their incomplete state-ness. The postimperial state is incipient, and the options for state building are both demanding and wide open. Contingency and choice defined pol-icy making in these moments. Foreign policy in newly independent states thus has always been about managing dependence, choosing a state iden-tity, and defining the nation.[160] One thing that is clear from these case stud-

[158] See, for example, Thomas Hodgkin, *Nationalism in Colonial Africa* (London: Frederick Muller, 1956).

[159] See L. Gray Cowan, *The Dilemmas of African Independence* (New York: Walker, 1964), 8–9; and Dharam P. Ghai, "Concepts and Strategies of Economic Independence," *Journal of Mod-ern African Studies* 11, 1 (1973): 21–42, especially 37–42. For a similar conclusion about Guinean socialism, see Kaba, "From Colonialism to Autocracy," 240.

[160] See especially Robert C. Good, "State-Building as a Determinant of Foreign Policy in the New States," in *Neutralism and Nonalignment: The New States in World Affairs*, ed. Laurence

ies is that the choice of an economic strategy has invariably depended on the identity of the society within a new state.

This finding is related to a more general, analytical claim: specific features of postimperial orders inherently politicize national identities. New statehood offers a pivotal moment of choice for a government to articulate an identity for its state. At the same time, dissatisfied successor states, as well as the former metropole, may object not only to the boundaries of newly independent states but also to the authority and autonomy their governments claim for them. These two features—new statehood and contested sovereignty—have caused national identity to be the central axis of debate about the reorganization of economic relations among postimperial states. The collapse of political authority, as well as the process of its reconstruction, thus politicizes social identities that in other times may be less salient in international relations. Postimperial moments in the twentieth century were defined by nationalist movements that were goal-oriented and sought to set the terms of societal debate about the political-economic future of the new state.

Related to this fact is another set of empirical conclusions drawn from the history of postimperial politics: nationalist movements have consistently been products of their ideological context, and nationalism, it turns out, is an extremely malleable form of politics.[161] As Bunce argues, nationalism has been linked to a wide variety of political projects and ideologies; nationalism, in other words, is wanton.[162] Anti-imperial nationalist movements tended, ideologically, to be antihegemonic. In postimperial Asia and Africa, nationalist movements were linked to socialism because capitalism, the economic system of the metropole, was what came before. In fact, as the case studies showed, nationalists in newly independent African and Asian states frequently equated imperialism and capitalism. But compare the socialist nationalisms of the 1950s and 1960s with the capitalist nationalisms of the 1990s in post-Soviet Eurasia, where Communism, imposed by a Moscow-based Soviet empire, was what came before—at least according to the nationalists. Thus, nationalist movements have had both a geographic and an ideological direction against which they defined their goals.

W. Martin (New York: Praeger, 1962), 5–10. On the issues of stateness and state building in postimperial states, see also Robert H. Jackson, *Quasi-States: Sovereignty, International Relations, and the Third World* (Cambridge: Cambridge University Press, 1990); and M. Crawford Young, *The African Colonial State in Comparative Perspective* (New Haven: Yale University Press, 1994).

[161] A related example is identified by Rupert Emerson, who showed that anti-imperial nationalisms were sometimes linked to democracy but at other times not. See his *From Empire to Nation: The Rise to Self-Assertion of Asian and African Peoples* (Cambridge: Harvard University Press, 1960), 213–54.

[162] Bunce, *Subversive Institutions*, 147–51.

Money and Trade

Newly independent states were not born with currencies and central banks. When there was political will to bear the costs of leaving the currency union, their governments created national moneys and national banks. Monetary dissolution often followed political disintegration, but not always.

The former metropoles of empires, if they were strong enough, frequently engaged in what Kirshner calls monetary entrapment, that is, they sought to create political acquiescence in member states of their currency unions.[163] To make entrapment work, the governments that sponsor a currency union must make membership attractive so that member states actually benefit substantially from the economic relationship. Thus, the core state must be "willing to make economic sacrifices to maintain the existence of a currency area."[164] France was willing to do so.

But as shown in chapter 3, by 1993 Russia was not willing to sacrifice for the sake of the ruble zone. Although the ruble zone had also had its cases of early exit, like Guinea's and Mali's exit from the franc zone, a number of post-Soviet states remained in the ruble zone and emphasized their intentions to do so indefinitely. And why not, since the implicit subsidies associated with ruble-zone membership, such as low-cost energy, were so large. Eventually, the Russian government, for several reasons, decided not to subsidize the ruble zone anymore and essentially expelled the rest of the members. But if Russia had been as willing as France to pay for its regional monetary hegemony, the ruble zone might have remained the economic center of gravity for as many as half the post-Soviet states.

All postimperial states would have benefited from free trade with one another. Their economies were unavoidably interdependent. Economists, both within and without, recommended free trade. Sometimes, as was the case with Austria, Senegal, Ivory Coast, and Belarus, the governments of newly independent states agreed to free trade, and when they did, they agreed to much more—customs unions, if other states were willing. But those who rejected free trade with the former empire—the vast majority of newly independent states—ruled it out completely. Political boundaries have always divided the imperial economy into smaller pieces. No proposal to put all those pieces back together has ever succeeded. The nationalists never allowed it.

Theories of IPE and the History of Postimperial Politics

These ten historical cases from interwar Europe (Austria, Hungary, Czechoslovakia, Romania, and Yugoslavia), 1950s southeast Asia

---

[163] Kirshner, *Currency and Coercion*, 117–18.

[164] Kirshner, *Currency and Coercion*, 153. See also 150, where Kirshner shows that "France attempted to make membership in the franc zone as appealing as possible."

(Indonesia), and 1960s Africa (Guinea, Mali, Senegal, and Ivory Coast) show that the relations among successor states of empires have been politicized more by national identities than by any other single factor. This was just as true in 1990s Eurasia.

Theories of international political economy derived in the Realist and Liberal traditions cannot explain the patterns of economic relations that emerged in any of these four postimperial political contexts. The central failing of Realist and Liberal theories of IPE is that nationalism creates a kind of nationalist politics for which they cannot account. Postimperial governments chose their strategies in ways that neither Realists nor Liberals could have predicted or explained.

Liberalism: Incentives and Institutionalization in Economic Cooperation. As in the post-Soviet cases described in chapters 3–6, however, there were cases for which Realist and Liberal theories were apparently useful. For example, Liberal theories seem potentially to explain the cases of acquiescence and economic cooperation, such as 1920s Austria and 1960s Senegal and Ivory Coast. These three states bore a striking resemblance to 1990s Belarus. All sought economic cooperation and integration with some other state or set of states, and the reason was simple: there were powerful material incentives for them to do so and no political commitment to inhibit them. In addition, with the exception of Austria's political-economic turn toward Germany, the institutionalization of economic cooperation influenced their preferences for cooperation. As we have seen, however, it was the ambiguity of Austrian national identity that allowed the Austrian economic problem to be framed in terms of forsaking independent statehood. Austrians did not lack a national identity. Instead, interwar Austrians lacked consensus on the meaning of their identity, and their state, as a result, lacked an agreed-on purpose.

Several other states, Senegal and Ivory Coast included, were prepared to strike the same bargain: political acquiescence and integration in return for subsidies. Although Senegalese and Ivorian nationalists complained bitterly about their governments' betrayal of the nation, their views were unpopular. Many Senegalese and Ivorians, including government elites, shared a francophone identity that did not rule out economic cooperation with France.

The causes of the Belarusian political and economic Anschluss with Russia during the 1990s were remarkably similar. As shown in chapter 6, Belarusian national identity was ambiguous and contested. Most Belarusians shared a pan-Slavic or Soviet identity that was complementary to Russian identity. As a result, the Belarusian government sought an external solution to the state's economic crisis. The Belarusian, Austrian, Senegalese, and Ivorian governments considered their states too small and too interdependent to exist on their own. Nevertheless, in post-Soviet Eurasia, interwar Europe, and postcolonial Africa there were smaller and more economically dependent states than these four, and they did not choose to trade political sovereignty for the potential of economic gain. The same incentives existed for many postimperial states. It was the ambiguity and fragmentation of national identity in these four states that caused their politics of acquiescence. The application of Liberal theories of IPE to postimperial politics depends on such a contested and ambiguous national identity and on the unpopularity of the nationalists, who never supported such cooperative policies with other successor states or former metropoles. Such cases thus were rare in the postimperial politics of the twentieth century.

Realism: Autonomy and Reorientation. Much more common were the governments that pursued autonomy at the expense of certain short-term economic gain. In these cases the nationalist political parties either made foreign economic policy themselves or did not need to because everyone else agreed with their external political-economic goals. Realist and Nationalist theories of political economy were the potential sources for an explanation of the economic discord of 1920s eastern Europe, 1950s southeast Asia, and 1960s Africa. The expectations of the two theoretical traditions overlap substantially. There are several reasons, however, to prefer a Nationalist explanation for these politics to a Realist explanation.

First, at least in post-Habsburg eastern Europe, a focus on power politics alone is underdetermining. Austria and Hungary were much too weak to warrant all the counterbalancing that Czechoslovakia, Romania, and Yugoslavia did during the 1920s and 1930s.[165] Although Vienna was still the financial center of the region, Austria, obsessed with its own internal weakness, clearly harbored no aggressive intentions to use its financial leverage on the politics of the successor states. And Hungary, though obviously resentful of the territorial redistributions of the peace treaties, was demilitarized; the Hungarian military threat was therefore unquestionably illusory. There is no doubt that it was the Austria and Hungary of the Habsburg past that Czechoslovakia, Romania, and Yugoslavia feared rather than the objectively feeble interwar rump states. Identity and ideology are necessary components of a determinate account of the 1920s international political economy.

Second, as indicated in previous chapters, a coherent economic nationalism results from societal consensus on the foreign economic policy goals embedded in nationalist ideology. Nationalists always have at least one external direction for their concerns about autonomy, an "other" against which identity is defined. Therefore, such a societal consensus gives

[165] See, for example, Deák, "Fall of Austria-Hungary," 97.

foreign economic policy the same direction—at least one state against which concerns for economic security are defined.

At the same time, the context of nationalist mobilization can orient foreign economic policy toward some other cultural or political space. The Lithuanian case illustrates this two-way directionality: economic nationalism oriented the country both away from Russia and toward the European Union. In 1920s eastern and central Europe, economic nationalisms in Czechoslovakia, Romania, and Yugoslavia were oriented against Austria and Hungary but not coherently toward any other states. Thus, in these cases the directionality of nationalism was one-way.

This variation reflects in part an important difference between the international political and economic contexts of the 1920s and 1990s. There was a wide range of legitimate and plausible theories of economic development earlier in the century, and interwar world politics were extraordinarily fragmented. Strategies of autarky were common during the interwar years, and protectionism was the rule in Europe. But inward-oriented economic strategies were profoundly delegitimized after the cold war, indeed by the end of the cold war itself. In the post–cold war world the relatively liberal, open economic development model is widely considered to have beaten protectionist, closed models in theory and in practice. In other words, the days of self-reliant and autarkic economic development seem, for now, to have passed. Instead, post–cold war governments tend to seek cooperation and integration with some group of states, whether that group is defined by politics, region, or issue area. It seems that economic integration with someone is necessary, even if it is not with everyone.

The directionality of economic nationalism was even more interesting in 1950s southeast Asia and 1960s Africa because of the additional component of ideological directionality. Indonesia, Guinea, and Mali clearly had one central direction away from which they intended to reorient their economies—Indonesia away from the Netherlands, and Guinea and Mali away from France. Both Realist political economy's balance-of-power considerations and Nationalist political economy's emphasis on identity would have expected these policies; therefore, this aspect of their reorientation is theoretically overdetermined. But recall that nationalism in those three states was linked to socialism and that Indonesia, Guinea, and Mali were, to a significant extent, interested in reorienting their economies away from all capitalist economies and toward socialist economies. Their policies certainly fell well short of any kind of alliance with the Soviet bloc, and each maintained its neutrality and nonaligned status. But in the most coherently nationalist governments of southeast Asia and Africa, there were important elements of directionality away from capitalism, represented by the former empire, and toward socialism, represented by a rejection of the economic institutions of imperialist Europe.

In addition, Guinea's and Mali's nationalists were also pan-Africanists and hoped ideally to integrate their economies into a pan-African economy that could unite them against France and the other imperialist powers. This is another element of directionality that is not captured by Realism's emphasis on statism and the pursuit of mere autonomy. For Indonesia, Guinea, and Mali, economic policies were reorientation with a purpose and a direction.

Moreover, even if that directionality was not as strong and as clear as in 1990s Eurasia, the issue of internal distribution is another way to distinguish economic nationalism from economic statism. In chapter 2 I showed that the internal distribution of income and wealth has traditionally been a central concern of nationalists and, therefore, an important element of economic nationalism. To date, distribution has not been as important as reorientation and autonomy in the economic nationalisms of the former Soviet Union. In contrast, in all the historical cases internal distribution rivaled autonomy as the dominant economic concern of nationalists. From nostrification in the 1920s to Indonesianization in the 1950s and Africanization in the 1960s, the politics of redistributing economic power from non-nationals to nationals was a central goal of postimperial governments led or influenced by nationalists. So although nationalists in postimperial states sought to make their state institutions more coherent, they also sought to make them more responsive to the national economy and to give their economic institutions national content. Realist political economy can explain only the state building, not its crucial intersection with nation making. In these cases the "national economy" always meant much more than a statewide economy; it meant an economy for the nation and, therefore, an economy for the sake of the population rather than for the state itself.

Third, the most important reason to privilege a Nationalist explanation for postimperial international political economy over a Realist explanation is the most straightforward: an explanation based on national identity can account for the variation in economic strategies as well as their motivation. That is, Realism can explain many of these postimperial cases, but there is an important set of cases (Austria, Senegal, Ivory Coast, and Belarus) that it cannot. There is also the problem of a state such as Mali, which, like Ukraine, retreated from its autonomy policies when the price turned out to be too high. And even if it were possible eventually to explain those cases with an ad hoc account based on variables drawn from Realist theory, such an explanation still would not be compelling. This is simply because the actual politics that determined postimperial economic strategies were about nationalism. When local nationalists were powerful and influential, strategy was ostensibly what Realist theories would have expected. When local nationalists were weak and marginalized, strategy was ostensibly what Liberal theories would have expected. I have argued that the success or failure of the nationalists reflected the content and contestation of national identity. And a systematic approach to international political economy based on national identity can make sense of the universe of postimperial cases, thus resolving an interesting set of empirical puzzles.

Chapter Eight

Conclusions

It is not a surprising conclusion that nationalisms and national identities influence the economic relations among states. But the contemporary study of international political economy lacks a fully articulated framework to explain those causal relationships. The field of IPE frequently treats nationalism and statism as equivalent concepts, but theoretical logic and empirical evidence suggest that they should be distinct and that scholars should revisit the Nationalist theoretical tradition. Thus, in this book I have put forward a theoretical agenda to distinguish a Nationalist perspective on IPE (based on national identity) from the Realist perspective (based on statism and power) and to advance the Nationalist perspective as an important explanatory paradigm in its own right.

The empirical puzzle of post-Soviet economic relations illustrates the theoretical arguments I have proposed. Understanding the national sources of foreign economic policies required research into the motivations and interpretations of post-Soviet governments. Describing the societal sources of those interpretations required an understanding of how post-Soviet societies created and contested their historical memories. Beyond the detailed analysis of the three states presented here, I draw several broader conclusions about nationalism after empire, the study of nationalism in IPE, and the nature of anarchy, identity, and realpolitik in the international system.

AFTER EMPIRE

Post-Soviet states inherited a material reality that was similar for all of them. Russia was clearly the dominant state in the region, and all the other fourteen were economically dependent on Russia. The governments of those fourteen states interpreted that material reality through their specific cultural lenses, which varied substantially among them.

By the end of the 1990s, ten years after the breakup of the USSR, post-Soviet states had sorted themselves into three groups defined by their stances toward the Commonwealth of Independent States and what they considered the "West." I have focused on Lithuania, Ukraine, and Belarus as representatives of these three patterns. The Lithuanian government interpreted economic dependence on Russia as a problem to be solved. So did the Ukrainian government, though much of Ukrainian society disagreed. And the Belarusian government interpreted economic dependence on Russia as part of its comprehensive, mutually beneficial economic relationship with a large neighbor that was also a military ally. By 2000, then, remarkable diversity had developed among post-Soviet states.

Diverse interpretations of the Eurasian regional economy had evolved within post-Soviet societies as well. Some people thought economic reintegration was prudent. Others considered it myopic and dangerous to their autonomy and looked to radical change and reorientation as a longer-term solution. Sometimes it seemed that political and economic actors had preferences that accorded with ostensibly objective material incentives. The organizations of industrialists throughout the former Soviet Union, for example, recognized their dependence on one another and on traditional markets and therefore pushed for economic reintegration. But other actors' goals seemed to be derived ideologically and retrospectively rather than materially and prospectively. A significant number of societal actors shared a leftover Soviet identity, for instance, and they still believed in the Communist union they had been promised. Some societal actors seemed to be influenced by unlikely outcomes and improbable incentives, relying on heroic assumptions about the region's economic future and their place in it. Others believed their economies would be saved by inexhaustible Russian subsidies or IMF membership. Each society engaged in an internal debate about what to do next.

Internal debates about the state's proper external economic orientation were linked to debates about the meaning of the nation, or the content of the national identity that a society collectively shared. National identity was without question the axis of debate. Nationalists in post-Soviet states interpreted economic dependence on Russia as a threat to the autonomy and security of the state. They derived that interpretation from their version of history, which treated the Soviet Union as a Russian empire that had subjugated them. The crucial issue was not the accuracy of these "national" histories but whether post-Soviet societies agreed about them. Those who disagreed with the nationalists' interpretation of Russia also tended to disagree with the nationalists' demands for economic autonomy. The outcomes of these societal debates about the meaning of the nation led to several of the most significant political results in the region as well, including which interpretation of the nation became ascendant, which interpretation of Russia influenced the government, and ultimately, which economic policies the government adopted. Thus, the single most important influence on the economic relations within and among post-Soviet states during the 1990s was national identity.

Parallels throughout the twentieth century abound. When empires collapsed, successor states were forced to choose between economic continuity and change. Similar debates arose within the societies of the successor states of the Habsburg, Dutch, and French empires. Each successor state became either polarized by contrasting interpretations of the nation or galvanized by consensus on national purpose. Viewing the reorganization of economic relations among post-Soviet states in a comparative, historical perspective therefore offers the possibility of evaluating the influence of highly politicized national identities on regional economies in several different contexts. These were good historical moments to understand nationalisms.

Postimperial nationalisms everywhere were linked to a wide variety of ideologies. Soviet and post-Soviet nationalist movements were linked to capitalist transition because Communism was putatively an exploitative economic system imposed by imperial rule. Nationalist movements in Indonesia and French West Africa were linked to socialist goals because capitalism was regarded as an exploitative economic system imposed by European colonizers. The formative contexts of various nationalisms—ideological as well as spatial—influenced their specific political and geographic directionality. Many nationalists apparently believed that if whatever came before was wrong, then its opposite must be right.

THE STUDY OF NATIONALISM

Surprisingly, a large divide exists between scholarship on nationalism as a cause and nationalism as a consequence. Scholarship specifically focused on the political-economic consequences of nationalism is comparatively rare, and it is frequently based on mistaken assumptions about the primordial origins of nations and the universal malevolence of nationalism. In contrast, the most influential and theoretically sophisticated scholarship on nationalism has traditionally dealt with the great question of origins: Why nationalism? Scholars such as Karl Deutsch, Ernest Gellner, E. J. Hobsbawm, and Benedict Anderson have explored why nationalism, and nationalist discourse, emerged throughout the world.[1] Their consensus, reached from different theoretical starting points, is that nationalism exists not because there are or have always been nations but because people believe in the existence and mythological timelessness of their nations. I have attempted to build on this consensus on the causes of nationalism by exploring the variety of nations as cultural symbols and national identities as social constructions. Rather than deal with the singular origins of nationalism, however, I have focused on the variety of consequences of nationalisms.

NATIONALISMS, NATIONAL IDENTITIES, AND IPE

Nationalisms are proposals for the content of national identity. National identities are collectively held understandings of a society's history and the purposes of its political authority and economic activity. National identities whose content is widely shared in a society have a number of influences on how governments approach the making of foreign economic policy. Consensually shared national identities endow policy with social purpose. A vision of the nation's future can engender sacrifice in pursuit of the fundamental goals connected to the nation and therefore can also lengthen the time horizons of a society and government. And national identities, because they are often defined in opposition to specific other nations and states, specify a direction for foreign economic policy, away from the nation's "other." At certain historical junctures national identities have been defined toward broader cultural spaces into which a nation was supposed to integrate.

I have used these premises to reformulate a distinctively Nationalist perspective on IPE. Thus, I have distinguished the causal logic of an approach based on national identity as the central explanatory variable from Realism's emphasis on the distribution of power. I have also distinguished the concept of economic nationalism, defined as economic policy that follows the national purpose and direction, from economic statism, which Realists understand as economic policy in pursuit of international and domestic autonomy and power, implemented by an autonomous state. Economic

[1] Karl W. Deutsch, *Nationalism and Social Communication*, 2d ed. (Cambridge: MIT Press, 1966); Ernest Gellner, *Nations and Nationalism* (Ithaca: Cornell University Press, 1981); E. J. Hobsbawm, *Nations and Nationalism since 1780*, 2d ed. (Cambridge: Cambridge University Press, 1992); and Benedict R. O'G. Anderson, *Imagined Communities: Reflections on the Origins and Spread of Nationalism* (London: Verso, 1991).

statism, often construed as simple mercantilism, is an important conceptual foundation of the Realist tradition in IPE. Economic nationalism, if it is related to *nationalism*, cannot serve a similar purpose.

There are limits to the usefulness of a Nationalist perspective on IPE because, like the other broad perspectives of Realism and Liberalism, it is based primarily on a single explanatory variable and a distinctive causal logic. Also like these other approaches, the Nationalist tradition is not a theory with specific causal relationships that can be tested and falsified; instead, it is a way to organize research to understand the influence of nationalisms and national identities on the economic relations among states.[2] What I have proposed is a way to think about the relationship between national identity and political economy.

I have not suggested that scholars should think only about that relationship when trying to understand patterns of monetary and trade cooperation and discord. Other important variables are involved, of course, as well as other influences on how governments interpret the material reality of the world economy and their actual and proper place in it. A Nationalist perspective is not general to all circumstances and contexts. This is not a shortcoming, for no approach to IPE can be universal. Nor should any strive to be. I suggest that the study of IPE and IR would benefit from greater attention to the contexts within which different theoretical perspectives are likely to be more useful or less so. Additional theoretical and empirical work on the usefulness of a Nationalist perspective is necessary, but it is already clear that the collapse of empires throughout the twentieth century—and the changing state identities that accompanied those postimperial moments—required that the contestation of national identities be more in the foreground of politics than is usually the case. When state identities are in flux, the influence of national identities becomes more obvious. National identities are often underlying social facts that are so taken for granted that we hardly notice their subtle and persistent influence. At times, however, debates about the nation become explicit, and the outcomes of those debates are consequential during succeeding decades. Future generations of Lithuanians, Ukrainians, and Belarusians, for example, will find that the choices their forebears made in the 1990s set them on trajectories and gave their nations and states identities that once institutionalized become difficult even to imagine to change.

This argument has implications for how IPE and IR scholars consider the task of theory building and the influence of context on the causal relationships they propose. The broad theoretical perspectives on IPE reviewed in this book—Liberalism, Realism, Nationalism, Institutionalism—are

---

[2] Specific falsifiable explanations can be derived within the Nationalist perspective as well, as I have shown.

useful for a number of reasons. They offer baseline expectations for emerging patterns of economic relations among states. They help scholars organize alternate explanations for specific empirical questions. These theoretical perspectives also fit within even broader analytical orientations, rationalism and constructivism, that distinguish modes of reasoning from one another. But they are not usefully conceived as abstract competitors. I have proposed the Nationalist perspective as a distinct causal logic and applied it successfully to several sets of cases. These are important cases, spanning nearly a century and covering four continents and twenty-four countries. There is reason to believe, therefore, that the causal logic proposed here will be useful for resolving many other empirical puzzles. But larger conclusions about the influence of national identities on the world economy must await the research questions and answers that produce them.

Constructivist approaches to IPE offer a great deal of promise. The dominant theories of IPE emphasize the influence of the material facts of the world economy—means, incentives, and regulatory institutions. Constructivist theories of IPE focus on the social facts of the world economy, which are no less important or influential. Collective identities, in particular, influence the purposes ascribed to economic activity, the meanings of economic relationships, and societies' and governments' interpretations of the world economy. The *national* identities analyzed here are just a part of the story.

ANARCHY, NATIONAL IDENTITY, AND STATE IDENTITY

The collapse of the Soviet Union raised issues of identity that are relevant to still other theoretical discussions in the field of IR. The work of Alexander Wendt and Iain Johnston sparked an interesting debate about the nature of state identities and realpolitik (the power politics of Realism) in the absence of centralized authority, or anarchy, that characterizes international politics. In an influential article Wendt argued that anarchy need not inherently produce the exclusively self-regarding, oppositional identities that Realist theorists assumed.[3] States, through the interaction among them, could in principle transform their identities, and their interests, even under anarchy. Power politics and the exclusively "self-help" international system in which states now find themselves, according to Wendt, could have turned out differently, and could yet still do so.

This argument led Jonathan Mercer to criticize Wendt using social identity theory (SIT) from social psychology. According to Mercer, even if the

[3] Alexander Wendt, "Anarchy Is What States Make of It: The Social Construction of Power Politics," *International Organization* 46, 2 (1992): 391–425.

anarchical structure of international politics itself does not lead necessarily to competitive identities and competitive relations among states, there are cognitive reasons for power politics and a system based on self-help. In particular, according to Mercer and the findings of SIT, intergroup relations under anarchy inherently create oppositional identities and a self-help international system.[4]

Iain Johnston raises similar issues in his work on Chinese strategic culture.[5] Johnston argues that Realist theorists have conflated their description of realpolitik with their structural explanation of it. In place of the Realists' assumption that anarchy leads to realpolitik, Johnston emphasizes the necessity of a "parabellum" strategic culture shared by state elites. Thus, Johnston proposes to study the ideational roots of realpolitik, or, in his phrase, "cultural realism." Although much recent work by constructivist IR scholars emphasizes political practices that deviate from the expectations of Realism, Johnston urges constructivists to challenge Realist theory more fundamentally by showing that even nondeviant power politics are derived from norms and identities.

Some of the abstract formulations offered in this book have implications for this theoretical debate about the nature of anarchy. I have emphasized the importance of distinguishing between national identities and state identities. National identities are the collective identities of societies that understand themselves to be nations; state identities refer to the polities that govern those societies. This distinction has generally been absent in the theoretical debate between Wendt and Mercer, who focus on state identities.

Nations and States in Post-Soviet Eurasia

The evolution of post-Soviet politics shows how important it is to include national identity in this discussion. According to Barry Posen, the collapse of a state or empire creates a situation of "emerging anarchy," and Realism "explicitly addresses the consequences of anarchy."[6] For neo-Realists, the relations among post-Soviet states should have become competitive, with power politics predominating, simply because of the absence of central authority. For Wendt, the identities of the fifteen new post-Soviet states were

[4] Jonathan Mercer, "Anarchy and Identity," *International Organization* 49, 2 (1995): 229–52. For Wendt's reaction, see his *Social Theory of International Politics* (Cambridge: Cambridge University Press, 1999), 241–43.

[5] Alastair Iain Johnston, *Cultural Realism: Strategic Culture and Grand Strategy in Chinese History* (Princeton: Princeton University Press, 1995), and "Cultural Realism and Strategy in Maoist China," in *The Culture of National Security*, ed. Peter J. Katzenstein (New York: Columbia University Press, 1996).

[6] Barry R. Posen, "The Security Dilemma and Ethnic Conflict," *Survival* 35, 1 (1993): 27–47, at 27–28.

open to alternative constructions, and competitive state identities combined with power politics were only one possible outcome. Mercer's conclusions from SIT suggest that in-group / out-group cognitive processes would lead to the same outcomes predicted by neo-Realism. And Johnston's analysis suggests that the identities and strategic cultures of new state elites would be most important for the evolution of post-Soviet international relations.

But the patterns of international relations among the successor states that actually emerged indicate that national identities were important influences on the state identities that governments chose and cultivated. Neither state-centered constructivism nor state-centered Realism provided enough guidance for how those newly international politics would develop because both seemed to leave nations out of the analysis.

The case of Belarus suggests several interesting conclusions about national and state identities in "emerging anarchy." Belarusian national identity was ambiguous with regard to potential overlap with the Russian nation and to broader societal categories such as Soviet and East Slavic. Belarusians believed themselves to be Belarusian and not Russian, but in general they did not believe that their Belarusian nationhood implied being separate politically and culturally from Russians. The anti-Russian content for Belarusian identity that the Belarusian Popular Front proposed was rejected by most Belarusians. As a result of these politics of national contestation, the meaning of the Belarusian nation was ambiguous and fragmented into incompatible visions of the Belarusian past and future.

The Belarusian government also sought an identity for the new Belarusian state. The only state identity that most other governments ascribed to Belarus was "post-Soviet." Otherwise, the identity of Belarus was in flux, and the government and society had an opportunity to choose their state's identity. Some of their Baltic neighbors proclaimed their states "European," a category that, they believed, excluded Russia. Belarusians made a different choice. They did not draw a sharp distinction between the Russian state and their own. Indeed, the identity that the government sought for Belarus included a broader political community with Russia. Neither Belarusian society nor its government wanted Belarus to become a Russian province. But they did seek to create a "community" and then "union" of states with Russia. Thus, neither Eurasia's emerging anarchy (its structural condition) nor the interaction among the new states (its process) created inherently competitive identities and relations. The reason lay in the domestic politics of the nation.

Still, there were some post-Soviet states, such as Lithuania, whose behavior was broadly consistent with what we might call an economic realpolitik, or the economic statism that Realist theorists projected for patterns of post-Soviet political economy. Johnston's theoretical logic suggests that something internal to Lithuania's politics must have led to its power politics.

The Lithuanian Case:
Two Conclusions about Anarchy, Identity, and Nationalism

I have suggested that national identity was the internal variable that influenced the directions that post-Soviet governments chose. It is possible to draw two somewhat different conclusions from the Lithuanian case. One is that a coherent, consensual national identity defined in opposition to Russia was the prerequisite for realpolitik in the former Soviet Union. Indeed, perhaps nationalists in the former Soviet Union have what Johnston would call parabellum strategic cultures. This conclusion is a significant challenge to the neo-Realist account of the power politics of the Baltic states in their relations with Russia. It is also an interesting empirical observation that sheds light on the debate among Wendt, Mercer, and Johnston because it suggests that national identities play an important role in the processes and strategic choices about which these scholars are concerned, in addition to the states and state elites they propose to study.

I prefer a stronger conclusion, one that relies on the conceptual distinction between economic nationalism and economic statism (or economic realpolitik). Lithuania's foreign economic policy is useful for distinguishing between economic nationalism and economic statism as empirical phenomena. One distinction is subtle: the politics of foreign policy making in Lithuania indicate that there was a national *motivation*, a social purpose derived from a shared sense of history, that underlay Lithuania's attempt to achieve economic autonomy. Another distinction is clearer, and that is the directionality of Lithuania's foreign economic policy. Lithuania was oriented not just away from Russia and the CIS but also toward the West and EU. Europe was not merely a refuge from Russia but a symbol of both the past and the potential future of the Lithuanian nation. Just as Lithuania's nationalism was anti-Russian and pro-European, so was its post-Soviet policy. The Lithuanian government's commitment to Europe went well beyond any balancing strategy. Thus, Lithuania's economic policy looked like economic realpolitik in one direction (east toward Russia) but the most benign liberal policy west toward Europe. In the end, Lithuania's economic nationalism did not turn the economy inward to create autonomy or build the power of the state. Instead, it led to the country's embrace of all things that seemed to be the opposite of its Soviet experience—capitalism, democracy, and Europe. Some policies that appear to be consistent with the power politics that Realist theories predict may on closer inspection turn out to be so purposeful and directional that a different description is more informative.

Either conclusion has implications for the research agenda of constructivist theorizing, which is likely to become more domestic, more national, and more pessimistic. Unlike constructivist theorizing at the level of the international system with its focus on the society of states, I have emphasized the importance of collective identities of domestic societies. Of these collective identities, the most significant has historically been national. A focus on the nation should be a welcome addition to constructivist theories that have, so far, explicated the identities of states. Finally, some rationalist critiques of constructivism hold that its theorists overstate the possibilities for positive change in the relations among states, which might be able to transcend the perils of anarchy through their interaction with one another. Such a critique is based on a mischaracterization of constructivist theory. Nevertheless, I have suggested that constructivist theory is both pessimistic and optimistic. The study of nationalisms and national identities certainly warrants both assessments.

These empirical and theoretical conclusions suggest several broader implications for how we understand the politics of the world economy. One is the importance of evaluating how societies interpret their economic relations with the outside world, and particularly with specific neighbors. Societies rarely interpret their economic activity and dependence on actors outside their state in purely material terms. More often, they endow their economies with national purposes. And societies view their external economic relations through a lens shaped by shared understandings of history and shared visions for the future. Societies' debates about what it means to be the nations they are influence those purposes, understandings, and visions. To understand the choices they make, it is as important to study what societies believe about themselves as it is to evaluate the distributional consequences of their policies. That is to say, political context and history are as important as economic reasoning for understanding what governments actually do in relation to the world economy.

Jacob Viner, the eminent Chicago economist, reached a similar conclusion in his classic analysis of customs unions:

> The power of nationalist sentiment can override all other considerations; it can dominate the minds of a people, and dictate the policies of a government, even when in every possible way and to every conceivable degree it is in sharp conflict with what seem to be and are in fact the basic economic interests of the people in question. To accept as obviously true the notion that the bonds of allegiance must necessarily be largely economic in character to be strong, or to accept unhesitatingly the notion that where economic entanglements are artificially or naturally strong the political affections will also necessarily become strong, is to reject whatever lessons past experience has for us in this field.[7]

[7] Jacob Viner, *The Customs Union Issue* (New York: Carnegie Endowment for International Peace, 1950), 105.

Fifty-odd years after Viner wrote these sentences, the contemporary world is full of both regional economic integration in Europe, North America, and Asia—and regional disintegration in the former Soviet Union and parts of Africa. As Viner likely would have argued, neither integration nor disintegration is being driven exclusively by societies' "basic economic interests," the purely material incentives they face. There is much more going on.

It is commonly said that globalization has changed the world economy and that one of the main threats to a world of free trade and capital flows is nationalism. In the judgment of some observers of the so-called new global economy, this tension pits the forces of modernity and cosmopolitanism against the backward and reactionary forces of "tribal," "ethnic," or even "suicidal" nationalism. I have shown, however, that it is quite problematic to assume, in Stanley Hoffmann's words, "a single and malevolent kind of nationalism." As Hoffmann argues, there is a variety of nationalisms, and we do not know the consequences of a particular nationalism until we have characterized it.[8] Some have asked, How will nationalism affect the global economy? But this question can be more accurately stated, because the answer to it depends—on the specific nationalism as well as on the nationalism's reception in society, its goals, and its history. It makes no more sense to have a single answer to that question than it would to similar questions, such as, How does culture affect the global economy? Or, How does ideology affect the global economy? The questions yield more insightful answers if stated in plural form—ideologies, cultures, and nationalisms.

Not all nationalisms are the same. They are not all harmful to economic cooperation, nor oriented against everyone, nor politically uncontested and influential. In this book I have offered a theoretical framework with which to create answers to specific empirical questions and to offer contingent generalizations about the influence of nationalisms and national identities. What societies want depends on who they think they are. Societies collectively believe that their national identities are important, that they have implications for their goals and means. In order to describe those identities and understand the economic choices that follow, scholars must study what nations mean to the people who invoke them.

[8] Stanley Hoffmann, "Nationalism and World Order," in his *World Disorders* (Lanham, Md.: Rowman and Littlefield, 1998), 209.

Index

Cornell Studies in Political Economy

A SERIES EDITED BY PETER J. KATZENSTEIN

National Interests in International Society
        by Martha Finnemore
Democracy and Markets: The Politics of Mixed Economies
        by John R. Freeman
The Misunderstood Miracle: Industrial Development and Political
  Change in Japan
        by David Friedman
Patchwork Protectionism: Textile Trade Policy in the United States, Japan,
  and West Germany
        by H. Richard Friman
Ideas, Interests, and American Trade Policy
        by Judith Goldstein
Ideas and Foreign Policy: Beliefs, Institutions, and Political Change
        edited by Judith Goldstein and Robert O. Keohane
Monetary Sovereignty: The Politics of Central Banking in Western Europe
        by John B. Goodman
Politics in Hard Times: Comparative Responses to International
  Economic Crises
        by Peter Gourevitch
Cooperation among Nations: Europe, America, and Non-tariff Barriers
  to Trade
        by Joseph M. Grieco
Nationalism, Liberalism, and Progress, Volume I: The Rise and Decline
  of Nationalism
Volume II: The Dismal Fate of New Nations
        by Ernst B. Haas
Pathways from the Periphery: The Politics of Growth in the
  Newly Industrializing Countries
        by Stephan Haggard
The Politics of Finance in Developing Countries
        edited by Stephan Haggard, Chung H. Lee,
        and Sylvia Maxfield
Rival Capitalists: International Competitiveness in the United States, Japan,
  and Western Europe
        by Jeffrey A. Hart
Reasons of State: Oil Politics and the Capacities of American Government
        by G. John Ikenberry
The State and American Foreign Economic Policy
        edited by G. John Ikenberry, David A. Lake,
        and Michael Mastanduno
The Nordic States and European Unity
        by Christine Ingebritsen

DATE DUE

OCT 1 7 2002			
OCT 1 4 2002			
OhioLINK			
AUG 0 2 REC'D			
OhioLINK			
JUN 2 4 REC'D			
GAYLORD			PRINTED IN U.S.A.

BOWLING GREEN STATE UNIVERSITY
DISCARDED
LIBRARY

HF 1557 .A23 2001

Abdelal, Rawi, 1971-

National purpose in the
 world economy